MARK
THE
EVANGELIST

MARK
THE
EVANGELIST

Studies on the Redaction History of the Gospel

Willi Marxsen

Translated by

James Boyce
Donald Juel
William Poehlmann

with

Roy A. Harrisville

Nashville   Abingdon Press   New York

MARK THE EVANGELIST

ISBN 0-687-23574-X

Library of Congress Catalog Card Number: 69-12022

SET UP, PRINTED, AND BOUND BY THE
PARTHENON PRESS, AT NASHVILLE,
TENNESSEE, UNITED STATES OF AMERICA

To my Mother
and the memory of my Father

Preface

When Conzelmann's investigations on the theology of Luke appeared early in 1954, my work was already in the hands of the theological faculty of Kiel University as a qualifications thesis. In the meantime, Conzelmann's results have been reviewed many times. Not all the reactions are positive, but we will not enter into that here. It seems to me that what is important in his work is the result of his formulation of the question. The present volume pursues a similar inquiry. The similarity between our studies does not appear to me to be accidental. After World War I, form history, stimulated above all by Gunkel's studies, was in the air, as it were. Following World War II, the same is true of redaction history. It is significant that here again Old Testament research led the way. In any event, I am grateful for stimulation received for this investigation from Gerhard von Rad's work on the Pentateuch. In this connection it naturally ought not be overlooked that ideas of other scholars have been appropriated and further developed, particularly those of Ernst Lohmeyer.

It is clear to me that the studies presented here must be carried further; that they must be extended to the entire

Gospel of Mark, and that they call for an interpretation of the Gospel as a whole. Perhaps several further studies, almost completed, should have been added to my qualifications thesis. I considered the question very seriously but for various reasons dismissed it. I did not want to postpone publication further—a prolonged substitute teaching job claiming my full attention would, unfortunately, have required it. I did not want the scope to become too large. Lastly, it seems desirable to me to get the discussion of Mark under way. Presumably, this discussion will be even more controversial than in Luke's case. The reason is that we undoubtedly have a poorer grasp of the oldest evangelist than of his successors. I would like to note, however, that the total picture which emerged for me has not altered in the meantime. For the publication I have incorporated several of Conzelmann's observations. For further details, the reader may refer to his work.

I now wish to meet my many obligations of thanks. Professor Wendland of Münster not only followed the development of the work with interest, but gave assistance in many areas not touching on the immediate task. The German *Forschungsgemeinschaft* granted a subsidy for printing costs. Professor Bultmann included the work in the series of *Forschungen*. Günther Ruprecht of Vandenhoeck & Ruprecht energetically expedited the printing. Vicars Helmut Baginski and Dr. Hans-Jürgen Brandt rendered assistance by proofreading, as did candidate of theology Mrs. Hannelore Frank, by preparing a register of Bible passages. I cordially thank them all.

The dedication page should express the deep gratitude I owe my parents. Regrettably, my father did not live to see the completion of the work whose development he followed with much interest. He was called home on February 7, 1954, only a few days before it was finished.

One further name I can only mention here with sorrow.

Professor Rudolf Schneider of Kiel died in the midst of full activity on March 14, 1956. Gratefully I recall in him a teacher who in difficult times played an essential role at the onset of my theological activity and attended it through the years with stimulation and help.

Preetz bei Kiel, March, 1956

Preface to the Second Edition

A second edition became necessary sooner than expected. At the moment, I can only have it reproduced photomechanically. Several errors were corrected.

Precisely because no other alterations have been made, I would like to single out for thanks all who, orally or in writing, have commented about this work, whether in criticism or agreement. I would like to have used many of the suggestions. Of course, the total picture would not be changed, for I believe I can maintain, even today, the theses of the first edition.

Bethel, August, 1958

Willi Marxsen

Contents

Introduction | Form History and Redaction History

On the whole, the so-called redactor always fares poorly in form history. He is readily characterized as "collector," and there is little inclination to concede to him any real share in the composition of his work, save in the matter of minor details. The remark of Martin Dibelius, e.g., is typical:

The literary understanding of the synoptics begins [!] with the recognition that they are collections of material. The composers are only to the smallest extent authors. They are principally collectors, vehicles of tradition, editors.[1]

What can such a characterization mean? The boundaries are necessarily fluid. Julius Schniewind unconsciously furnishes proof of this.[2] With Martin Dibelius and Karl Ludwig Schmidt he protests the application of the modern idea

---

[1] Martin Dibelius, *From Tradition to Gospel,* trans. Bertram Lee Woolf (New York: Charles Scribner's Sons, 1935) , p. 3.

[2] Julius Schniewind, "Zur Synoptiker-Exegese," *Theologische Rundschau,* Neue Folge 2 (1930) , 151.

"author-personality" to the evangelists. Yet only a few lines later he calls Mark an "author." It is much the same when, in the wake of Papias and Justin, the synoptic writers are viewed as "biographers." The unanimous and indeed uncontested opinion today is that Mark in no way deserves this title. But the case is different with Luke. As Hans Conzelmann has shown, the third evangelist certainly intends to write a *vita*.[3] Of course, the question is whether or not he succeeds. We must deny that he does, but the intention is still there. Luke and his work must be judged and characterized from a different point of view, depending on whether his intention is taken into account or whether the result of his work is measured according to historical fact. So we do well to postpone any classification for the time being.

On the other hand, there is another more pressing question. Again and again, form critics have implicitly or explicitly stressed the "anti-individualistic" and "sociological" orientation of their research. This gave much emphasis to the anonymous character of the individual pieces originating in the oral tradition. We cannot deny that form history correctly viewed traditional material as used by the Synoptists. But is it correct to say that the composition of the Gospels "involves nothing in principle new, but only completes what was begun in the oral tradition"? [4]

The results of form history directly contradict this assertion. Form history indicated the diversity of forms and, in this connection, the various "life situations" of the individual tradi-

---

[3] Hans Conzelmann, *The Theology of St. Luke,* trans. Geoffrey Buswell (New York: Harper & Row, 1960).

[4] Rudolf Bultmann, *The History of the Synoptic Tradition,* trans. John Marsh (New York: Harper & Row, 1965), p. 321 (hereafter referred to as *History*); similarly Conzelmann, *op. cit.,* pp. 10-11, who extends the first phase of the collection of the traditional material, illumined by form history, up to the redaction of the Gospel of Mark.

tions. This means, however, that the traditional material scatters in every direction! We can group together *similar* forms. We could point, e.g., to the parable source available to Mark.[5] But it is not at all obvious that this totally disparate material should finally find its way into the unity of a Gospel.[6] We could, of course, point with Harald Riesenfeld to the fact that "from the beginning there was an overarching, cohesive factor in the tradition which in part coincides with what is customarily denoted by the term kerygma." [7] Here "mention of the earthly life of Jesus has its proper place." Hence it follows that by their very nature "kerygma and Gospel tradition must have been connected." But this is true only of the individual traditions concerned. If, according to Riesenfeld, it is certain that "a Gospel may not be viewed as a chronicle to be evaluated for biographical purposes, nor as an itinerary of Jesus' sojourns," we can only agree. But in opposition to Riesenfeld, this insight does *not* have as

its necessary counterpart the assumption that proclamation and instruction in the primitive church dealt not only with isolated pericopes, but also with a total picture of Jesus' life. This picture was certainly anchored in the faith of the communities and beyond that in the reality experienced and attested by persons still living.

In reference to Acts 10:37-39; 13:31, Riesenfeld seeks to single out the guideposts of an itinerary and assumes we could be dealing here with "an original feature of the life of Jesus." [8] But this ignores the fact that Luke has appropriated this

---

[5] Cf. Willi Marxsen, "Redaktionsgeschichtliche Erklärung der sogenannten Parabeltheorie des Markus," *Zeitschrift für Theologie und Kirche,* 52. Jahrgang (1955) , 255 ff.

[6] The only exception is the passion narrative.

[7] Harald Riesenfeld, "Tradition und Redaktion im Markusevangelium," *Neutestamentliche Studien für Rudolf Bultmann* (Berlin: A. Töpelmann, 1957) , p. 158.

[8] *Ibid.,* pp. 159-60.

17

scheme from its creator, Mark—of course with a totally different intent, as I shall try to show later.[9]

To a degree, Riesenfeld's ideas are reminiscent of the protest which Karl Holl raised against form history: "The whole,
the *unity* of the picture is not a subsequent creation; it is
there from the outset."[10]

This is certainly correct. But we must ask wherein this unity
consists—in the person or in his biography? For this reason,
Holl's objection is no argument against form history or its
results. The total picture of the life of Jesus, his person and
significance, has its deposit in each individual piece of tradition. But this occurs in various circles of the primitive community, in various forms and for various purposes. Multiplicity
thus results from the unity. This unity exists prior to the
synoptic tradition and is still mirrored in it, though often in
a refracted way. But the individual tradition scatters in different directions.

The unity subsequently created by the evangelists—first of
all by Mark—is something else again. It is a systematically
constructed piece which cannot be understood as the "termi-
nation" of the anonymous transmission of material.[11] The
transmission leads rather to ultimate "fragmentation." The
redaction, on the other hand, counteracts this natural development.

This counteraction cannot be explained without taking into
account an individual, an author personality who pursues a
definite goal with his work. We must now inquire into this.
While the scope and limit of our evangelists' sources and their

---

[9] Riesenfeld himself is not quite certain here, but concedes (*ibid.*, p.
159) that "the actual or stylized (!) course of Jesus' life" may underlie
this scheme.

[10] Karl Holl, "Urchristentum und Religionsgeschichte," *Gesammelte
Aufsätze zur Kirchengeschichte* (Tübingen: J. C. B. Mohr, 1928), II, 15.

[11] Riesenfeld is correct: Mark's redactional work is "the deliberate construction of a single person" (*op. cit.*, pp. 158-59). Conzelmann, *loc. cit.*,
convincingly shows that this is also true of Luke's reconstruction.

share in the revision of the material can scarcely be determined with final certainty (unfortunately, we cannot get a glimpse of their writing desk) ; while ultimately we cannot know even the names of our authors, their backgrounds, or their careers, we must still emphasize that we are dealing with authors. Whenever the anti-individualistic view of the Gospels is elevated to a dogma, it is absolutely *impossible* to get a glimpse of the evangelists themselves.

Mark's situation differs from Matthew's and Luke's. From the outset, Matthew and Luke had access to a presentation which somehow was already formed. It consisted of an enlarged sketch which formed a unity created by one individual. In addition, Matthew and Luke used anonymous tradition. (At this point, we can pass over the question of the so-called logia source.) Mark, on the other hand, has at his disposal only anonymous individual traditions, except for certain complexes and a passion narrative. Mark's achievement in shaping the tradition is thus incomparably greater. As far as we can tell, Mark is the first to bring the individualistic element to the forming and shaping of the tradition.

Does form history pay sufficient attention to this fact? We sometimes wonder whether form history really takes seriously the two-source theory it presupposes.[12] If it makes no difference in which source a piece appeared, and if, at the same time, the whole of the synoptic material is to be drawn upon,[13] is not the traditional material at least in danger of being leveled out? The material which penetrated the "major Gospels" [14] via Mark was *also* influenced by the oldest evangelist, though there may be differences in detail. For this reason we cannot avoid reckoning, at least, with the individualistic element here.

[12] Bultmann, *History*, pp. 1 ff.; Martin Dibelius, "Zur Formgeschichte der Evangelien," *Theologische Rundschau*, Neue Folge 1 (1929), 187.

[13] Bultmann, *History*, p. 3.

[14] This term will be used often in what follows, so as to contrast Mark most simply with his two co-evangelists.

Failure to do so *can* mean a regression to Gieseler's traditions hypothesis. At this point in the analysis there is a gap which is almost always overleaped.

The situation is no different with the constructive sort of form history. Dibelius states (unfortunately only in a footnote) quite correctly:

What is given to us are not the facts, but rather what was handed down. We approach the facts as we reconstruct the world of this traditional material, because in so doing we learn to understand the tradition in its true concerns.[15]

Dibelius concludes:

Our primary (!) task is to arrive at *the tradition* which lay before the collector (!), and thus to reconstruct a narrative in its original, isolated condition, a speech in the form which gives it its point.[16]

But is this correctly evaluated? Tradition is indeed the primary factor which we encounter, but it is the tradition of the evangelists, that is, the tradition laid down in the Gospels. When we reconstruct their world (and that means the world of the evangelists) we approach the individual tradition. Can it then be our first task to proceed to an investigation of the material of synoptic tradition, ignoring the evangelists? Is not our primary task twofold—that of arriving at redaction *and* tradition?

To a degree, this has of course been done in literary criticism. But if only literary factors are taken into account, could we not fall prey to the prejudice that the evangelists were "only" collectors? And would we not have to examine whether and to what degree a conceivably orderly redaction, carried

---

[15] Dibelius, *Die Formgeschichte des Evangeliums*, 4te Auflage (Tübingen: J. C. B. Mohr, 1961), pp. 29-30, n. 1.

[16] Dibelius, "Zur Formgeschichte der Evangelien," p. 210.

out from a specific point of view, has shaped or reshaped tradition?

Fortunately, the ignoring of this gap is not so disastrous in its effects since the stylistic means used by the evangelists are in fact quite simple. But this must not tempt us to draw conclusions as to subject matter on the basis of stylistic means alone, with the result that motifs dealing with subject matter are not taken into account. Form history which bypasses the authors of the Gospels is somehow left hanging in the air.

For this reason, form history as carried on till now needs to be supplemented by a "form history of the Gospels." If the former is oriented to individual pieces, the latter is oriented to each Gospel as a whole. The former would be more accurately described as "form history of the material of synoptic tradition." But this would only create confusion, since the nomenclature has already been fixed. Hence it will be best to range redaction history alongside what till now has been called form history.[17]

Redaction history is not merely the continuation of form history. It was simply taken up at a later date. It can in turn learn much from work previously done. Theoretically, it would have been possible for redaction-historical research to have begun immediately after literary criticism.[18] It is really quite

[17] Among other things, we choose this term so as to use the most common expression possible (cf. Dibelius, "Zur Formgeschichte der Evangelien," pp. 198-99) . We hold, of course, that *all* the evangelists were considerably more than mere "redactors," but by naming the method do not wish to anticipate the result. (Strictly speaking, we are not dealing with one "method" but with a combination of several for redaction-historical purposes. Only in this sense can we speak here of a method.) The term "redaction history" is especially appropriate because we can begin with the general agreement that the evangelists were redactors. The investigation itself must determine to what extent they were redactors (there is considerable distance between "collector" and "theologian") .

[18] Cf. Johannes Weiss, *Die Schriften des Neuen Testaments* (Göttingen: Vandenhoeck & Ruprecht, 1906) , I, 62: "The task of the Gospel expositor is many-sided. He must first [!] understand the author, recognize what he intends to say to his readers. . . ."

astonishing that it did not, for soon after Wernle's[19] fixing
of the two-source theory, beginnings were made which should
have led automatically in that direction. We need only refer
to Wrede[20] and Wellhausen.[21] Yet it seems that their *results*
robbed scholars of the courage to pursue their *methods* in
thoroughgoing fashion.[22] Nevertheless, it is generally conceded
that the theory of the messianic secret belongs to Mark's point
of view.[23] It should have occurred to the scholars to search
for further motifs originating in his point of view. Instead,
the evangelists were examined almost exclusively from literary
standpoints.[24] Measured against Wrede's understanding, this
is a regression, for he had already emphasized that Mark is
"in a certain sense a creative personality." [25]

[19] Paul Wernle, *Die synoptische Frage* (Freiburg i. Breisgau: J. C. B.
Mohr, 1899).

[20] Wilhelm Wrede, *Das Messiasgeheimnis in den Evangelien*, 3te Auflage
(Göttingen: Vandenhoeck & Ruprecht, 1963).

[21] Julius Wellhausen, *Das Evangelium Marci*, 2te Auflage (Berlin:
Georg Reimer, 1909); *Einleitung in die drei ersten Evangelien*, 2te Auflage
(Berlin: Georg Reimer, 1911).

[22] Cf. the very instructive study of H. J. Ebeling, *Das Messiasgeheimnis
und die Botschaft des Markus-Evangelisten* (Berlin: A. Töpelmann, 1939),
esp. in part one (part two requires corrections at many points).

[23] Among others, cf. Bultmann, *History*, p. 346; Dibelius, *From Tradition to Gospel*, pp. 72-73, *passim*.

[24] E.g., a remark of Bultmann is typical of this (*History*, p. 345). He
thinks Mark's redactional work rests chiefly on literary motifs "even
though they are mixed with dogmatic motifs in the picture of Jesus . . ."
(cf. also *History*, p. 1). Is it not just at this point that the question of
the relationship between the two motifs arises? We must inquire further:
are "literary motifs" really motifs? Are they not rather a means Mark
uses to implement a (dogmatic?) motif? We will deal with this question
repeatedly.

[25] Adolf Jülicher, "Wrede," *Realencyklopädie für protestantische Theologie und Kirche*, herausgegeben von Albert Hauck (Leipzig: J. C. Hinrichs'sche Buchhandlung, 1928), XXI, 509. Cf. also his other evaluation:
"In lieu of an atomistic study of individual synoptic pericopes whose sole
concern was the question of the tradition's usefulness for our knowledge of
Jesus, Wrede set himself the task of *understanding each individual Gospel
as a whole;* evaluating its components chiefly for an understanding of the
whole book; setting the Gospel within the history of the life-of-Jesus tradi-

We grasp Mark's share of the work and thus his actual achievement (as well as that of the other evangelists) not in the material primarily[26] but in the "framework." This term is to be taken quite loosely. Not only the itinerary and scenic links are included but also textual transformations, to the extent we can recognize them. This framework should not be dismantled from a merely historical standpoint, as is almost always the case with form history, but should be examined for its "situation-in-life" from the standpoint of redaction history.

Here we can see the great similarity between redaction history and form history. Of course, their similarity ought not deceive us as to their differences. If Joachim Jeremias[27] differentiates the "first situation-in-life" located in the unique situation of Jesus' activity, from the "second situation-in-life" mediated by the situation of the primitive church (which form history seeks to ascertain), we are dealing here with the *"third situation-in-life."*

With this approach, the question as to what really happened is excluded from the outset. We inquire rather how the evan-

---

tion, and *viewing it as a witness to a specific stage in the development of this history of faith.* This was a real step forward." (Italics mine.)

Markus Barth has recently stated his views on the problem ("Die Methode von Bultmanns 'Theologie des Neuen Testaments,'" *Theologische Zeitschrift,* XI (1955), 1 ff.). He maintains that Bultmann (among others) holds to the "complicated and contrived thesis of the messianic secret with which Wrede aims to explain Mark's Gospel" (p. 5). Later (p. 8) he laments the fact that the atomizing of the material has obscured a "view of the total [!] Mark, Matthew and Luke." This is correct—but he overlooks the fact that it was Wrede who was on the way to the total Mark (and precisely via this messianic secret).

[26] So, e.g., it is most problematic to assume, on the basis of a few Latinisms in Mark's text, that the Gospel originated in Rome. These are almost accidental features which, next to Jewish and Hellenistic motifs, never assume any real place. At best they allow us to deduce the origin of each traditional piece—or we would have to prove they are of Markan origin.

[27] Joachim Jeremias, *The Parables of Jesus,* trans. S. H. Hooke (London: SCM Press, 1954), p. 18.

gelists describe what happened. The question as to what really occurred is of interest only to the degree it relates to the situation of the primitive community in which the Gospels arose. We basically agree with Bultmann[28] who saw Wellhausen's special contribution in his stating

that a literary work or a fragment of tradition is a primary source for the historical situation out of which it arose, and is only a secondary source for the historical details concerning which it gives information.[29]

Thus we inquire into the situation of the community in which the Gospels arose. The community ought not to be unqualifiedly viewed as located in a specific place, though we shall keep in mind the possibility of defining it exactly. Our concern is much more with what is typical in this community, its views, its time, perhaps even its composition. Hence a sociological element is present throughout. But over against form history this element is joined to an "individualistic" trait oriented to the particular interest and point of view of the evangelist concerned.[30]

[28] *Journal of Religion,* VI (1926), 341 (according to H. J. Ebeling, *op. cit.,* pp. 32-33).

[29] It should be emphasized that the aim here is not to contest the validity of the quest of the historical Jesus as such. On this point, cf. Ernst Käsemann, "The Problem of the Historical Jesus," *Essays on New Testament Themes,* trans. W. J. Montague (London: SCM Press, 1964), pp. 15 ff.

[30] Though analogies most often break down, and though we do not prefer to draw inferences from our present situation, we can still refer to the modern sermon. It too is sociologically oriented in its relation to the congregation, and at the same time receives its peculiar stamp from the preacher. To great extent, the preacher's and hearer's points of view can (and will) coincide. But the analogy goes still further. All things being equal, I can get a very clear picture of the preacher and his congregation from a volume of sermons covering, say, a year. In *this* respect historical documents are involved. But at best I get information on the facts reported in the sermon only at second hand.

The variety of forms within the individual pieces of tradition leads to a further consideration. Can we speak of a Gospel "genre"? Could not each community or period in which the evangelists live develop a quite distinct "form" from out of its own problems and for its own ends? For example, the words or concepts which the evangelists use at the beginning of their Gospels are striking. The βίβλος in Matt. 1:1 and the διήγησις in Luke 1:1 correspond to the εὐαγγέλιον in Mark 1:1. Do these give us any clues? If so, then we must not let ourselves be deceived by material which is so very similar. Criteria for determining the genre of the work will have to be drawn from the "framework" rather than from the reworked material.

This third life-situation is thus thoroughly differentiated, though it is not as complex as the second, since we have three (or four[31]) fixed points in our extant Gospels. And if we examine the development from one to the other, a very vivid picture of the history of the early church results.[32]

Finally, we should note the circular character which redaction-historical work also shares. The form of the Gospels should help us to draw inferences as to the author's point of view and the situation of his community. On the other hand, when these two factors come more clearly into focus, they can help explain the history of the redaction leading directly to this form.[33] Thus both the analytic and constructive approaches have their proper place.

The present inquiry is concerned primarily with the Gospel

[31] If, in addition to John's Gospel, we add the apocryphal Gospels, the number is not greatly increased.

[32] Such a comparison would really be a "form history of the Gospels," oriented to the Gospels as a literary type.

[33] With Erich Fascher, we ought not describe this as a "vicious circle" ("Die formgeschichtliche Methode, eine Darstellung und Kritik," *Zeitschrift für die neutestamentliche Wissenschaft*, Beiheft 2, XXIII (1924), 214, n. 1). That would ignore the nature of historical research. Cf. Bultmann, *History*, p. 4; Dibelius, "Zur Formgeschichte der Evangelien," pp. 212-13.

of Mark. Without throwing open the "question of genuineness," we shall designate Mark as author. Several difficulties arise here with which we must briefly deal. If the evangelist's work is to be explained, we must know the material he had at his disposal. Things are much simpler with Matthew and Luke, since Mark and his outline provided one specific source. For that reason, we more easily gain an insight into the *altered* points of view of the major evangelists. Still, there are uncertainties even here, for the exemplar which Matthew and Luke used can hardly have been our present Gospel of Mark. This does not absolutely require that we accept the hypothesis of an Ur-Markus—there are also later synoptic assimilations. And yet, the dependence of the later evangelists is not entirely literary. Matthew and Luke still stand within the living tradition of an oral and later probably more stereotyped written transmission. This also influenced their material to great degree, even where a Markan exemplar lay before them. So in any case, we must be cautious about hasty conclusions.

But the same holds true for Mark, perhaps to even greater extent. For here we depend on literary-critical analyses for separating tradition from redaction. It is quite clear that *final* certainty can hardly be achieved. But this insight does not exempt us from the attempt.

There is considerable agreement today "that the process of the origin of our Synoptic Gospels was certainly more complex than the oversimplifying abstraction of the two-source theory" describes it.[34] We are a long way from even a partial consensus. The last rather significant attempt by Emanuel Hirsch is extraordinarily penetrating.[35] But his desire to reconstruct the sources of the sources (and the sources of these

[34] Eduard Schweizer, "Eine hebraisierende Sonderquelle des Lukas?" *Theologische Zeitschrift*, XI (1950) , 161 ff.

[35] Emanuel Hirsch, *Frühgeschichte des Evangeliums*, Erster Band, 2te Auflage (Tübingen: J. C. B. Mohr, 1951) ; Zweiter Band, Erste Auflage, 1941. Cf. also Helmbold, *Vorsynoptische Evangelien*, 1953.

sources in turn) leads to a vacuum. We cannot engage in detailed debate with Hirsch here.[36] And it is not absolutely

[36] A few remarks on Hirsch's analysis of Mark (all quotes are from Vol. I). Mark I was first written in Aramaic, then "once and for all" translated into Greek. It has no "tendency." "One year after Jesus' death this narrative already existed" (pp. 188 ff.). Mark II (originating "in the Christian community at Rome toward the end of the sixties," p. 205) arose because Mark I no longer corresponded with the ideas of the community. Its desire now is to recognize in the Gospel "the picture of the Lord it worships." For this reason, Mark II has "gone over the first narrator's report as with a hedge clippers" (p. 192), and at the same time works in pieces from the "Source of the Twelve" originating in the sixties and reflecting a second generation interpretation (pp. 200 ff.). The Redactor [R] created our present Gospel of Mark (apart from a few later glosses) from Mark I and Mark II. But we ask: Why from Mark I, whose utterances were superseded? Hirsch replies that the community wished to have "collected in *one* Gospel everything it owned now or owned at one time" (p. 205). So the work of R presupposes "a very distinct type of piety: whatever is transmitted is sacred." We reply: Why then is *only* Mark I appropriated and not *everything* which for Hirsch existed at that time (the entire Source of the Twelve, Q, etc.)? But Hirsch works with a second presupposition which appears alongside the piety of R: a "quite specific local connection," i.e., Rome. Only the Roman traditions were collected. But if that is so, then it was not a "local connection" but rather—if the reader will pardon the expression—rigid provincialism. Then R not only meticulously separated alien from local tradition, but also disregarded alien tradition which was appropriate to the time (!) because it answered to the latest needs of the community. On the other hand, he appropriated parts of Mark I which had already been eliminated because they did not suit the time. This is most improbable. If R (and, if his work arose at the behest of the community, then this community as well) had obviously little feel for theological needs and requirements, his literary work was still such an astonishing achievement that it demands even Hirsch's admiration, for R accomplished the feat of "including almost every word [!] from Mark I in Mark II without doing damage to Mark II . . ." (p. 205). This too is highly improbable. Further difficulties arise when we inquire into the number of exemplars present from each stage. (On this, cf. W. Michaelis, *Die Erscheinungen des Auferstandenen*, Basel: H. Majer, 1944, p. 131, n. 3). Hirsch's undoubtedly penetrating analysis lacks the corrective of a synthesis—which must, however, lie in the realm of possibility! In addition, his analysis has a limit. "Hirsch (as well as other source critics) errs throughout by proceeding from the tacit but far from certain assumption that what is always involved is merely the relationship between text forms present in only *one* exemplar" (Michaelis, *op. cit.,* p. 8). Small wonder that R combines Mark I and II almost completely.

necessary to do so, since no one can dispute *that* Mark had sources. How accurately they can be singled out, however, is not too important for the *final* redaction which concerns us. At any rate, we will start from the presupposition that Mark "nowhere used a source which itself had already portrayed a thoroughly coherent life of Jesus which could have been called a Gospel." [37]

We will now attempt to approach Mark's point of view from two aspects. First we shall go back behind Mark and separate tradition from redaction, then by way of construction, illumine and explain his composition. Afterwards we shall include the major Gospels in our investigation and pay special attention to their (altered) points of view. Some results can perhaps be gained for a redaction-historical description of the Gospels of Matthew and Luke.[38] But no great weight should be laid

---

Dibelius' statement regarding the basic problem of separating the sources over and above the two-source theory is still valid ("Zur Formgeschichte der Evangelien," p. 190) : ". . . the most important phenomena these source hypotheses are set up to explain can be interpreted in other ways. First of all, they can be traced to the discrepancy existing between the material and the framework created by the evangelist. . . . So additional source constructions lack the certainty which would accord them equal status with the two-source theory." Most probably, redaction-historical work on all the Gospels will shed light on the question of sources as well. Recognition that the evangelists were more independent than generally assumed till now will obviate many attempts at further separation of sources. But to call these attempts "blind alleys which cannot lead us on to an understanding of the Gospels" is probably an exaggeration (cf. Kendrick Grobel, *Formgeschichte und synoptische Quellenanalyse,* Göttingen: Vandenhoeck & Ruprecht, 1937, p. 120) .

[37] On this, cf. Bultmann, *History,* p. 338.

[38] In the meantime, redaction-historical studies (besides those by Conzelmann and Riesenfeld) already include: Günther Bornkamm, "Matthäus als Interpret der Herrenworte," *Theologische Literaturzeitung,* Jahrgang 79. (1954) , cols. 341 ff.; Eduard Lohse, "Lukas als Theologe der Heilsgeschichte," *Evangelische Theologie,* Jahrgang 79 (1954) , 256 ff. In "Zweck des 4. Evangeliums," *Zeitschrift für Systematische Theologie,* 22. Jahrgang (1953) , 257 ff., C. K. Barrett indicates that the problems in John's Gospel are in many respects similar. Lohmeyer, of course, conducted the most significant preliminary studies. Above all, we must refer to his *Galiläa und Jerusalem, Forschungen zur Religion und Literatur des*

on this aspect. We wish rather to try to get a clearer grasp of what is typically Markan on the basis of later formation. The developments beyond Mark are significant for us due to the inferences we can draw from them.

The four studies which follow were begun with the intent of applying redactional-historical investigations to the Gospel of Mark from the most distinct and variegated starting points. They were to have been independent essays with their results combined at the conclusion. Each essay was to furnish a demonstration of the fruitfulness of the method and prepare for redaction-historical investigations on the whole Gospel. It became apparent, however, that the problems interpenetrate to greater degree than was originally assumed. The result is much overlapping which restricts the independence of each study, but which may nevertheless facilitate a total picture.

The first study deals with the Baptist; the second examines the geographical data of the Gospel; the third deals with a concept, and the fourth with a coherent "speech complex."

Alten und Neuen Testaments, herausgegeben von Rudolf Bultmann, Neue Folge, 34. Heft (Göttingen: Vandenhoeck & Ruprecht, 1936). In this volume, the framework and the geographical data are examined from new points of view. A comparison with K. L. Schmidt, *Der Rahmen der Geschichte Jesu* (Berlin: Trowitzsch und Sohn, 1919) (hereafter referred to as *Rahmen*) shows the advance which has been made over form history. This does not render Schmidt's volume superfluous; but after he proved that the Gospel's framework cannot answer the question regarding the historical Jesus, Lohmeyer now attempts to get a picture of the primitive community from that framework. His failure clearly to see the evangelist behind his work leads to several premature conclusions, to which we will return toward the end of the second study. [Much of the material in Barrett's "Zweck des 4. Evangeliums" is contained in his commentary, *The Gospel According to St. John* (London: S.P.C.K., 1955). To Marxsen's list should be added the volume by Bornkamm, Barth, and Held, *Tradition and Interpretation in Matthew,* trans. Percy Scott (Philadelphia: The Westminster Press, 1963). Translators' note.]

Study One | John the Baptist

We turn now to the question as to how Mark deals with the Baptist tradition available to him. We will try to determine from the way in which he composes and (re-) shapes this tradition whether we can recognize the motives underlying his redaction. This requires that we single out the material at the evangelist's disposal so far as is possible.

A. Analysis and Findings in Mark

Because of its problematic character, the first verse of the Gospel does not provide an appropriate starting point for our analysis. This verse will meet us quite often in the course of our investigations and will probably become entirely clear only in the third study. Martin Kähler had already stated— "somewhat provocatively," as he himself put it—that we can call the Gospels "passion narratives with an extended introduction." [1] Thereby he intended first of all to describe their content. But to a degree this is also true of the Gospels as lit-

---

[1] Martin Kähler, *The So-called Historical Jesus and the Historic, Biblical Christ,* trans. Carl E. Braaten (Philadelphia: Fortress Press, 1964), p. 80, n. 11.

erature. The passion narrative admittedly represents the first stereotyped written unit in the tradition of Jesus. The tradition then developed backward. This is true at least of the Gospel of Mark—naturally not of every individual piece of tradition, but certainly of the complexes. Mark thus prefixes the passion narrative with the tradition of Jesus, and prefixes that tradition with the tradition of the Baptist. The section in 1:9-11 then forms, so to speak, the connecting link.

Did the evangelist have access to a coherent Baptist tradition, which he prefixed to his Gospel? This is assumed, e.g., by Lohmeyer, who regards vss. 1-8 as comprising this traditional unit.[2] He asserts that vss. 4-8 are a line-for-line commentary on the prophecy in vss. 2-3, and that the prophecy was fulfilled in the Baptist. Both prophecy and fulfillment intend to give force to the previous clause: "The beginning of the gospel of Jesus Christ." As linguistic support for his hypothesis, Lohmeyer refers in particular to the phrase ἐν τῇ ἐρήμῳ (1:4) which he assumes contrasts with Mark's usual ἔρημος τόπος.

These arguments, however, are not convincing. First of all, vs. 1 must be excluded. It can hardly have appeared as it does now in an isolated piece of tradition. What meaning would it have had there? The traditional material would have had to continue on to vs. 13. But in that case the verse still says too much. In addition, Lohmeyer's hypothesis shatters on the independent character of the pericopes in vss. 9-11 and vss. 12-13.[3] Secondly, it would be very difficult to point to a life-situation for this unit of tradition. Further, the literary argu-

[2] Ernst Lohmeyer, *Das Evangelium des Markus, Kritisch-exegetischer Kommentar über das Neue Testament*, herausgegeben von H. A. W. Meyer, 12te Auflage (Göttingen: Vandenhoeck & Ruprecht, 1953), p. 10; *Urchristentum* (Göttingen: Vandenhoeck & Ruprecht, 1932), I, 13. In "Die Zusammensetzung des Markusevangeliums," *Acta Academiae Aboensis Humaniora*, IX (1934), 6-7, J. Sundwall also reckons with this possibility, but in the main leaves the question open.

[3] Dibelius, *Die urchristliche Überlieferung von Johannes dem Täufer* (Göttingen: Vandenhoeck & Ruprecht, 1911), p. 47, applies the superscription (only in Mark's context, of course) to vss. 1-8.

ment cannot carry the burden of proof. The use of ἔρημος and of ἔρημος τόπος is not uniform in Mark,[4] at least at first glance.[5] Finally, we should mark the oft-noted syntactical difficulty in the connection of vss. 1+2 f.+4 ff. The difficulty can be accounted for if the verses were connected here for the first time. On the other hand, if the redactor is following a written exemplar, it is obvious he has done some polishing.

What seems decisive, however, is that it is not at all apparent that vss. 4-8 are a "line-for-line" commentary on vss. 2-3. Quite the other way around! If we recognize that vss. 2-3 are a "formula quotation,"[6] and that these verses together with the Old Testament prophecies are a commentary on vss. 4-8, then not only the syntactical difficulties become plausible, but we also catch a glimpse of the evangelist's method. So there is no reason for departing from the conclusion of K. L. Schmidt who regards the introduction as the evangelist's own composition.[7] We can be even more precise: Mark composes backward.[8] The individually edited pericopes are clearly differentiated. Pericope 1:12-13 (καὶ εὐθὺς . . .) precedes 1:14 (καὶ μετὰ . . .);

[4] Ἐρημία occurs in Mark 8:4 (as in the parallel Matt. 15:33); in Mark 1:12, 13 (thus in a piece of tradition originally independent at least of vss. 1-11) and also ἔρημος (cf. parallels in Matt. 4:1 and Luke 4:1). On the other hand, the "typically" Markan ἔρημος τόπος occurs at best in 1:45. In the other passages in which this expression appears, the other Synoptists include it: Mark 1:35 (Luke 4:42); Mark 6:31, 32 (Matt. 14:13, parallel only to vs. 32). The last passage which Lohmeyer cites, Mark 6:35 (Das Evangelium des Markus, p. 10, n. 1) is not suitable for comparison, since the aim here is to stress the τόπος as ἔρημος.

[5] Cf. further below.

[6] It is the only "formula quotation" in Mark. Cf. H. J. Holtzmann, Die Synoptiker, Handcommentar zum Neuen Testament, herausgegeben von Holtzmann, et al., 3te Auflage (Freiburg i. Breisgau: J. C. B. Mohr, 1901), I, 1, 112.

[7] Rahmen, pp. 18-19. Cf. Erich Klostermann, Das Markusevangelium, Handbuch zum Neuen Testament, herausgegeben von Hans Lietzmann, et al., 4te Auflage (Tübingen: J. C. B. Mohr, 1950), p. 3; Sundwall, op. cit., p. 6 (with the above mentioned qualification).

[8] Further development in Matthew and Luke indicates we have correctly viewed Mark's direction.

1:9-11 (καὶ ἐγένετο . . .) precedes 1:12-13; 1:7-8 (καὶ ἐκήρυσσεν . . .) precedes 1:9-11; and 1:4 ff. precedes 1:7-8.[9] Already one important clue emerges from this observation. Just as the "life of Jesus," i.e., the tradition prior to the passion narrative, must be seen from the viewpoint of the cross, so the narrative of the Baptist must be read with Jesus as point of reference. It is most often true of a literary work that what follows interprets what precedes. We will also find examples of this in Mark, when he comments on the pieces of the tradition available to him. But here, where we are dealing with the arrangement of "complexes," the reverse is true —precisely because of the direction which the arrangement gives. What precedes (the Baptist) takes its shape from what follows (Jesus.) This means that the Baptist has no significance in himself. There can be no "doctrine" of or about the Baptist. Rather, the statements concerning the Baptist are christological. As such they interpret the Jesus event in a certain way, but by qualifying it. The Baptist, who has become forerunner, identifies the one who follows as the one awaited.

We can pursue this one step further back. The same relationship exists between the Baptist and the Old Testament. This is quite clear when we examine vs. 4. Here, in fact, we have a key, perhaps *the* key to an understanding of the entire introduction in Mark. We note first of all the textual variants which obscure the original reading.[10] In the main, preference is given Vaticanus: ἐγένετο 'Ιωάννης ὁ βαπτίζων ἐν τῇ ἐρήμῳ κηρύσσων . . . .[11] When ὁ βαπτίζων was no longer construed as

[9] We may not rule out the possibility that the original corrector of Sinaiticus has preserved the original reading in the καὶ ἐγένετο. The καί was later deleted so as to set up a more intimate connection with what precedes. On this, cf. Schmidt, *Rahmen*, p. 18; Bultmann, *History*, p. 246.

[10] At this point, Nestle vacillates almost from edition to edition!

[11] Thus among others, Bernard Weiss, *Die Evangelien des Markus und Lukas, Kritisch-exegetischer Kommentar über das Neue Testament*, herausgegeben von H. A. W. Meyer, 9te Auflage (Göttingen: Vandenhoeck & Ruprecht, 1901), *ad loc.*; J. Weiss, *Das älteste Evangelium* (Göttingen:

a title, the article was accordingly deleted (the Koine family, etc.).[12] K. L. Schmidt[13] thinks the Hesychian family could have altered the text for the same reason: the two participles were connected by καί. Still, a problem poses itself here, at least with regard to 6:24.[14] We probably cannot solve it by assuming only one reason for the changes. There was also a second: the baptism in the wilderness appeared offensive. This may perhaps explain the transposition in Beza. Finally, the further difficulty arises that the ἐγένετο can be interpreted in various ways.[15] We will have to forego drawing up a genealogy of the variants. The fact that the reading given in Vaticanus can at least to some degree explain the others speaks for its originality. But it will be good to keep in mind the three motives which, following the hypothesis presented above, together or singly occasioned the copyist's alterations: misunderstanding of the title, the connection of wilderness and baptism, and the ἐγένετο.

We now pursue the reading in Vaticanus: ἐγένετο Ἰωάννης ὁ βαπτίζων ἐν τῇ ἐρήμῳ κηρύσσων. . . . But when the following verse states that "all" come to him and are baptized, without any account of the Baptist's journey to the Jordan, we cannot

---

Vandenhoeck & Ruprecht, 1903), p. 127, n. 1; Schmidt, *Rahmen*, p. 20; Klostermann, *op. cit.*, and Lohmeyer, *Das Evangelium des Markus, ad loc.* Wohlenberg, G., *Das Evangelium des Markus, Kommentar zum Neuen Testament*, herausgegeben von T. Zahn, 1ste und 2te Auflage (Leipzig: A. Deichert'sche Verlagsbuchhandlung, 1910), *ad loc.*, reads καί before κηρύσσων.

[12] It is not true that ὁ βαπτίζων appears only once in place of ὁ βαπτιστής which elsewhere is "always" used in the New Testament (contra Lohmeyer, *Das Evangelium des Markus*, p. 13, n. 1). Cf. Mark 6:14, 24. At any rate, both these passages are of interest for our discussion. In 6:14 ὁ βαπτίζων is uniformly transmitted; but in 6:24 C and D make alterations (due to the βαπτιστής in 6:25?), whereas the Hesychian and Caesarean families do not oppose it.

[13] *Rahmen*, p. 20.

[14] Cf. note 12 above.

[15] Lohmeyer, *Das Evangelium des Markus*, p. 12, n. 4.

help but ask what the reference in vs. 4, "in the wilderness," is supposed to mean. It would appear that we should follow the hypothesis of K. L. Schmidt who assumes Mark is combining a dual tradition.[16] The one tradition harks back to the wilderness preacher, the other refers only to the Jordan baptizer. In fact, vs. 6 is an entirely new beginning. These references really belonged in vs. 4. But not only literary-critical factors appear to indicate such a separation. The Fourth Evangelist is evidently not aware of a wilderness tradition, though in 1:23 he cites Isa. 40:3.[17] The same is probably true of the Gospel of the Ebionites.[18] The tradition of the Jordan baptizer is therefore the only authentic one.

In addition, K. L. Schmidt believes the wilderness motif is of a more recent date than that of the Baptist; indeed, that it is very probably the evangelist's own creation:

For upon closer scrutiny, the report of the wilderness (viz., in vs. 4 which refers to locale, and in vs. 6 which describes the Baptist's mode of life) indicates that it is an outgrowth of the prophetic quotation in vs. 2 f. This hypothesis stands the test insofar as insertions can be easily and smoothly removed from the context.

Let us test the arguments. To be sure, vs. 6 gives us pause. The verse has scarcely any "redactional" character[19] and can hardly, as Bultmann supposes, be construed as an exegesis of Isa. 40:3. Above all, it might not have originated as such. The verse, which we can also identify in the Gospel of the Ebionites,[20] was probably transmitted independently (perhaps to-

---

[16] *Rahmen*, pp. 21-22; also Bultmann, *History*, p. 246; Klostermann, *op. cit., ad loc.*

[17] According to John 3:23, John also baptized in inhabited regions. (Cf. Lohmeyer, *Das Evangelium des Markus*, p. 13, n. 1).

[18] Cf. Epiphanius, *Haer.* 30, 13, 6 (Holl, *op. cit.*, I, 350, 8-12).

[19] Contra Bultmann, *History*, p. 246. For the rest, Bultmann is primarily concerned with determining the growth of the tradition.

[20] Epiphanius, *Haer.* 30, 13, 4 (Holl, *op. cit.*, I, 350, 2-6).

gether with vs. 7), and will already have been at Mark's disposal.[21] But it has been given its position by the redactor, as here, too, the introductory καί shows.

The situation is different in the case of the ἐν τῇ ἐρήμῳ (vs. 4). By a textual-critical comparison we saw that here *also* difficulties were felt which the other evangelists removed in similar fashion.[22] They are fairly easily solved if this phrase is removed and viewed as a redactional supplement. Accordingly, vs. 4 of Mark's material might have read: καὶ ἐγένετο Ἰωάννης ὁ βαπτίζων κηρύσσων βάπτισμα. . . . It could be translated in Semitic fashion: "And John appeared who was preaching a baptism . . . ," or (ἐγένετο as paraphrase[23]): "And John began by preaching a baptism. . . ." Now vs. 5 follows without difficulty. Men do not go out to the wilderness to be baptized, but to the Jordan.

This procedure should help us arrive at the motives underlying Mark's composition. It is best to proceed from vs. 6, which of course cannot be clearly interpreted.[24] Yet this much appears to emerge with relative certainty: the diet points to a vegetarian ascetic; the clothing, and especially the leather girdle, to Elijah (II Kings 1:8).[25] Perhaps in that day such garb was required of a prophet. In any case, as Lohmeyer suggests, "all these details" confirm the narrator in his conviction "that John is the 'One crying in the wilderness.'" But this

[21] Cf. also Matthew, who sets this verse at 3:4 instead of after 3:6.

[22] Cf. Matt. 3:1 (with the addition τῆς Ἰουδαίας); further, Luke 3:2, where the word of God comes to John in the wilderness. Only in 3:3 does John go to the Jordan to preach and baptize.

[23] Blass-Debrunner, *A Greek Grammar of the New Testament*, trans. Robert Funk (Chicago: University of Chicago Press, 1961), § 354.

[24] Cf. the commentaries, esp. Lohmeyer, *Das Evangelium des Markus*, ad loc.; also his *Urchristentum*, I, 49 ff.; Dibelius, *Die urchristliche Überlieferung von Johannes dem Täufer*, p. 48.

[25] Cf. H. L. Strack and P. Billerbeck, *Kommentar zum Neuen Testament aus Talmud und Midrasch* (München: C. H. Beck'sche Verlagsbuchhandlung, 1922), I, 98.

means that prior to Mark the wilderness tradition was at least implicitly connected with the Baptist.[26]

Now the evangelist's compositional work can also be explained. He combines both traditions. In vs. 4 the phrase ἐν τῇ ἐρήμῳ is lacking, but the wilderness motif is at least echoed in vs. 6.[27] At this point, the Baptist tradition requires corroboration from the Old Testament. For the sake of the traditional features, Mark fashions a mixed quotation. The idea of the forerunner and the Elijah analogy well known from tradition induce the evangelist, while reflecting, to combine Mal. 3:1 and Exod. 23:20 at vs. 2. The idea of the wilderness (vs. 6), of the one crying and, again, of the one preparing the way occasion the quotation from Isa. 40:3 at vs. 3.[28]

Mark now prefixes this "backward-directed prophecy" to his Baptist tradition. But this tradition contains the phrase ἐν τῇ ἐρήμῳ (LXX) *expressis verbis*. This induces him to adjust the tradition to the prophecy by repeating this phrase in vs. 4. Now it is quite clear: the one who appears—in the wilderness—is the one who was already announced by the prophets. Thus in fact the ἐν τῇ ἐρήμῳ in vs. 4 is an Old Testament quotation.[29] The wilderness is not a locale. We ought not speculate as to its location. The phrase does not intend to specify the Baptist's abode (not even in the most general way as adverbial).[30] Rather, ἐν τῇ ἐρήμῳ qualifies the Baptist as the fulfiller of Old Testament predictive prophecy. Put in exaggerated form, the Baptist would still be the one who

the wilderness is not a locale!

---

[26] It also appears in Q. Cf. Matt. 11:7 ff.; Luke 7:24 ff. Cf. below note 45.

[27] It is possible that the εἰς ἄφεσιν ἁμαρτιῶν (vs. 4) was also lacking in Mark's source. Cf. Lohmeyer, *Das Evangelium des Markus, ad loc.*

[28] Verse 2 is thus not a later insertion but is the evangelist's own contribution. Cf. Lohmeyer, *Das Evangelium des Markus*, p. 11, n. 2.

[29] Lohmeyer, *Das Evangelium des Markus*, p. 13, n. 2.

[30] Contra W. Schmauch, "In der Wüste; Beobachtungen zur Raumbeziehung des Glaubens im Neuen Testament," *In Memoriam Ernst Lohmeyer* (Stuttgart: Evangelisches Verlagswerk, 1951), pp. 202 ff., esp. pp. 204, 213. We will return to this study.

appears "in the wilderness" even if he had never been there in all his life.

We do not want to generalize yet, but in connection with this verse we must assert that Mark uses a datum which in itself is geographical, but not, as we might first suppose, with geographical but with theological intent. The question as to whether such a phenomenon occurs only here will have to be answered later.

Following the "reference to place," we turn now to a reference to time. Verse 14 records that Jesus made his first public appearance after the Baptist had been "delivered up." As is well known, John's Gospel is apparently of another opinion. It records at least a simultaneous appearance of John and Jesus (3:22 ff.; 4:1). It is usual to ask which account is historically correct, and the obvious answer is to point out that the Fourth Evangelist's description is tendentious, i.e., polemical. But that is no argument against the historical reliability of the report which underlies it. More importantly, can we really play off Mark's account against the Fourth Evangelist's? Is Mark free of "tendency"?

What is the nature of those time references? After Jesus' baptism (vss. 9-11) the Spirit εὐθύς hurls him into the wilderness (vss. 12-13). A forty-day duration is indicated. Then immediately follows the report of Jesus' first public appearance.

Was the Baptist arrested immediately after the baptism, i.e., within those forty days? Or is Mark silent about the interval between Jesus' temptation and public appearance? [31] The evangelist certainly understands the baptism and wilderness sojourn as immediate preparation for Jesus' public appearance. So there is a close topical connection here. This is what concerns Mark.

And the reference to time? Certainly John's arrest at the hand of Herod is reflected in that παραδοθῆναι (1:14). But

[31] According to K. L. Schmidt, *Rahmen,* p. 34, there is a seam between 1:13 and 1:14.

if this were its only meaning, then it would be natural to insert the description of the Baptist's arrest and execution at this point, and not wait till 6:14 ff. But then, as Lohmeyer already indicated, an addition such as "into prison" would hardly have been omitted.[32]

If, however, the παραδοθῆναι is used absolutely, then that expression has "the same meaning which it has elsewhere in the Gospels: as the Son of man is delivered up, so also is John. Both fulfill the same divine decree."[33]

First of all, this prohibits our understanding the phrase in purely historical fashion. Further, we must keep the eschatological aspect in mind. It could be that Mark interprets eschatologically a traditionally historical account of John's imprisonment. In that case, a "tendency" would also be present in Mark, though different from that in the Fourth Gospel. Both evangelists—at times in different ways—give theological weight to their statements. But then it is especially interesting that different, even contradictory, statements underlie their theological goals. It is this which first gives rise to the question as to the actual course of events. It is just as conceivable that the Fourth Evangelist invented Jesus' simultaneous appearance with the Baptist so as to furnish a polemic against the Baptist sect, as it is that Mark invented a succession.[34] The question is, what purpose he could have had for doing so.

---

[32] Lohmeyer, *Das Evangelium des Markus, ad loc.;* cf. *Rahmen,* p. 33.

[33] Here are the findings in Mark: παραδιδόναι (except for this passage) is used in the absolute only of Jesus: 3:19; 14:11, 18, 21, 42; 15:10 (in D, Theta, etc., also in 14:10). It is also used of Jesus with some supplementation in 9:31; 10:33; 14:41; 15:1, 15. In reference to other persons, παραδιδόναι never appears in the absolute. Cf. 13:9, 12 (13:11 is only an apparent exception—it merely resumes 13:9). The exception is 1:14.

[34] So we must ask whether we can learn anything at all here of the historical sequence of events. Lohmeyer thinks the Fourth Evangelist is better informed than the Synoptists (*Urchristentum,* I, 26, n. 4; cf. p. 27, n. 2 and p. 41); further, Schmidt, *Rahmen,* p. 34. For a different view, Bultmann, *History,* p. 203, n. 1; Dibelius, *Die urchristliche Überlieferung von Johannes dem Täufer,* pp. 111, 140. But are we not in danger here of making an "aesthetic judgment"?

Here again we must note the direction of the evangelist's arrangement. He prefixes the Jesus complex with the Baptist complex. This is for the purpose of expressing a topical and not a chronological sequence. Though later on Mark will still say something about the Baptist,[35] he sets the report of his arrest at this point. By applying to the Baptist the terminology of early Christianity (cf. I Cor. 11:23), he intimately connects the Baptist's fate with that of Jesus. For if the point is to give the Baptist theological rank, then, as far as subject matter is concerned, his "delivering up" belongs right here.[36]

The intention behind Mark's redaction then becomes clear. K. L. Schmidt speaks of a "heilsgeschichtlich schematization" here.[37] This describes the situation exactly. The Baptist is Jesus' forerunner. What is to be said of him is said prior to Jesus' appearance. The reason is not that he was arrested before that time. That may indeed be true, but not necessarily. The reason is rather that topically John belongs before Jesus. In this sense the Baptist is the "pre-history" of Jesus. The μετὰ τὸ παραδοθῆναι thus gives support to the idea that John is Jesus' (announced) forerunner.

We must realize that the Baptist in turn has a prehistory, viz., in the prophetic utterances of the Old Testament. But just as the Baptist, so this Old Testament prophecy is so closely tied to Jesus that the entire work can be titled ἀρχὴ τοῦ εὐαγγελίου Ἰησοῦ Χριστοῦ.

This first verse is at times quite skeptically viewed.[38] Bult-

---

[35] The aim of Mark 6:17 ff. is to give expression to christological elements. When we compare also 8:27 ff., we recognize both the similarity and dissimilarity of the utterances concerning Jesus and the Baptist.

[36] It is therefore an error (even the question is falsely put) to attempt to use this datum to establish a contradiction of or agreement with a historical reality.

[37] Rahmen, p. 24. What is involved is an "unchronological chronology." Cf. also J. Weiss, Die Schriften des Neuen Testaments, I, ad loc.

[38] Cf. Ragnar Asting, Die Verkündigung des Wortes im Urchristentum (Stuttgart: W. Kohlhammer Verlag, 1939), p. 323, n. 1.

mann regards it as an "old gloss";[39] Friedrich believes it is "perhaps" a later addition.[40] Difficulties always emerge at this passage when exposition of the Gospel begins with 1:1. But as far as the evangelist's arrangement is concerned, we are dealing, so to speak, with the "last word." This is what interpretation must keep in mind. The word ἀρχή here, as elsewhere in Mark, does not mark a point of departure for a development in sequence, but rather the starting point to which a given datum can be retraced.[41] The fact that in Mark's *presentation* such an ἀρχή harks back to the beginning, obscures the origin of the concept and hence, if Mark is to be interpreted, leads to abridgment, since the compositional work is disregarded.[42]

What follows must still be modified later, but something can be said by way of summary. By his arrangement Mark indicates he not only resumes the old pre-Pauline historical-theological point of view, but also that he enlarges upon it in a peculiar way. The κατὰ τὰς γραφάς (I Cor. 15:3-4) not only symbolizes Christ's death for our sins and his resurrection on the third day. There is more—his public appearance, his work and "life" lead back beyond the forerunner to the Old Testament. However, it is not a temporal sequence which is at

[39] Bultmann, *Theology of the New Testament,* trans. Kendrick Grobel (New York: Charles Scribner's Sons, 1955), II, 125. Earlier, Bultmann regarded the verse as the evangelist's redactional work (*History,* p. 245).

[40] Gerhard Kittel, *Theological Dictionary of the New Testament,* trans. G. Bromily (Grand Rapids: Eerdmans, 1964), II, 727, n. 52.

[41] Of course, passages such as 10:6 and 13:19 (though they are inserted here) cannot prove that this is a typically Markan usage. 13:8 can do so, however. What is quite obviously involved here is a formulation on the part of the evangelist. The tribulation endured in the present is not the end—as the community, in accordance with apocalyptic predictions, might expect—but only the ἀρχὴ ὠδίνων. The tribulation is thereby separated from the end, but it is also defined by it. The end qualifies the present as ἀρχή. For details, cf. below in the fourth study.

[42] This is true, e.g., of Delling ("Ἀρχή" in Kittel, *op. cit.,* I, 482) who in reference to 1:1 speaks of a "temporal starting point of the evangelical preaching of Jesus." In any event, it is clear also here that the two Gospels require another kind of interpretation, at least in those passages where they follow Mark's *sequence.*

issue here. Indeed, we can scarcely speak of a *Heilsgeschichte* in terms of a sequence of events; for the concept of time is, as it were, eliminated from the παραδοθῆναι (1:14). We are dealing with "blocks" (Jesus—the Baptist—the Old Testament) which are juxtaposed so as to be understood together. The connection is topical, that is, it is made from a theological or, strictly speaking, christological point of view. However the tradition at his disposal looked, Mark looses the Baptist from his historical context and sets him in front of Jesus by describing him, viewed from Jesus, as the forerunner of the Coming One. There is not any reflection on temporal sequence. Viewed from Jesus via the Baptist, even the Old Testament prophecy can now become the ἀρχὴ τοῦ εὐαγγελίου 'Ιησοῦ Χριστοῦ. Put in another way, viewed from Jesus, the preliminary event is qualified in a totally new way and can for the first time become true prophecy and John a true forerunner. But we must keep in mind that the prophecy as well as the forerunner "belong" to the gospel.

Thus Jesus' ministry begins with the ministry of the Baptist. For both, the wilderness plays a decisive role (1:4; cf. 1:12).[43] The baptism of John is already a baptism for the forgiveness of sins (1:4).[44] Both preach.[45] Both in corresponding fashion

---

[43] Note the passage!

[44] Lohmeyer thinks this phrase constitutes the narrator's interpretation (*Das Evangelium des Markus, ad loc.*). But it appears that cannot be established with sufficient certainty. Yet it suits Mark's point of view perfectly.

[45] When Kümmel ("Die Eschatologie der Evangelien, ihre Geschichte und ihr Sinn," *Theologische Blätter*, XV (1936), cols. 225 ff.) states: "There is, of course, no direct witness to Jesus' appropriation of the Baptist's eschatological call to repentance, but it may indeed be assumed to be the case" (col. 227), then the question arises whether the situation was not just the reverse. Because Jesus and John preach the same message, John is closely associated with Jesus. We established above that the wilderness tradition very probably lay at Mark's disposal. The tradition of the wilderness *preacher*, however, might indeed originate with the evangelist. In this sense K. L. Schmidt's thesis must be improved upon (*Rahmen*, pp. 21-22).

are "delivered up." According to the evangelist's view, the Baptist genuinely belongs to the gospel.[46] Again we must emphasize that *here* we cannot be concerned with establishing how it really was. Important for our inquiry is the way in which Mark views it. We might describe his work by the term "consolidation." The individual pieces are not only juxtaposed, they are also connected. The concept "wilderness," in itself geographical, is emptied of its geographical content; the reference to the "delivering up," in itself historical, is emptied of its historical content. Both are pressed into the service of a theological statement. Mark does not make use of his sources by adding formula quotations to them (as, e.g., Matthew in the matter of Old Testament quotations), but rather interprets his sources by his arrangement of them.

This arrangement, however, is in no way intended to express temporal sequence. At the same time, the evangelist *cannot* report without the aid of sequence. And this sequence always appears to be temporal.[47] Here lies the "ideal" starting point for later corrections, ideal since it is simply given with the means of reporting. What has been consolidated requires only to be separated.

This is what actually occurs with Mark's successors. We shall

[46] Cf. Adolf Schlatter, *Markus, der Evangelist für die Griechen* (Stuttgart: Calwer Verlag, 1935), p. 9. Bultmann appropriately describes the Baptist as a "figure of the Christian interpretation of history" (*Das Evangelium des Johannes, Kritisch-exegetischer Kommentar über das Neue Testament,* herausgegeben von H. A. W. Meyer, 13te Auflage [Göttingen: Vandenhoeck & Ruprecht, 1953], p. 121). It should be noted that this figure not only makes various interpretations possible, but that such interpretations are actually given. Each evangelist uses the Baptist to present his own point of view. Cf. also below.

[47] It would, e.g., be entirely conceivable (though I regard it as improbable) that Mark knew something more of a ministry carried on simultaneously by the Baptist and Jesus. His composition does not militate against it. Did the Fourth Evangelist interpret the Synoptists in a temporal sense here? John 3:24 appears to be a correction. As much as we would like to fix the actual event, nothing in the way of certainty can be achieved.

indicate this at certain points—not, as noted, so as to describe the major evangelists with any finality, but in order that Mark might be more clearly recognizable against their background. When they make changes, something in Mark must not have "pleased" them or must have been too obscure *for their purposes.* Thus the alterations in turn illumine the oldest evangelist.

B. Alterations in the Major Gospels

Some things can be learned merely from the way in which the major Gospels use the term and concept "wilderness." For there is a quite obvious disparity here between the evangelists, overlooked by Schmauch in his essay "In der Wüste." [48] His piece offers a series of good observations, but unfortunately harmonizes in a synoptic comparison and thus does not do justice to the various interpretations in the first three Gospels.[49] First of all, Schmauch's thesis, leading to a differentiated

[48] *In Memoriam Ernst Lohmeyer,* pp. 202 ff.

[49] Schmauch (*op. cit.,* p. 213, n. 18) himself sees the restricted character of "Findings in the New Testament" which do not "consider the problems of tradition-history." Unfortunately, he does not see the consequences. We also take issue with him here because this "error" in observation is very common. For the most part, Kittel's *Theological Dictionary of the New Testament* presents findings in the Synoptic Gospels in one section. Naturally, the Synoptists have not used or understood all the concepts in different ways. But that they interpret them in identical fashion should really be the end result and not a tacit assumption. We will try to demonstrate this later in connection with εὐαγγέλιον. When we speak of Synoptists, synoptic usage, synoptic theology, etc., we must differentiate more sharply than heretofore between synoptic material and the evangelist. We will also have to demonstrate that. It will become apparent that the findings in the synoptic material by no means always coincide with the interpretation advocated by the evangelist. And if a separate chapter is most often devoted to John (as, e.g., in Kittel), each Synoptist will often require the same. The fact that in the Fourth Gospel original material and author share largely the same point of view may not lead us to conclude prematurely that such should also be true of the Synoptic Gospels.

understanding of the concept "wilderness," is important in the context of our discussion, depending, of course, on whether this datum is used in connection with Jesus or the Baptist. Schmauch is of the opinion that in reference to the Baptist the place is geographically defined. But "as for Jesus, none of the three Synoptic Gospels containing reports of the temptation indicate where this place is to be found." [50] To understand Schmauch we must observe his threefold distinction. From the concrete references to place, he culls out those which furnish no clue as to content but still contain an adverbial reference to place.[51] He sees this second meaning as given with the Baptist.[52] On the other hand, where Jesus is concerned, a third meaning is characteristic. Here the wilderness has "become an empty vessel, the locale of the eschatological event." The wilderness has "as it were . . . been abandoned; it is *wherever this event has to do with Jesus.*" [53] Salvation is thus no longer realized "in the wilderness," as is the case with the Old Testament or even with the Baptist, but in Jesus. He has taken its place.[54]

No doubt, Schmauch has correctly seen that there is such a thing as a reference to place which is not really such but is rather a statement with theological content. But—at least in our case—this is not determined by the question as to whether the datum is applied to Jesus or the Baptist. Moreover, this understanding is confined to Mark; his two successors are not acquainted with it.

We saw earlier that we may not put to 1:4 questions as to

[50] *Op. cit.,* p. 213.
[51] Cf. *ibid.,* p. 204.
[52] For this reason we may not give one-sided attention to naming a specific name (e.g., in Matt. 3:1) for, even when the name is lacking (e.g., in Mark 1:4) a reference to place (precisely in this second sense) is involved, according to Schmauch.
[53] *Op. cit.,* p. 214 (italics mine).
[54] Cf. *ibid.,* pp. 221-22. Later, the New Testament concept "in Christ" displaced and replaced the Old Testament concept "in the wilderness" (*op. cit.,* p. 223).

place or locale. Nor are we dealing with an adverbial reference to place. In 1:4 the phrase "in the wilderness" is an Old Testament quotation describing the Baptist. It is John's certification, singling him out as the eschatological forerunner of the Coming One. Or, in other words, it is not the Baptist's appearance in the wilderness which characterizes his function as forerunner. Quite the contrary, since he is the eschatological messenger, it is said of him that ἐγένετο . . . ἐν τῇ ἐρήμῳ. . . . [55] Only *after* the Baptist has been described in this fashion does the "concept" wilderness become an adverbial reference to place, at first without, then later with localization. This is how the copyists understood it when they encountered the "baptism in the wilderness." [56] This is how Matthew and Luke understood it and, under their influence, the commentators on Mark. [57]

Matthew adds the supplement τῆς Ἰουδαίας (3:1), which would have made no sense in Mark. Luke separates the act of baptizing from the Baptist's "call" (3:2), which occurs in the wilderness. From there, John moves into the region of the Jordan (3:3). We see clearly how the development proceeds beyond Mark.

This is true not only where the wilderness is noted in connection with the Baptist but also where Jesus is described as being in the wilderness. Schmauch's assertion that the wilder-

[55] Thus (from Mark's point of view) what Schmauch says of Jesus is actually true of the Baptist: Wherever the Baptist is, there is the "wilderness."

[56] Cf. above. The objection could be raised that the wilderness often extends to the Jordan and that the "baptizing in the wilderness" can therefore have worked no hardship or furnished any reason for correction. But that presupposes that the geographical relationships were known to the copyists, which in most cases can hardly be assumed.

[57] Cf. Klostermann, *op. cit.*, on 1:4. Wohlenberg's comment is both interesting and typical (*op. cit.*, pp. 40-41, n. 14) : "In Mark's language we see a feature which suggests that his home was not far from the wilderness referred to here. That being the case, it would require no further localization."

ness has lost all the aspects of a locale is true enough of Mark
1:12. We ought not define its site. Are we perhaps to think
in terms of an adverbial reference? Schmauch says we ought
not inquire "after any other circumstances" nor after "other
persons than those named or other events in the same area." [58]
In light of this statement Mark 1:13 seems to go somewhat
further, though with restraint. But the "wild beasts" are here
the allies of Satan. They are mentioned so as to intensify the
horror "expressed by the wilderness as the realm of the
Satanic." [59] All geographical significance appears in fact eliminated.[60]

But contrary to Schmauch, this is true only of Mark. In Matt.
4:1 and Luke 4:1 the idea "wilderness" is doubtless changed to
a reference to place. Schmauch overlooks the fact that two
other data follow which parallel the εἰς τὴν ἔρημον (Matt. 4:
1), i.e., εἰς τὴν ἁγίαν πόλιν (4:5) and εἰς ὄρος ὑψηλὸν λίαν (4:
8). The same is true of Luke. To the ἐν τῇ ἐρήμῳ (4:1) corresponds the mention of Jerusalem (4:9), and behind the
ἀναγαγὼν αὐτόν (4:5) there is naturally the idea of a change
of *place*. Of course, we must not ignore the fact that all the
places noted have theological significance for the major Gospels as well. But in our context it is of primary importance
that the wilderness of the temptation is only *one place among
others*. The meaning of the term in Mark is changed into a
locale by his two co-evangelists (or at least is changed into a
term which includes the geographical element).

Here is where Schmauch's thesis breaks down. It cannot be
proved (and this was Schmauch's real concern) [61] that the term

---

[58] *Op. cit.*, p. 214.

[59] Lohmeyer, *Das Evangelium des Markus*, p. 27.

[60] This, of course, is not Mark's doing, since he hands down the tradition transmitted to him without perceptible alteration. His work may be
simply the arrangement.

[61] The other passages in Mark's Gospel which report of Jesus' sojourn
in the wilderness (or in a desert place) yield nothing for our investigation. Schmauch also regards them as largely references to place.

was transferred to Jesus. In the content of the word ἔρημος there is no gulf between Jesus and the Baptist—but there is a gulf between Mark and his successors. For the oldest evangelist there is no great difference between Jesus and the Baptist at this point. Since what is decisive for both is bound up with the wilderness,[62] they are once more intimately related. By their alteration of the Markan exemplar, it is clear that Mark's co-evangelists are of another view.

We glance first of all at *Matthew*. The way in which he appropriates and reshapes the Old Testament prophecy already indicates the degree to which he moves beyond Mark. The compound quotation in Mark 1:2-3 takes on a totally different character in Matt. 3:1-2. It is no longer a backward directed prophecy, or at least is no longer recognizable as such. It is rather a corroborative prophecy.[63] It no longer belongs, as for Mark, within the gospel, but precedes it. Since what the prophet foretold has taken place, what has occurred is demonstrated to be the fulfillment of the promise. There is much more reflection involved here.[64] This is generally true of the way in which Matthew *uses* his Old Testament proof texts. He *finds* them (to the extent he has no available models)

[62] We can also indicate Old Testament parallels to Jesus' wilderness sojourn. In the wilderness Moses and Elijah prepared for their work. In both instances (1:4 and 1:12) specific features point to the Old Testament, though they penetrated the Gospel in quite different ways. But now when we examine Mark's point of view, there is no correspondence between the wilderness in connection with the Baptist (1:4) and the wilderness in the context of Jesus' ministry (1:12). The latter no longer has such decisive significance for our evangelist. Another "geographical" term occupies the foreground—Galilee. More about this in the next study.

[63] The reflection presented above can be called "inorganic" (Wendling, *Die Entstehung des Marcus-Evangeliums*, Tübingen: J. C. B. Mohr, 1908, p. 2) only if the goal of Mark's composition is missed and Matthew's method of quoting is made normative for Mark.

[64] The deletion of Mark 1:2b also arises from such reflection. There is no quotation from Isaiah here. For the rest, the same motive is present in the Koine family, which corrects Mark 1:2 to read: ἐν τοῖς προφήταις.

much as Mark did, and, of course, by moving back into the Old Testament from the event to be corroborated. But he proceeds a step beyond Mark by constructing a temporal sequence. For Mark it is as if the event itself proclaims; for Matthew the proclamation lies in the Old Testament, in the prophecy qualifying the New Testament event. This means that Matthew is concerned with the factuality of the report.[65] This is indicated by 4:14-16, where Galilee loses the meaning it has in Mark 1:14 and becomes the actual place of Jesus' appearance.[66]

Another phrase in Matt. 4:12 points in the same direction. The evangelist smooths out the seam before Mark 1:14 with the introductory remark ἀκούσας δὲ. . . . The eschatological content of the παραδοθῆναι is changed to one which at least can *also* be construed temporally. Strictly speaking, Mark's description of the Baptist's arrest as a "delivering up" is a statement of faith. For Matthew it becomes an event which can be "heard." For him, the Baptist's arrest, understood as a point in time, becomes the motivation for Jesus' public appearance.[67] The complexes in Mark, topically connected and intended to express "theological sequence," now take on a temporal sequence, for only ἀπὸ τότε ἤρξατο ὁ Ἰησοῦς κηρύσσειν (4:17).

But when the Baptist is described after the style of Matthew, i.e., as preceding Jesus in time, then it follows that he must also be described as materially distinct from Jesus. The ἄφεσις

[65] This has to do with Matthew's penchant for creating speech complexes. Mark does not need to create such complexes, since for him the event itself does the speaking. In Matthew, however, event and speech are differentiated. What is decisive is the (proclaiming) speech. If the event is to be qualified, it requires proof that it fulfills Old Testament prophecy.

[66] Details on this in the following study.

[67] Schmidt's observation (*Rahmen*, p. 35) must be improved upon along these lines.

ἁμαρτιῶν (Mark 1:4) is deleted. It does not apply to the forerunner, but only to the Christ.[68]

Another feature is seen in Matthew's reshaping of the phrase ἐν δὲ ταῖς ἡμέραις ἐκείναις. In Mark (1:9) this phrase connects Jesus' appearing for baptism with the Baptist's sojourn at the Jordan. The connection is quite "natural," but in Matthew it is moved up to 3:1 so as to connect the prehistory with the Baptist, though vaguely. If Mark establishes a material connection between the prehistory and Jesus, the phrase in Matthew reflects his concern for the temporal by furnishing a prehistory to be construed temporally. Matthew's genealogy which sets up a connection with the patriarchal period is especially typical. There is no longer an ἀρχή in the Markan sense; only a genealogy beginning with Abraham. Finally, Mark writes an εὐαγγέλιον and Matthew a βίβλος. It will be our task later to show that this is typical.[69]

The alteration of Mark's point of view is almost more clearly visible in *Luke*. The essential points in evidence have already been gathered by Conzelmann.[70] Only a few characteristic traits will be noted here.

In Luke, much more emphatically than in Matthew, the historicizing element plays a dominant role.[71] This does not mean that Luke was better informed regarding the actual event. Rather, he uses his historicizing description to convey a theo-

[68] Klostermann, *Das Matthäusevangelium, Handbuch zum Neuen Testament,* herausgegeben von Hans Lietzmann *et al.,* 2te Auflage (Tübingen: J. C. B. Mohr, 1927), *ad loc.* Yet we should note the identical content of the Baptist's (Matt. 3:2) and Jesus' preaching. But this preaching does not qualify the preacher. It aims merely to express the fact that "John and Jesus pursue the same goal" (Dibelius, *Die urchristliche Überlieferung von Johannes dem Täufer,* p. 49).

[69] Cf. below in study 3.

[70] *The Theology of St. Luke,* pp. 18-27.

[71] Of course, the fact that Matthew already reveals this tendency does not appear in Conzelmann in just this way. We shall see that it is this Gospel which occupies a unique position between Mark and Luke. This should not lead us to assume an intermediate stage, say, in terms of Luke's literary dependence on Matthew.

logical, i.e., *heilsgeschichtlich* point of view. The Baptist is clearly contrasted with Jesus. With Jesus' public appearance, indeed already at his baptism, John's history is concluded. The sequence Mark furnishes is corrected. Between the Baptist's preaching and Jesus' baptism Luke inserts the brief report in 3:19-20. The result is the anachronism according to which the baptism follows the arrest. Luke helps himself out of the difficulty by omitting to mention the Baptist in connection with the baptism, in contrast to Mark 1:9 (and Matt. 3:13). The significance of the Baptist for Jesus' baptism is eliminated.[72]

Luke's historicizing description is his way of making a (first of all, negative) theological statement. The eschatological significance of the Baptist in Mark is omitted. He is only a prophet and no longer, as in Mark, belongs to the gospel. Thus (with the exception of the prehistory)[73] Luke no longer recognizes any typological correspondence between John and Jesus.[74] He achieves his portrait of the Baptist by "transforming" Mark's eschatological utterances "into objective history."[75] John's significance lies at a distinct point of salvation history, i.e., immediately prior to the "center of history." He himself does not belong to the βασιλεία; he *precedes* it.[76]

---

[72] Thus according to Dibelius, *Die urchristliche Überlieferung von Johannes dem Täufer*, p. 60, and Conzelmann, *op. cit.*, p. 21. It is an error to compare Luke with Matthew at this point and assert that his description of the baptism is "totally unbiased" (contra J. Weiss, *Die Schriften des Neuen Testaments*, I, on Mark 1:9; *Das älteste Evangelium*, p. 123).

[73] This is a special problem which we cannot enter into here. Morgenthaler, via word statistics, has recently contested Conzelmann's thesis in "Statistische Beobachtungen am Wortschatz des Neuen Testaments," *Theologische Zeitschrift*, XI (1955), 97 ff.; cf. 110 ff.

[74] Conzelmann, *The Theology of St. Luke*, p. 24.

[75] *Ibid.*, p. 26, n. 3 [our translation]. The μετὰ τὸ παραδοθῆναι (Mark 1:14) is not taken over in Luke 4:14.

[76] Cf. Luke 16:16 with Matt. 11:12-13. Conzelmann, *op. cit.*, pp. 23-24. One passage should be given attention here. Lohmeyer (*Das Evangelium des Markus, ad loc.*) observes that the note in Mark 1:5 ("*all* the country of Judea, and *all* the people of Jerusalem" went out to John), viewed historically, is an exaggeration. He then points to its eschatological sig-

C. Summary

Naturally, no "result" can be constructed on the meager basis examined till now. But a few points should be noted which we must attend to later.

Mark's greatest consolidation appears at the beginning of his Gospel. This is also true in regard to the transmission of the individual material. Mark's achievement lies not only in collecting pieces from his sources and combining them by adding material of his own, but rather in connecting them from a topical viewpoint. This means that a unity emerges despite the diversity of material. "Pre-history" and "forerunner" enter the gospel.

Later on, these connecting devices are loosened. Geographical and temporal data as well as sequence are no longer viewed within this topical-theological consolidation. The shift of emphasis to the "original literal sense" gives rise to the notion of temporal sequence and of geographical reference. Mark's theological statements completely recede or are greatly modified.

So Mark's very consolidation provides the occasion for the later evangelists' alteration, since it always makes possible the elimination of a motif. The process of dissolution is facilitated by the fact that the later evangelists possess material which did not undergo consolidation.

Basically, very little manipulation is required to undo Mark's arrangement, or at least to dismantle or unravel it.

---

nificance, since Isa. 48:20 and 52:11 speak of the necessity of such a journey. Luke changes it to objective history. To be sure, he emphasizes that "all" were baptized (3:21), but also that the leaders refused baptism (7:28-30). Certain inconsistencies result which Conzelmann notes (*op. cit.*, pp. 20-21). In any case, this view may not be countered with the argument that neither Mark's, Matthew's, nor Luke's point of view is always consistent. The tradition shines more clearly through the major Gospels than through the oldest Gospel. But then the peculiar intent of the evangelists stands out all the more clearly.

Bultmann has established that Mark was not yet master of his material.[77] Measured against John, this is undoubtedly true. And yet we may not ignore the fact that Mark does not simply collect. On the other hand, his slight reworking of the material facilitates later reconstruction. The material can be taken over almost without alteration; it requires only to be reshaped and combined afresh in the redaction. The outline still shines through. A comparison of the synoptic materials is a relatively simple task, as the fact of synopsis itself indicates. Nevertheless, when dealing with the evangelists we deal with men whose points of view are more disparate than a superficial comparison leads us to suppose.

[77] *History*, p. 350.

Study Two | The Geographical Outline

The observations made above in connection with the wilderness concept suggest a closer examination of the geographical data in Mark. Ours will certainly not be the first such examination. We are dealing here with one of the oldest problems posed by the Gospels. It was an all but inevitable result of the difference in synoptic and Johannine outlines. The problem (greatly oversimplified) may first of all be reduced to this formula: How often was Jesus in Jerusalem during his public ministry? From this, all things being equal, the length of his ministry might be calculated.[1]

In its earliest stage, form history thoroughly dismantled the framework of the Synoptic Gospels. Redaction and tradition were separated. If the results are correct—and, allowing for corrections in the matter of detail, we will not dispute them—the consequence must be an abandonment of the *old* historical inquiry after the course of Jesus' life.[2] There are two possible explanations for Mark's geographical framework. One is that he constructs it for historical purposes but cannot achieve his goal, due to his ignorance of the territory or to the incomplete-

[1] Schmidt (*Rahmen*, pp. 1 ff.) records the controversies and attempts at solution up to the beginning of form-historical research.

[2] From this standpoint, it is not easy to see how such a book as K. Buchheim's *Das messianische Reich* (München: Hegner-bücherei im Kösel Verlag, 1948) could be written.

ness of his materials.[3] In that case, the historical question is disposed of, since it led to the result that Mark was in error.[4] The other explanation is that with his outline Mark has in mind a purpose other than the historical and uses the geographical data to express it. But then we must put the question in another way, since we can get an answer to our question only if the object of our inquiry at least implies it. The proper question is not the one which happens to interest us, but the one to which the person or thing interrogated aims to give the answer. Right here, this means that it is Mark who decides how the question ought to be put. But it is to be gleaned from the framework, from the redaction.

Lohmeyer has given atention to this problem area. In *Galiläa und Jerusalem,* he examines the references to place in Mark's framework (and in the individual pieces of the tradition). On this basis he attempts to draw inferences as to the situation (from a form-historical standpoint we could say, as to the geographical-theological sociology) of the primitive community. His commentary on Mark [5] contains the assertion that *"the second Gospel scarcely notes one biographical detail which does not have theological significance."* [6]

[3] From the standpoint of method, Riesenfeld's notion that he can extract from Acts 10:37-39 and 13:31 a possibly "original basic feature of the life of Jesus" would be open to serious question (Riesenfeld, *op. cit.,* pp. 159-60). The "schema" (so also Riesenfeld!) Galilee-Jerusalem which we encounter here must first of all be examined as to its source. The essays, e.g., by Dibelius (*Studies in the Acts of the Apostles,* trans. Heinrich Greeven [London: SCM Press, 1956]) and Conzelmann seek to make clear the part played by the author of Acts. We have a rather good grasp of his point of view here. But it is a point of view which harks back to Mark's (though greatly modified).

[4] Naturally, where *isolated* pieces of the tradition are concerned, we can continue to look for place designations. But where the framework is concerned, this method leads us no further.

[5] Lohmeyer, *Das Evangelium des Markus,* p. 162 (on 8:27).

[6] Martin Kähler had gone still further: "Every detail of the apostolic recollection of Jesus can be shown to have been preserved for the sake of its religious significance" (*The So-called Historical Jesus . . . ,* p. 93).

This attempt seems fruitful for our inquiry. Still, we must distinguish, perhaps even more sharply than Lohmeyer, the traditional material from the work of the evangelist himself.[7] The references to place in the first group are the concern of form history and those in the second of redaction history. Moreover, it is possible that the tradition influenced the framework and, conversely, that the framework led to revision of the tradition. This must be tested in the individual instance, though it will not always be determined with certainty. But then the framework must be taken seriously as *Mark's framework;* the tradition leads back to an earlier period.

In Mark's framework two epochs are differentiated: the beginning in Galilee and the end in Jerusalem. It is difficult to make a clear distinction. Perhaps it is best to take chapters 1–9 as the first and 11–16 as the second complex. Chapter 10 would then be a transition. But here details are not yet important. There is every indication that we are dealing with *one journey* from the original site of activity (which clearly involves an extended sojourn) toward the capital city for the passion.

This outline, as we said, was created by Mark. This is true even when he is historically "correct." On the other hand, a series of references within pieces of the tradition indicate the possibility of another outline. These include first of all the oft-discussed passages[8] in 10:46-47; 11:2-3; 14:3; 14:13 ff.; 14:49; 15:43. Somehow they all betray the idea that Jesus had already been in or about Jerusalem since he had acquaintances there or they describe him as familiar with the locale. Even the traditional material appropriated by the major evangelists indicates this.[9] But this means that if Mark had followed the

[7] This is also true of R. H. Lightfoot's monograph, *Locality and Doctrine in the Gospels* (New York: Harper & Bros., 1938).

[8] Schmidt, *Rahmen*, pp. 301-2; Lohmeyer, *Galiläa und Jerusalem*, p. 28; Lightfoot, *op. cit.*, pp. 125-26, and the commentaries on these passages, esp. Lohmeyer, *Das Evangelium des Markus.*

[9] Matt. 23:37-39 and parallels. Cf. Schmidt, *Rahmen*, pp. 271 ff.; Dibelius, *Jesus*, trans. C. Hedrich and F. C. Grant (Philadelphia: The Westminster Press, 1949), pp. 62-63; and perhaps also Luke 19:44.

material available to him it would have been quite possible for him to construct another outline, one similar perhaps to the Fourth Gospel.

This is underscored by the fact that more than half the passages cited occur in the context of the Markan passion narrative already compiled before Mark's time.[10] If he expands this narrative in backward direction, then—without contradicting it; quite the reverse, by actually taking up its starting point— he could have allowed Jesus' path to lead him repeatedly toward or in the vicinity of Jerusalem. Thus when Mark creates the "Galilean epoch" and prefixes it to the passion narrative, a certain inconsistency results.

This leads us to inquire into the reasons for such a procedure. Our first study suggests one explanation. There we saw that Mark prefixed the John complex to the Jesus complex, but he connects the two complexes topically and without regard to temporal sequence. Could topical considerations be determinative here also? No opinion should be expressed before the passages concerned are examined. The chief object of our concern is the place-name which has given this complex its title—Galilee.

A. Analysis and Findings in Mark

1. Galilee Prior to the "Journey Report"

In the old tradition, Jesus and Nazareth are connected. In Mark the connection is always adjectival: Ναζαρηνός (1:24; 16:6), a usage heightened in 14:67 where Jesus appears as *the* Nazarene absolutely. All these passages contain references which more precisely define men of the same name. Mark

[10] This does not mean that here Mark made no alterations, additions, etc. On this subject, cf. below. In addition, cf. Sundwall, *op. cit.*, pp. 78 ff., who combines commentaries and individual studies.

found them in the tradition.[11] The situation is different in 1:9. Here ἀπὸ Ναζαρέθ is not added to the name but is to be joined to the verb.[12] Jesus proceeds from his home city, described as situated in Galilee. It is uncertain whether this verse is to be credited to the evangelist (Lohmeyer[13] thinks it probable but K. L. Schmidt[14] does not). At any rate, the redactor's hand must be seen at least in the connection.[15] Most probably, the piece of the tradition at Mark's disposal merely reported that Jesus (or Jesus Ναζαρηνός) came to John to be baptized. From this Mark then created the point of departure—Nazareth in Galilee. Not only Jesus' ministry began there (1:14); he also came from there. This is most likely true historically, but it is unimportant in our context. It is much more important to note that at the very first mention of Jesus' name (apart from 1:1), the evangelist also refers to Galilee.[16]

The next passage is 1:14. This verse is certainly redactional.[17] The fact that it describes for the first and only time the "content" of Jesus' preaching underscores the significance which this verse has for the evangelist. Jesus' preaching occurs in Galilee. Viewed geographically, this datum is quite "inexact," since it does not explain but only raises the question, Where? That we must still inquire after the locale despite the reference indicates that Mark's concern lies elsewhere.[18] When we add to this the fact that 1:16 reports the disciples' calling by

---

[11] Instead of this term Matthew has Ναζωραῖος, which could be due to the formula quotation in 2:23. Luke is not uniform.

[12] Klostermann, *Das Markusevangelium, ad loc.*, contra Lohmeyer, *Das Evangelium des Markus, ad loc.*

[13] *Galiläa und Jerusalem*, p. 26, n. 2.

[14] *Rahmen*, p. 29.

[15] Bultmann, *History*, p. 339; Sundwall, *op. cit.*, p. 7.

[16] Matthew did not at all omit the ἀπὸ Ναζαρέθ here but moved it up to 2:23.

[17] Whether with Sundwall (*op. cit.*, p. 8) we can reconstruct a pre-Markan torso seems most unlikely.

[18] Cf. below on 1:39.

the Sea of Galilee, Galilee[19]—or actually the entire reference[20]—being obviously the evangelist's own creation,[21] a first,
preliminary impression results.

We turn for a moment to what was reported of the Baptist
at the beginning of the Gospel. Now we see a correspondence
which supplements Mark's earlier description of the Baptist.
John appeared—in the wilderness (1:4); Jesus comes—to
Galilee. The preaching of both is summarized in one short
phrase (1:7; 1:15).[22] *i.e. "wilderness" + "Galilee"*

Both place-names are redactional, inserted into an already
existing context. Does this not suggest that Galilee, just as the
wilderness, has some kind of theological significance? The
wilderness (since it was foretold in the Old Testament) is
the "place" of the Baptist. Galilee is Jesus' "place." He comes
from Galilee; his preaching takes place in Galilee; he calls
his first disciples in Galilee. But now we must ask, Why in
Galilee? We can of course reply: Because that is the way it
was. And, in the main, that answer will very likely be correct.
But this was also true of the Baptist (cf. 1:6); yet in his case
it did not suffice to explain the term ἔρημος in 1:4. Is there
behind the term "Galilee" more than meets the eye? Lohmeyer
thinks Jesus "made Galilee the home of his gospel and his
community."[23] It is probably correct that this is the *purpose*
Mark's description aims to pursue. But what induces the *evan-*

[19] Schmidt, *Rahmen*, p. 43.

[20] Lohmeyer, *Das Evangelium des Markus, ad loc.*

[21] Again, we will not discuss whether the call is chronologically in the
"proper" place, a notion which Lohmeyer disputes (*Galiläa und Jerusalem*, p. 29) and which cannot be proved from the outline. What is
certain is merely that Mark inserts an isolated piece here, thus intending
to bring up the matter of the call. When Luke delays his report of the
calling of the disciples (5:1 ff.), he clearly betrays his concern to achieve
a lucid, chronological sequence. So Luke is much further on the way to a
vita Jesu than Mark, who—this time we can put it negatively—does not
have a chronological but a topical, i.e., theological, principle of arrangement.

[22] Cf. Lohmeyer, *Das Evangelium des Markus*, p. 29.

[23] *Galiläa und Jerusalem*, p. 30.

gelist to fix this area so categorically? Where can we find a reason for this?

At this juncture no final answer can be given. But we may at least make a conjecture, which results from the analogy between the redactional work done here and that done in connection with the Baptist. In 1:4 the wilderness tradition has been appended to the Baptist tradition without detriment to (probable) historical accuracy. If this is correspondingly true of Galilee, perhaps Lohmeyer's statement could be reversed. That is, *Galilee* becomes the place of Jesus' activity because *it has special significance for Mark;* it plays a special role. We will have to keep this in mind.

The Galilee passages noted till now are carried forward and supplemented in 1:28. Again, the reference to place is redactional [24]—but, surprisingly enough, only this reference.[25] To the teaching in the Capernaum synagogue, resulting in the astonishment of all (1:22) Mark adds the healing narrative which—by itself without reference to place—he now localizes in the synagogue. In 1:27-28 the evangelist then found a final choral statement expressing this astonishment and subsequently reporting the spread of this miraculous event παν-ταχοῦ.[26] Of course, the aim here is to emphasize that Jesus' fame spreads to the widest possible area. But when Mark supplements this with the datum "Galilee," the result is precisely

---

[24] Klostermann, *Das Markusevangelium, ad loc.*; Sundwall, *op. cit.*, p. 9; similarly J. Weiss, *Die Schriften des Neuen Testaments*, I, *ad loc.*; cf. also Wohlenberg, *op. cit., ad loc.* Contrariwise, Schmidt, *Rahmen,* p. 51.

[25] Cf. Lohmeyer, *Das Evangelium des Markus,* p. 38, n. 4.

[26] Both features also appear singly. A glance, e.g., at Luke 4:14*b* is instructive. Mark's source for vs. 28 might have looked something like it. Also in the parallel to this verse (Luke 4:37) Galilee is lacking. This is probably an intentional abbreviation resulting from Luke's point of view. Indeed, in the first period he allows Jesus to appear in Galilee, but "in contrast to Mark, Jesus' ministry covers the whole of Jewish territory, and is all the more rigidly restricted to this" (Conzelmann, *op. cit.,* p. 41).

that of a limitation. It was taken to be such by copyists and gave rise to corrections.

The section 1:35-38 cannot be analyzed unequivocally. Because of the various linguistic peculiarities, it is best understood as a piece of tradition handed down to the evangelist [27] by which he concludes the "day" in Capernaum.[28] Verse 1:39 is then a summary report originating with Mark.[29] Just such a combination is typical of Mark. In 1:38 Jesus' task was described simply as κηρύσσειν. This is taken up in the first half of vs. 39. Then follows Mark's characteristic emphasis on Jesus' activity as exorcism.[30] The report is a bit awkward, since not every healing occurs in a synagogue.

This redactional note contradicts what precedes and follows. Jesus has just left Capernaum (1:35) to preach in the synagogues throughout all Galilee (that is why he "came out," 1:38) and to expel the demons. We expect the report of his activity "throughout all Galilee." But after the healing of

---

[27] Lohmeyer, Das Evangelium des Markus, ad loc.; thus, though for another reason, Sundwall, op. cit., p. 10.

[28] Moreover, that "day" is a very puzzling factor, esp. when we consider that the Jewish day begins at evening. It is also hard to see how everything should have occurred on the Sabbath (1:21). But where is there really any talk of a "day"? It can be inferred only from 1:32 in connection with 1:35. If we wish to retain the expression, then we should not be concerned with proximity in time and on that basis attempt hazardous constructions. (Wohlenberg, op. cit., p. 63, assigns Peter's fishing expedition in 1:16 ff. to a Friday!) What is involved is merely a combining of various traditional pieces from a topical interest. More recently, J. Schmid offers another opinion in "Markus und der aramäische Matthäus," Synoptische Studien: Alfred Wikenhauser zum 70. Geburtstag (München: K. Zink, 1953), p. 157. If, moreover, the triadic scheme developed by Lohmeyer in his commentary holds true, then this too indicates that the evangelist is obviously not thinking of one "day," since it ends at 1:31. For this reason, Albertz, whose division is similar to Lohmeyer's, actually concludes for two days: a Sabbath (1:21-31), followed by a weekday (1:32-45). M. Albertz, Botschaft des Neuen Testaments (Zollikon-Zürich: Evangelischer Verlag, 1947), I, 1, 191.

[29] Schmidt, Rahmen, p. 59; Sundwall, op. cit., p. 10; Lohmeyer, Das Evangelium des Markus, ad loc.

[30] Cf. Klostermann, Das Markusevangelium, ad loc.

the leper (1:40-45) Jesus returns to Capernaum (2:1).
Though Mark clearly has no interest in the names of cities
and though almost all references to place (except for Galilee)
are already anchored in the tradition,[31] he is concerned with
Galilee! As soon as Jesus leaves Capernaum, he moves (according to Mark) in or toward Galilee.

Again a very marked impression results. The obvious intent
of vs. 38 is to open wide the door for Jesus' ministry; yet in
vs. 39 *Mark* again sets limits. Jesus comes from Galilee (1:9);
there he begins his public ministry (1:14) and calls his disciples (1:16); in Galilee Jesus' fame spreads throughout all
the surrounding region (1:28), though he himself does not
go there, for men must come to Galilee to hear him (3:7).
Jesus works in one city of Galilee—Capernaum. But if he
leaves it to go ἀλλαχοῦ (1:38), then his journey proceeds
throughout all Galilee (1:39). After 1:14, but also after 1:28,
this is an intensification,[32] whose motif Mark quite appropriately derives from his sources. But now we must add that
despite the range which 1:39 intends to express, Jesus' ministry
takes place *only* in Galilee. We get the impression that Mark
is anxious not to allow Jesus (at least not yet) to go beyond
Galilee, and yet takes pains to describe *all* Galilee as the area
of his activity.

From this angle, light is again shed on 1:14. If we do not
inquire into the precise location or into the time in terms of
an *initial* preaching, this summary takes on fundamental significance. *This decisive preaching always occurs in Galilee.*

Further, 3:7-8 is particularly informative. Here we encounter
a summary report which was certainly first compiled by the

---

[31] In 2:1 the redactional work cannot be clearly distinguished from the
tradition (Bultmann, *History*, p. 341). As Schmidt (*Rahmen*, p. 78)
states, probably only the πάλιν and perhaps also the δι' ἡμερῶν are Mark's
own. But the reference to place is anchored in the narrative.

[32] Coming after 1:28, since Jesus now expands the radius of his
ministry and in a certain sense follows his *fame.*

evangelist.[33] The punctuation of this passage, however, is unclear and has given rise to many a correction. Precise definition of Mark's materials also poses problems.

Jesus' withdrawal together with his disciples (vs. 7a) must be understood as concluding the previous pericope (vs. 6).[34] In the tradition was this already a withdrawal to the sea? Then the sea would denote a solitary region.[35] But it is more appropriate to attribute the reference to the evangelist who is setting the scene here for vs. 9. Mark's source did not record that people accompanied Jesus on this flight. So we may assume that the Sea (naturally, of Galilee; cf. 1:16 and later 7:31) and the great multitude from Galilee are to be assigned to the redaction.

Thus a foundation is laid from the original conclusion for a new beginning.[36] Added to Galilee from which a multitude *follows* Jesus on his withdrawal, there is a rather long list of places from which people *come to Jesus at the Sea*—Judea, Jerusalem, Idumea, beyond the Jordan, and about Tyre and Sidon.

Of course, the purpose of this list could have been to demonstrate Jesus' success.[37] Yet nothing is actually said of that. Rather, these people are witnesses. They witness to what for Mark lies at the heart of the gospel—the expulsion of spirits who cry out *the* confession, "You are the Son of God." [38]

[33] J. Weiss, *Die Schriften des Neuen Testaments*, I, ad loc.; Schmidt, *Rahmen*, p. 105.

[34] Schmidt, *Rahmen*, p. 107; Klostermann, *Das Markusevangelium*, ad loc.

[35] We meet this idea elsewhere in the tradition; cf. Mark 4:35 ff. and 6:30 ff.

[36] In what follows the evangelist practically overlooks the reason for the withdrawal. So he evidently puts no value whatsoever on this feature in 3:1-6.

[37] Thus J. Weiss, *Die Schriften des Neuen Testaments*, I, ad loc.; Schmidt, *Rahmen*, p. 106.

[38] The entire section 3:7-12 appears to be a summary composition of the evangelist, which prepares for the calling of the twelve (vss. 13-19).

But how does Mark arrive at this combination? He has made a point of limiting Jesus' "fame" to Galilee (1:28). In light of everything we have observed till now, it cannot possibly be the evangelist's view that Jesus "worked in all these areas," as K. L. Schmidt supposes.[39] So he must have a specific purpose for listing the names "which represent all the Jewish people."[40] This suggests that in Mark's day Christians were living in all these places or in all these regions.[41]

From this standpoint, the summary report takes on primary importance. These Christians have a meeting place—the Sea of Galilee. And, indeed, *Mark* lets them assemble there. Among the communities Galilee enjoys first place. With Lohmeyer we can call this passage "paradigmatic," "binding on believing Christendom."[42] But this statement must be improved upon so as to apply *to Mark's time*.

This carries what has been established till now one decisive step further. We must now ask whether "Galilee" played any role at all in the Jesus tradition available to Mark. *Places* in and around Galilee are named. But it is clearly Mark who first gives the name of the territory itself. For him Galilee is the place of Jesus' activity. This apparently coincides with the fact that Galilee, or the Sea of Galilee, has special significance for the primitive community of Mark's day. Hence, not only Jesus' activity is concentrated in this area; the communities as well are directed here; indeed, they come here.

Till now the reason for this is not clear. Still, we can take up the thread left lying earlier and carry our hypothesis a bit further, since we have uncovered a motive for Mark's redactional work. It is conceivable that, for some reason still to be

[39] *Rahmen*, p. 106. Where is there any hint of that for Idumea? The other data are at least secured in the tradition.

[40] Lohmeyer, *Das Evangelium des Markus*, p. 71.

[41] *Ibid.*, p. 72; Conzelmann, *op. cit.*, p. 35. It is noteworthy that Galilee is lacking in Luke 6:17. Does this indicate an anti-Galilean tendency? Cf. further below.

[42] Lohmeyer, *Das Evangelium des Markus*, p. 71.

ascertained, the primitive community was directed to Galilee and assembled there. That Galilee should serve as this meeting place *may* correspond with the fact that Jesus' home was there and that reminiscences of it were carefully preserved. But for Mark the situation is such that this orientation is already present or is just being completed. So the historical question at best provides only an indirect motive for his presentation. On the other hand, the real stimulus is a community situation prevailing in his time. This situation furnishes the evangelist his occasion for focusing in paradigmatic fashion upon Jesus' ministry in Galilee.

We could formulate our observation in this way: The past is viewed and shaped from the standpoint of the present. This statement is correct to a degree but does not quite touch the heart of the matter. The "framework" (Galilee) has present significance, but may not covertly be made a thing of the past. Its task is rather to traject into the present the material, the tradition, which has the past as its content. The interpretation of a piece of literature must begin with the latest stratum which brings the reworked material up to date. This is true of the growth of traditional material within the Synoptic Gospels. Supplementation and redaction "stretch" into the present.[43]

This, of course, may not be construed to mean that what is reported is taking place right now. But it is narrated or reported not for the sake of the past which speaks out of the tradition, but for the sake of Mark's own time. In other words, Mark does not write from a biographical interest, but because these stories have something to say to the present and are proclaimed in the present. There is a kerygmatic interest here.

What was said earlier in connection with 1:14-15, viz., that this preaching "always" occurs in Galilee, can now be put more precisely. This summary preaching appears at the begin-

[43] I have tried to indicate this for Mark 4 in Marxsen, *op. cit.*, pp. 263 ff.

ning as a paradigm. The examples the evangelist takes from the tradition indicate the kind of preaching carried on in Galilee in his own time. To a degree, 1:14-15 titles whatever individual preaching is to follow; indeed, as we will see, it summarizes the entire gospel.

Finally, Galilee itself has this summarizing significance. Just as many isolated pieces point to local tradition, so there is a local tradition in Mark's Gospel as a whole. It is the "Galilean Gospel." This gives rise to an important question which can only be thrown open here: Does not this local tradition really point to the place of the Gospel's origin? Must we not at least put a question mark after the old churchly tradition which allows that the Gospel was written in Rome? [44]

2. The Geographical Data of the "Journey into Gentile Territory"

We can now ask whether the evangelist is consistent in his orientation to Galilee. It is clear, of course, that the Gospel's conclusion with Jerusalem as its midpoint forms an exception. The passion narrative is firmly localized in the tradition. Yet, as we shall see, the Jerusalem "epoch" does not entirely demolish the evangelist's point of view. We can also see that the passion narrative in turn drew to itself various traditions and thus already tended to grow in a backward direction. Verses 10:46 ff., e.g., would be characteristic of that. The sources cannot be clearly marked off there.

But even in the Galilean "epoch," thus in the complex preceding the passion narrative, report is made of Jesus' sojourns and activities outside Galilee. Mark's Gospel is often divided into three periods: Galilee/Journey/Jerusalem. We no longer

[44] The oft-named Latinisms in Mark's Gospel have scarcely any significance here, since they are a part of the tradition, not the redaction. The Hellenistic and Jewish elements in the isolated pieces give just as little indication of the place of composition. If such information is to be had, only the redaction can supply it.

need to prove that the middle section lacks a coherent itinerary. There is not even any sharp delineation. This fact gives rise to the question as to whether Mark really intended to depict a journey.

Briefly pursuing the individual references, Mark locates Jesus' only extended discourse (in addition to chap. 13) at the Sea (4:1-2). Here 3:7-8 is taken up again.[45] In 4:35 ff., the boat introduced in 3:9 is used for the journey to the other side. The stilling of the storm recorded here naturally requires the Sea as its scene of action, but the Sea reappears as the place of terror. In 5:1 Jesus and his disciples are on the other side of the Sea. Again, the tradition furnishes the story of the expulsion of the spirits into the swineherd with its locale. Verse 20 in chap. 5 is interesting. Does the reference to the Decapolis originate with the evangelist? A stylistically appropriate conclusion (cf. 1:28; 1:45) would report merely that Jesus preached in the surrounding region. That is still true here. But whether from the tradition or by Mark himself, a feature is inserted here which largely coincides with the localization at the Sea. Lohmeyer indicates that subsequently "the Decapolis and Galilee, previously separate territories, were the single home of the Jewish-Christian community." [46] But this means that the reference can be explained from the evangelist's own time, which in turn indicates that "Galilee" is not to be taken strictly as the area west of the Sea, but as including the territory around the Sea.[47]

Verses 5:21 ff. again have their setting on the other side and 6:1 ff. have their setting in "his own country." These localiza-

[45] Cf. Marxsen, *op. cit.*, p. 262.

[46] Lohmeyer, *Das Evangelium des Markus*, p. 99.

[47] Verse 3:8 already reported that, among others, men from "beyond the Jordan" came to Jesus. Taking that report in isolation, it is only now that Jesus' fame spreads there. But we may not inquire in such fashion. There is no real sequence here. For Mark these events are simultaneous and take place in his own time: The word is being preached in the Decapolis, and the communities are assembling by the Sea.

tions (6:4) are probably firmly fixed in the tradition. For some time no references to place appear. In 6:30 ff. the apostles rest in a lonely place which must be reached by boat. Again we may ask whether the tradition construes the Sea as a "lonely place" whereas Mark views it as a lively center toward which men soon run from all sides (6:33).

After the first feeding, Jesus makes his disciples get into the boat in order to go before him to Bethsaida (6:45). Contrariwise, they land at Gennesaret (6:53). It is hard to see Mark's hand in the geographical note of 6:45 since here he has obviously pieced together two originally independent stories (6:45-52).[48] We glance ahead at 8:22 which records the arrival in Bethsaida which we had expected back in 6:53.[49] Did Mark insert the reference to Bethsaida in 8:22? If we take vs. 22a as the introduction to the following pericope,[50] we could make such an assumption, especially since the name of the city contradicts the reference to the village which follows. But it is questionable whether we may urge this kind of argument here. What reason could the evangelist possibly have had for introducing the name? We cannot infer from 8:22b-26 that in the tradition at Mark's disposal this piece must have dealt with a healing in Gentile territory[51] and that for this reason he added Bethsaida here. Another explanation is more to the point. When we note that the journey after the first feeding has Bethsaida as its goal (6:45), we then discover the conclusion to the dual account of the feeding. Verse 8:22a is thus still a part of 8:21. To this extent, the tradition contains a broad parallel. The feedings included the tradition of a voyage to

[48] Bultmann, *History*, p. 216; Sundwall, *op. cit.*, pp. 40-41; a good analysis in Lohmeyer, *Das Evangelium des Markus, ad loc.*

[49] If not, then we should read "Bethany" here with D and the Old Latin witnesses. But then the problem would be completely confused and could only be solved via such dubious hypotheses as Schmidt refers to (*Rahmen*, pp. 205-6).

[50] Bultmann, *History*, p. 338; Lohmeyer, *Das Evangelium des Markus, ad loc.*

[51] Thus Schmidt, *Rahmen*, p. 207.

Bethsaida, the goal òf the first and the debarkation point of the second voyage. Events on the voyage are variously shaped. We need not decide whether this shaping was done by Mark or by the tradition at his disposal. The reference to place which Mark appropriated was preserved.[52]

Till now the Sea and its environs are not yet abandoned; but now the problem of the journey emerges. We must inquire whether Mark constructed it.[53] In 7:24 Jesus enters the region of Tyre.[54] Though Mark may have shaped vss. 24-25 on his own, the reference belongs to the tradition available to him, as a glance at vs. 26 shows.[55] This also explains the reference to "Tyre" in 7:31. The episode is past. But the other data in this verse are unclear.[56] First of all, it seems as if the pericope of the deaf-mute originally began with vs. 32 and was thus without reference to time or place. Verse 31 would then be Mark's creation. But the verse is too cumbersome for that, quite apart from the geographical difficulty of this "journey." Why this heaping up of references to place which are only a contrived connecting of the two pericopes? This strongly suggests

[52] That might also be true of the data in 6:53 and 8:10. As to Gennesaret (6:53), it has been conjectured that this reference is to prepare for the appearance of Pharisees and scribes from Jerusalem (7:1 ff.), an event hardly conceivable outside Palestine (Schmidt, *Rahmen*, p. 195). But is that the case? Could we not rather assume that the original locale of 7:1 ff. was "Gennesaret," that Mark prefixed this pericope with his own summary report (6:54-56), which he in turn joined to what preceded via the reference taken from 7:1 ff.? Because of the well-known textual difficulties, we can scarcely give an opinion regarding Dalmanutha (8:10).

[53] This is assumed by Lohmeyer, among others (*Das Evangelium des Markus,* p. 144).

[54] The addition of "Sidon" in a series of manuscripts can stem (subsequently) from Matt. 15:21 or be a faulty correction on the basis of Mark 7:31.

[55] So also Bultmann, *History*, pp. 64-65; Schmidt, *Rahmen*, pp. 198-99; Klostermann, *Das Markusevangelium, ad loc.* Lohmeyer (*Das Evangelium des Markus, ad loc.*) is evidently of a different opinion.

[56] This was in turn the cause of various "improvements" on the text, made by copyists first of all but due also to Wellhausen's proposal (*Das Evangelium Marci, ad loc.*) that Saidon, i.e., Bethsaida, should be read here instead of Sidon.

the attempt to divide up the references. We already noted that Tyre forms the conclusion of 7:24-30.[57] In the tradition, Sidon seems closely connected with Tyre (cf. Mark 3:8).[58] And what of the Decapolis? Some have assumed there is a connection here with vss. 32-37.[59] That is indeed obvious. We need only prefix the reference to place with the καί of vs. 32 to see how the piece of tradition once began: (καὶ) ἀνὰ μέσον τῶν ὁρίων Δεκαπόλεως φέρουσιν αὐτῷ κωφόν. . . .

In midst of these references, the Sea of Galilee again appears, but the reference to it is clearly redactional. This gives an interesting insight into the evangelist's method. For the first time he uses a piece of tradition which clearly has Gentile territory as its locale (7:24-30). What follows takes place in (ἀνὰ μέσον) the Decapolis, which at least still borders on the Galilean Sea. Mark now seizes this opportunity to correct his "inconsistency," wends his way back and restores the connection with Galilee. Many an inconsistency remains—first of all, the journey from Tyre northward (without an incident in Sidon), then the reference to the region of the Decapolis as extending to the Sea. But such inconsistencies naturally occur whenever an author elects to combine his own with traditional ideas. Mark puts up with them so as to carry out his point of view regarding Galilee in any event, and even where the tradition obviously resists it.[60]

The final question arises in regard to the datum in 8:27. The fact that opinions are rather diverse here is due largely to the significance of the following pericope which we will not

[57] Bultmann views the entire verse as such a conclusion (*History*, p. 211).

[58] Wellhausen (*Das Evangelium Marci, ad loc.*) thinks it possible we have here a conflation of two different data regarding the scene of the healing of the deaf-mute.

[59] Thus Schmidt, *Rahmen*, p. 201.

[60] In addition, cf. Lohmeyer's remark (*Das Evangelium des Markus*, p. 144) that among the stories told of this "journey" none (except for 7:24-31) need be associated with a sojourn in Gentile territory. They could just as well take place on Palestinian soil.

treat in detail. According to Bultmann, vs. 27a belongs to the preceding section.[61] On the other hand, K. L. Schmidt regards the ἐξῆλθεν as introducing an originally independent pericope which was also geographically fixed.[62] This distinction is only of secondary importance to us, since—whether as conclusion or introduction—our concern is to establish whether or not Mark invented the reference. Both solutions answer this question in the negative.

H. J. Ebeling makes a different evaluation.[63] He believes the datum results from the consistency of the journey route Mark adopted. "In contrast to Jesus' experience among the Jews, the aim is to describe the success of his activity among the Gentiles." [64] Finally, Ebeling refers to Luke and John who indicate how uncertain this reference is.[65]

What of the consistency of the "journey route"? Even Ebeling sees the confusion. The popular division of Jesus' ministry into two areas—Galilee and Gentile territory—runs aground

---

[61] *History*, pp. 64 and 257 ff.; likewise Sundwall, *op. cit.*, p. 54. A certain difficulty arises for Bultmann here, since he regards Mark's pericope as broken off. Matthew, on the other hand, supposedly preserved the original conclusion to the "Easter narrative." If this is true, he must have had access to a complete tradition which he used in lieu of the torso in Mark. But this contains a reference to place which belongs to Matthew's pericope in any event, since he connects his material quite differently than Mark. In Matthew, Caesarea Philippi cannot at all be connected with what precedes. Naturally, there is an explanation for this too, which still allows for Bultmann's thesis: Matthew fused Mark with his own material. But the question can only be solved when Matthew's literary method is examined. [Cf. Bornkamm, Barth and Held, *op. cit.*, pp. 46 ff. Translators' note.]

[62] *Rahmen*, p. 216; cf. also Mundle, "Die Geschichtlichkeit des messianischen Bewusstseins Jesu," *Zeitschrift für neutestamentliche Wissenschaft*, XXI (1922), pp. 307-8.

[63] Ebeling, *op. cit.*, pp. 213-14.

[64] This (popular) contrasting of Jewish and Gentile territory easily ignores how widely Galilee itself was populated by Gentiles in Jesus' time. Cf. Bauer, "Jesus der Galiläer," *Festgabe für Adolf Jülicher zum 70. Geburtstag* (Tübingen: J. C. B. Mohr, 1927), p. 22.

[65] *Op. cit.*, p. 214, n. 1.

on 9:30 (and 9:33) .[66] Therefore, we cannot really insist that the second section (the journey) merges "imperceptibly" with the third (Jerusalem) .[67] From a geographical standpoint, the second section leads back to the first. It would be more correct to say that *all* the epochs set up merge imperceptibly. They are not to be precisely defined and so are hardly intended to be "epochs." Is not the attempt to arrive at these epochs of a piece with the division of Mark à la the outline of Luke? If we wish to speak of a "journey" in Mark, we must immediately add that it leads back *at once to* Galilee, indeed, that in light of 7:31 it ought to be divided into two "journeys." Schniewind's title "Scattered Reports," might be the most appropriate description of the section.[68] We must avoid establishing a geographically oriented arrangement. We are dealing with a "gleaning" of the evangelist, containing pieces which already attracted local traditions.

This is also true of Caesarea Philippi. Contrary to Ebeling's opinion, Luke does not construct a counterargument, for he consistently omits all of Jesus' activity outside Palestine. In general, John goes his own way here. Further, we cannot speak of a "climax in Gentile territory," for the scene in this pericope is quite incidental, since it takes place exclusively within the circle of the disciples.

It is the same here as elsewhere in Mark. The locales which he occasionally furnishes his pericopes derive entirely from his sources.[69] We must note the fact that at a very early stage

[66] The Capernaum reference evidently belongs to the tradition at Mark's disposal. Cf. Schmidt, *Rahmen*, p. 230.

[67] Thus Wellhausen, *Einleitung in die drei ersten Evangelien*, p. 45.

[68] Julius Schniewind, *Das Evangelium nach Markus, Das Neue Testament Deutsch*, herausgegeben von Paul Althaus und Johannes Behm, 5te Auflage (Göttingen: Vandenhoeck & Ruprecht, 1949), on Mark 6:1 ff.

[69] Cf. Schmidt, *loc. cit.* A few characteristic remarks: "That Mark at times localizes his scenes (sometimes to lesser, sometimes to greater degree) and at times does not, indicates that he found these references in the tradition at his disposal" (p. 53). "Topographical notices, which casually appear in the individual narratives, cannot be the invention of the evangelist" (p. 209, n. 1).

local traditions were formed which may be associated with Christian communities in these places. We must also reckon with the probability that the geographical data may be historically reliable. But this is irrelevant to our inquiry.

Galilee, however, is *the* exception! Here we must return to two passages. It is most likely that the "leading men of Galilee" in 6:21 is a note Mark appropriated from the tradition. On the other hand, 9:30 is redactional.[70] The redaction occurs at a significant passage. The first passion prediction is already furnished its locale in 8:27; the same is true of the third (10:32 ff.); only the second is without any reference to place (9:31-32). So only here can Mark provide the locale himself. In Galilee, therefore, Jesus' passion and resurrection are proclaimed.

Now a brief look at the transition to the Jerusalem sojourn. The passion narrative already provided Mark with a locale. We can give no clear-cut answer to the question as to where Mark's source begins. But it can still be shown that it grew in backward direction (and prior to Mark).[71] Three times Jesus comes to Jerusalem before entering the city for Passover (14:17) —in 11:27; 11:15; 11:1 ff. From these references the various "days" are inferred. Prior to this occurs the healing of the blind man (10:46 ff.) which probably in origin, or at least in

[70] Bultmann, *History*, pp. 331-32; Sundwall, *op. cit.*, p. 60; Lohmeyer, *Das Evangelium des Markus, ad loc.*

[71] In dependence on Bousset (*Kyrios Christos, Geschichte des Christusglaubens von den Anfängen des Christentums bis Irenäus*, 3te Auflage [Göttingen: Vandenhoeck & Ruprecht, 1926], p. 34; cf. the first ed. of 1913, p. 43), at least one possibility should be weighed. Mark could have found connected with the passion narrative the passages in 10:46-52 (?); 11:1-11, 18, 19; 12:41-44 (?) and 14:1 ff. (The temple as the locale of 12:41-44 was a part of the traditional piece itself. If the evangelist had access to it as an isolated piece, he could hardly have inserted it anywhere else than here.) To this "beginning" of the passion narrative Mark would then have added a good deal which could have its setting at other places as well.

73

Mark's sources, took place before the gates of Jericho.[72] Even the name of the person healed suggests that the story attracted local tradition. But vs. 46a (the entry into Jericho) could be credited to the evangelist;[73] perhaps also the reference to the disciples (vs. 46b). So the overloading of the verse can be explained from the redactional addition. The passage falls automatically into place.

Much of what precedes is, of course, still open from a geographical standpoint. Besides 10:1 there is no definite datum.[74] It is quite generally recognized that this verse comes from the pen of the evangelist, since the subsequent pieces of the chapter are without reference to place.[75]

But where is Jesus going? To Judea and Perea (beyond the Jordan)? The sequence is striking. Unless we rule out a journey to Judea through Samaria, we should have expected the reverse. So it has been assumed that we are not yet dealing here with a journey to Jerusalem for the feast, but rather with a ministry in both the territories named.[76]

But the passage is disputed from a textual point of view. Most probably, the Western text contained the original. Jesus then comes εἰς τὰ ὅρια τῆς Ἰουδαίας πέραν τοῦ Ἰορδάνου.[77]

---

[72] Cf. Bultmann, *History*, p. 213.

[73] Dibelius, *From Tradition to Gospel*, pp. 52 ff.

[74] Verse 10:32 is not a specific reference. This (redactional) verse is quite generally retained and is occasioned by vs. 33.

[75] Schmidt, *Rahmen*, pp. 238-39; Bultmann, *History*, p. 344; Klostermann, *Das Markusevangelium, ad loc.*; Sundwall, *op. cit.*, p. 63.

[76] Lohmeyer, *Das Evangelium des Markus*, p. 198.

[77] This can explain both corrections. The interpolation of a καί before πέραν τοῦ Ἰορδάνου (Sinaiticus, B, etc.) is due to the awareness that Judea (viewed from Galilee in 9:30 and Capernaum in 9:33) does not really lie beyond Jordan (note the passage). The result is an activity in two different regions. The διὰ τοῦ πέραν . . . (the Koine family and most mss.) sprang from acquaintance with the avoidance of a journey through Samaria and eliminates the "false" sequence (it is thus scarcely original; contra Wohlenberg, *op. cit., ad loc.*). Lohmeyer, *Das Evangelium des Markus, ad loc.*, thinks the καί was omitted because Matthew does not include it. But the reading without the καί is certainly the most difficult, and Matt. 19:1 is clearly the earliest witness to the original form in Mark.

We can cite Matt. 19:1 in support of this. Matthew's reference corresponds exactly with Mark's. Jesus thus comes to Judea east of the Jordan. This geographical note is of course uncertain.[78] Still, it is supported by Matthew, and that speaks for it, at least indirectly.[79] But even if this is open to debate, 10:32 to a degree interprets the reference. "Somehow the aim is to make clear that Jesus travels through East Jordan to Judea."[80] No particular "epoch" (Judea/Perea) is thus involved. Rather, what follows takes place beyond Jordan, hence in Perea.[81] Chapter 10 is then in the nature of a transition, as vss. 46 ff. also indicate.

3. Galilee in the Passion Narrative

Mark 14:28 and 16:7 are intimately related. This relation is given formal expression in the use of the future tense in the first and the use of the present tense in the second passage. The verses relate to each other as prophecy to fulfillment. There is extensive agreement regarding 14:28, to the degree it is assumed we are dealing with an individual saying inserted into the content at this point. In addition to the context, the connection of σκανδαλισθήσονται with σκανδαλισθήσεσθε seems to indicate that vs. 29 did in fact originally follow vs. 27. Whether this insertion is an isolated dominical saying[82] or

[78] It is advocated by Schlatter, *Der Evangelist Matthäus* (Stuttgart: Calwer Verlag, 1929), on 19:1; cf. Wellhausen, *Einleitung in die drei ersten Evangelien,* p. 12 (ἡ 'Ιουδαία ἡ περαία) ; but Theodor Zahn, *Das Evangelium des Matthaeus, Kommentar zum Neuen Testament,* herausgegeben von T. Zahn, 4te Auflage (Leipzig: A. Deichert'sche Verlagsbuchhandlung, 1922) on 19:1, is of another opinion.

[79] A comparison with Matt. 4:25 is interesting. Here Matthew alters his Markan exemplar (3:8). Judea and πέραν τοῦ 'Ιορδάνου, appear alongside each other as independent references connected by the καί. But in 19:1 the καί is lacking.

[80] Schmidt, *Rahmen,* p. 239.

[81] In this connection, Schlatter's note that the region adhered politically to Galilee (*Der Evangelist Matthäus,* on 19:1) deserves attention.

[82] Lohmeyer, *Das Evangelium des Markus, ad loc.;* but cf. also his *Galiläa und Jerusalem,* p. 14.

was formed by Mark or the community[83] is for the moment irrelevant to our inquiry. But it is significant that we can see Mark's hand here as he uses this verse to prepare for 16:7.[84] The evangelist, however, made alterations in the final chapter as well. Very probably he appended 16:1-8 to the passion narrative furnished him by the tradition, since this pericope conflicts with 15:42-47 in many details.[85] How the original ending (prior to Mark) read can at best be conjectured, and is of no importance for us.

A whole series of questions attaches to 16:1-8. They focus first of all on the long-noted contradiction between vss. 7 and 8. The women's silence disobeys the angel's command to tell the disciples and Peter that Jesus goes before them to Galilee. It is hardly the intention of Mark's conclusion to emphasize this disobedience. How then do we account for the contradiction?

Wellhausen[86] conjectured that the silence is intended to ex-

---

[83] Bultmann, *History*, pp. 266-67.

[84] There is a textual-critical problem here to the extent 14:28 is lacking in the Fayoum Fragment. So it has been suggested that this verse first entered the text after Mark (Bultmann, *History*, p. 267, n. 1; Lohmeyer, *Das Evangelium des Markus, ad loc.*, is of another opinion). But Matthew sets the verse in the same context. This means, however, that there is not sufficient time for an interpolation. Cf., among others, Holtzmann, *Die Synoptiker*, p. 174; Klostermann, *Das Markusevangelium, ad loc.;* Sundwall, *op. cit.*, p. 80; von Campenhausen, *Der Ablauf der Osterereignisse und das leere Grab, Sitzungsberichte der Heidelberger Akademie der Wissenschaften, Philosophisch-historische Klasse*, 4te Abhandlung (Heidelberg: Carl Winter Universitätsverlag, 1952), p. 35, n. 116. Dibelius offers a plausible explanation. He believes the fragment is "to be regarded as a chria-like abbreviated reproduction of a bit of tradition." Then, "it appears in no way surprising that Mark 14:28 does not correspond with the Fragment, for Mark 14:28 is only in place in a connected description" (*From Tradition to Gospel*, p. 181, n. 1).

[85] Bousset, *op. cit.*, pp. 64-65; Bultmann, *History*, p. 285; Lohmeyer, *Das Evangelium des Markus*, p. 348.

[86] *Das Evangelium Marci, ad loc.* (cf. on this von Campenhausen, *op. cit.*, pp. 24-25); likewise Bousset, *op. cit.*, p. 7, n. 1, and p. 65; Dibelius, *From Tradition to Gospel*, p. 190, *passim*.

plain why this resurrection narrative became current at such a late date.[87] In that event, the "legend of the empty tomb" would have originated at some time or other in the primitive community. But mention of it so long after the event reported requires support. This is given in an inference (one could call it a negative, etiological inference) drawn by the Gospel writer by way of a correction at vs. 8.[88]

But, we must now ask, why is such an apology necessary only at this point in the context of the Gospel? If Wellhausen views the motive correctly, then vs. 8, just as it reads now (in substance, at least) must from the outset have formed the conclusion of this legend. This does not explain the contradiction at all. If vs. 8 (still assuming Wellhausen is correct in the main) cannot have been altered, then the problem is vs. 7! But vs. 7 does not even belong to the report of the empty tomb and, in addition, can be easily removed from the context.[89] The apologetic motif then already lay in the tradition prior to Mark in vss. 1-6, 8. But this means that the real difficulty in the text did not at all originate with the alteration of vs. 8 but with the insertion of vs. 7.

Naturally, the difficulty may not be eliminated by deleting one of the "unsuitable" verses. It must be explained. But it is another question entirely whether, by means of literary criticism, we can peel off the sources which the evangelist arranged. The examination of each of these sources can first of all allow us to infer the original meaning of the ancient pieces of tradition, and then can help to fix the apparent discrepancies in an utterance of the extant text. Whoever is content with sepa-

[87] Lindton thinks we should not attribute "such clever ideas" to the evangelist ("Der vermisste Markusschluss," *Theologische Blätter*, VIII [1929], col. 231) . Cf. also R. H. Lightfoot, *The Gospel Message of St. Mark* (Oxford: At the Clarendon Press, 1950) , p. 92.

[88] Wellhausen regards the author as the originator of this apology because "16:8 is an indispensable conclusion" (*loc. cit.*) .

[89] Cf. also Dibelius, *From Tradition to Gospel*, p. 191.

rating out the sources has left the crucial work undone.[90] For our inquiry this means that even if vs. 7 should be a "troublesome insertion," vss. 1-8 must be capable of explanation. Of late, von Campenhausen has defended the originality of vs. 7, and—despite his difference from Wellhausen—has offered a solution very similar to his.[91] He also sees the evangelist's work in the alteration of vs. 8. He also believes that vss. 1-8 reflect apologetic motifs which gave rise to the contradiction in the text.

In contrast to Wellhausen, von Campenhausen does not view the goal of this apologetic as explaining the late currency of the report by a concentration on its age, but sees the crux of the apologetic in the subject matter itself. This is debatable, as a comparison with the other Gospels, especially with Matthew, shows. The women's silence so strongly emphasized *by the evangelist* aims to express the fact that the disciples had "nothing at all to do with the empty tomb." [92] We are dealing with "an event in and of itself," [93] totally independent of the appearances von Campenhausen (following vs. 7) assigns to Galilee. But precisely because it occurred so independently of the disciples' experiences, it is proved to be especially trustworthy.

Here too we must raise suspicions (as in Wellhausen's case). We must state first of all that we scarcely arrive at von Cam-

---

[90] One has the impression that not merely the past but the present as well gives too little attention to these points of view. Hirsch's amazingly penetrating analysis (*Frühgeschichte des Evangeliums*) suffers precisely from the fact that the compositional work fares badly, that far too little explanation is given for it. In the development of our Gospels, literary criticism does not play such an exclusive role. The "redactors" were a bit more reflective than Hirsch would like to concede. On the other side, it is completely groundless to be "fearful of the scissors." If the scissors are properly handled, they do not cut the Gospel to pieces but help to understand it better as a *unity*, because the work of the evangelist comes more clearly to the fore.

[91] *Op. cit.*, pp. 24 ff.; 34 ff.

[92] *Ibid.*, p. 34.

[93] *Ibid.*, p. 35.

penhausen's view solely from an observation of 16:1-8. This can only be inferred (and this is just how von Campenhausen proceeds). Only in later sources are apologetic motifs connected with the empty tomb. This does not absolutely prohibit our assuming such motifs for Mark 16:1-8. And yet there is a difficulty here. In the last analysis, von Campenhausen assumes what he wants to prove. Because of the contradiction between vss. 7 and 8 such an interpretation is possible only if we assume a correction of vs. 8 *on the part of the evangelist.* In other words, because von Campenhausen assumes the same tendency for Mark as e.g., for Matthew, Mark therefore must have reshaped vs. 8. It is just this which is problematic.

Now if we look carefully, it is not really vs. 8 which causes the difficulty, but rather vs. 7. If we again assume Mark's source did not contain this verse, von Campenhausen can still interpret vss. 1-6, 8 as he does. This hypothesis would also be much simpler. The narrative of the empty tomb would have been apologeticaly oriented from the very outset. Later, Matthew would have reshaped this apology in his own peculiar way.

There is another reason why von Campenhausen is obviously much concerned with 16:7 (something we shall have to discuss later). He thinks it is "no longer necessary" to regard the verse as an insertion, and adds: "These words are absolutely indispensable here, especially if Mark 16:8 was really the conclusion to the old Gospel." [94] The observation is quite correct. But does that not speak again for the fact that the *evangelist* inserted this verse which was so "absolutely indispensable" to *his* conclusion? [95]

---

[94] *Ibid.,* p. 35, n. 116.

[95] At this point, von Campenhausen does not distinguish clearly enough between an insertion by the evangelist or a later interpolator. The parallels indicate that the latter is out of the question. Von Campenhausen is quite correct about this. For Mark's Gospel 16:1-8 is a unity. Lohmeyer is not quite clear here. He regards the narrative as "self-contained" *(Das Evangelium des Markus,* p. 357). But this is true only to the degree we are dealing with the report in the framework of the Gospel. For Lohmeyer

After all the discussion to this point, there seems to be no other solution than that the contradiction resulted from Mark's insertion of vs. 7 into the context of vss. 1-6, 8.[96] Why did he do this?

The question is closely tied to the question concerning Mark's conclusion. We do not intend to take up the discussion in its entirety here but will treat the most important arguments. Here again we must sharply distinguish the ending of a pre-Markan passion narrative from the Gospel's conclusion. How the former appeared can at best be conjectured. We do not get beyond dubious hypotheses. If Mark abandoned his sources at 15:47, they still must have contained some sort of resurrection account. What that account looked like we do not know.[97]

Did the Gospel itself once have a resurrection narrative

---

too this is the decisive thing. But it is an entirely different question whether this "self-contained quality" is original or was first produced by Mark. Nor can von Campenhausen resolve the contradiction which the evangelist supposedly did not see, due to his one-sided pursuit of an apologetic goal (*op. cit.*, p. 35). It is true that Matthew also created inconsistencies in the parallel passage (cf. von Campenhausen, *ibid.*, pp. 26-27), but not such a harsh contradiction. We shall see later that this "contradiction" in Mark need not remain such but can be thoroughly explained.

[96] Thus, among others, A. Merx, *Die Evangelien des Markus und Lukas nach der syrischen im Sinaikloster gefundenen Palimpsesthandschrift erläutert* (Berlin: Verlag von Georg Reimer, 1905), p. 170; Bultmann, *History*, pp. 284-85; Dibelius, *From Tradition to Gospel*, p. 192, n. 1; Klostermann, *Das Markusevangelium, ad loc.*; Michaelis, *op. cit.*, p. 62.

[97] On this, nothing can be gleaned from Mark 14:28, since this verse (in this context) originates with the evangelist. Contra Dibelius, *From Tradition to Gospel*, p. 190. Lightfoot (*Locality and Doctrine in the Gospels*, pp. 21-22) explains the conclusion by suggesting that Mark's Gospel should not be viewed so much "as an individual composition," but "as the culmination of a considerable process of growth." From a practical viewpoint, this shifts the problem into the area of form history, and there can be no serious talk of a *Markan* ending, at any rate not in the sense that the Gospel is strictly speaking a "literary work." That is true only of Luke (cf. Lightfoot, *ibid.*, pp. 43 ff.).

(apart from 16:1-8) ? We have *no* literary evidence for it. The fact that Vaticanus and Sinaiticus, the Sinaitic Syriac and Armenian versions break off at 16:8 speaks as clearly as possible against it.[98] If the conclusion had been "in strong contradiction to the later Easter legend (s) ," as Bultmann supposes,[99] then it would sooner have been replaced than removed. The supplement later added to vs. 8 indicates precisely that a gap was felt here.[100] When Bultmann postulates a lost ending which allegedly reported appearances of the Risen Lord in Galilee, this squares with his other hypothesis according to which "the old tradition" supposely told of the disciples' flight to Galilee where the first appearances of the Risen Lord were localized. This flight was supposedly deleted. For this reason, in 16:7 (and 14:28) they are *sent* to Galilee on the basis of a command. But where is there anything about the *disciples' flight to Galilee?* [101]

[98] We should note with Lindton (*op. cit.*, col. 229) that the hypothesis of a Markan ending always turns up because the conclusion following 16: 8 is felt to be intolerable. Instead of attempting once for all to solve the riddle at this point, there is immediate preoccupation with the question as to "what the original ending could have contained and how it was lost." On the problem of the Markan ending, cf. also Michaelis, *op. cit.*, pp. 7 ff.

[99] *History*, p. 285.

[100] Lightfoot describes it "as a kind of canon that a gospel must end with a narrative of one or more manifestations of the risen Lord," but then continues, "Let us put this canon to the test." (*The Gospel Message of St. Mark*, p. 93.)

[101] This idea has been haunting the literature for a long time. Referring to Mark 14:50; 14:27-28; 16:7 (the last two passages "already secondary" in nature), and further to John 18:8 (and 16:32), Bousset (*op. cit.*, first ed., p. 44) maintained: "There is a very old and irrefutable tradition that after Jesus' imprisonment the disciples immediately fled to Galilee." How is it with these proof passages? There is no reference to locale in 14:50. This passage contains no other suggestion than that the disciples forsake Jesus who must go the way of suffering alone. Nor is there reference to locale in John 18:8. It is impossible to infer a flight *to Galilee* from John 16:32, though this verse supposedly prepares for the disciples' flight at Jesus' arrest (cf. Bultmann, *Das Evangelium des Johannes*, p. 456) —but without destination. The remaining passages, Mark 14:28 and

We must inquire still further. Where, but in these two passages, do we gain any clue that the disciples saw Jesus in Galilee? Matthew is dependent on Mark here and must be ruled out first. Luke knows of Easter events only in or about Jerusalem.[102] The same is true of John 20. Only in 21:1 ff. is the Sea of Tiberias the scene of an appearance. Here it is evidently a case of the author's wanting "to combine with the Johannine description the Markan-Matthaean tradition of a Galilean appearance of the Risen Lord." [103] Finally, the notion that the appearances reported in I Cor. 15 at some point referred to Galilee since the appearance to the "five hundred" could "scarcely take place in Jerusalem" is without substantiation.[104] We must simply be content with the fact that no reference to locale can be derived from I Cor. 15.[105]

16:7 (also designated by Bousset as "secondary") are to be explained in entirely different fashion. But even if our exegesis is not followed, these passages offer no proof for the hypothesis (contra Bultmann, *Theology of the New Testament*, I, 45; cf. J. Weiss, *Die Schriften des Neuen Testaments*, I, on 14:28; further Albertz, "Zur Formgeschichte der Auferstehungsberichte," *Zeitschrift für neutestamentliche Wissenschaft*, XXI [1922], p. 261; Michaelis, *op. cit.*, pp. 65 ff., and p. 140, n. 71). *The fiction of the disciples' flight to Galilee should now be laid to rest!* On this point, von Campenhausen (*op. cit.*, p. 46, n. 160) correctly states that such a judgment would result from a preconceived notion and not from the text itself.

[102] Luke 5:1-11 is no proof to the contrary. Even if there should be an Easter motif here, even if Peter's calling as the *first* disciple should be related to Jesus' appearance to him as the *first* disciple, the parallel is to be seen in *that* fact. But the locale of the calling is simply given in Peter's occupation and home (contra von Campenhausen, *op. cit.*, pp. 14-15). Hence, if there is any motif, it is present in Mark 1:17 (cf. Bultmann, *History*, p. 217).

[103] Bultmann, *Das Evangelium des Johannes*, p. 546.

[104] Thus von Campenhausen, *op. cit.*, p. 12.

[105] At the most we can ask whether I Cor. 15 suits references to place found elsewhere or whether it contradicts them. Support for other references, as von Campenhausen seeks, cannot be found here, and in no case can we agree that "the reports which Paul gives secure the Easter events for Galilee" (*op. cit.*, p. 19). On the problem, cf. Michaelis, *op. cit.*, pp. 41 ff.; 55 ff.

The result is that only one lone passage points to Galilee—Mark 16:7 (together with 14:28). But this verse is also at the root of the (subsequent!) hypothesis of the Galilean appearances. Perhaps still more can be said. It is questionable whether the Galilean tradition of the resurrection narrative would ever have existed if *Mark* had not taken 16:7 up into his Gospel, since this verse forms the sole basis for locating the appearances in Galilee, and since all subsequent tradition can be traced to it.[106] It is not at all certain whether this saying originates with Jesus, the community, or the evangelist. If Mark appropriated the (isolated) saying, it is possible (but improbable; more on this presently) that he was preceded by a tradition which knew of appearances in Galilee. But this in no way changes what we established above. The authentication of this tradition rests on this verse.[107] Still, we can pass over this question here. The question which concerns us is how Mark understood this verse (whether already extant or constructed by him is immaterial) and what *he* intended to say by it, provided he inserted it here where it is really not compatible with the following verse.

As is well known, Lohmeyer argued that ἐκεῖ αὐτὸν ὄψεσθε does not refer to appearances of the Risen Lord, but to the Parousia.[108] He indicates that the technical term for appearances of the Risen Lord was ὤφθη, whereas "you will see him" was the stated expression for the Parousia. But it is not quite certain whether the linguistic evidence is sufficient or can sup-

---

[106] Von Campenhausen is correct: "Matthew simplified and condensed the Easter narrative . . . in very radical fashion," i.e., into "one single, massive appearance to all the disciples, occurring on a mountain in Galilee to which Jesus ordered them" (*op. cit.*, p. 15). But it is clear from this that the geographical reference originates with Mark (Mark 16:7 = Matt. 28:7). Cf. further below.

[107] This is the case even if there *actually* were appearances in Galilee. On the improbability of this assumption, cf. Michaelis, *op. cit.*, p. 72. At best, John 21 could be referred to as an exception.

[108] *Galiläa und Jerusalem*, pp. 10 ff.; also *Das Evangelium des Markus* on 16:7.

port this contention.[109] Matthew, e.g., who in chap. 28 no doubt aims to report appearances of the Risen Lord, uses for this purpose not only the phrase in vs. 7, taken over from Mark 16:7, but also a corresponding phrase in vs. 10 (which, of course, can be derived from vs. 7) and vs. 17. The situation is similar in John's Gospel.[110] But these are only a few exceptions which for the most part can be easily explained.[111] Besides, we must determine that this usage is also illustrative of the Parousia, particularly in Mark's Gospel (9:1; 13:26; 14: 62).[112] Thus, whether Lohmeyer's hypothesis is correct or whether we must follow the traditional interpretation can only be decided by other arguments. The linguistic considerations only lend probability to his exegesis.[113]

Now we must note that in this context 16:7 is redactional. As we assumed, Galilee has special significance for Mark's day. This significance seems to be associated with the community in the evangelist's own time. If this is correct, it follows that

[109] This has been disputed by von Campenhausen (op. cit., p. 45, n. 158), who calls it "sheer arbitrariness." " Ὁρᾶν means simply 'to see' and nothing more. The context determines whatever the content of this seeing may have been." Michaelis, who himself sees a connection with the Parousia in these passages, is also in doubt as to whether the terminological basis alone suffices. He begins his argument with Mark 14:28 (op. cit., pp. 137-38, n. 58; cf. also his article on " Ὁράω" in Kittel, op. cit., V, 361, n. 222). More on this presently. On ὤφθη, cf. K. H. Rengstorf, Die Auferstehung Jesu; Form, Art und Sinn der urchristlichen Osterbotshaft (Witten-Ruhr: Luther Verlag, 1952), pp. 34 ff., 83 ff.; Michaelis, op. cit., pp. 104 ff., and Kittel, op. cit., V, 385 ff.

[110] Cf. John 20:18, 25, 29. But because of the peculiarity of the Johannine usage, conclusions can scarcely be drawn for Mark.

[111] On this cf. Kittel, op. cit., V, 358, esp. lines 30 ff.

[112] On ὁρᾶν in connection with the Parousia, cf. Kittel, op. cit., V, 360-61.

[113] It is questionable whether the Test. Zeb. 9:8 (Lohmeyer, Das Evangelium des Markus, p. 356, n. 2) really supports Lohmeyer's thesis. If Mark 16:7 refers to the Parousia, that is no longer the case in the parallel passage in Matt. 28:7. On the other hand, this also means that the other usage in Matt. 28:7 (and in vss. 10, 17) proves nothing for Mark.

the mention of Galilee does not allow us to conclude first of all for a historical reminiscence or to view the content of the report in isolation. We must, rather, be aware that by his redaction Mark intends to interpret his own time. We are not primarily concerned with interpreting an isolated piece of the tradition *as* tradition; rather, the tradition, precisely because of its redactional adaptation, serves the interpretation which is oriented to the evangelist's own time.

We have further observed that the communities in Mark's time are somehow directed to Galilee, or assemble there.

If, therefore, Mark inserts 16:7 into an already existing context, then we are dealing with the latest stratum reflecting the evangelist's own situation. *But then this redactional note cannot deal with an appearance of the Risen Lord awaited in Galilee; in Mark's context this passage can only refer to the expected Parousia.* If this is correct, several questions are immediately taken care of. The interruption at vs. 8 becomes intelligible. If Mark intends to prepare for the Parousia in vs. 7, then its coming *cannot* be referred to after vs. 8. The phrase "see him" is future for Mark. The Parousia is still to occur. At the same time, we understand the Gospel's orientation to Galilee. It is there that Mark awaits the Parousia. We see why Galilee is a midpoint, why (in Mark's time) the communities "gather" by the Sea. This explanation is compatible with the text as we have it and no longer requires that we postulate a lost conclusion whose content would in any case be open to serious question.

We cannot say that Mark had no Easter narrative. True, he does not speak of appearances and we might ask whether he has a particular view of the resurrection. But it is always precarious to work with an argument from silence (as 16:9-? in its "Markan" form indicates). What is to prevent our understanding 16:1-6, 8 as an "Easter narrative"? Perhaps the evangelist felt this to be much "clearer" than a report of appearances.[114] In any case, if with von Campenhausen we assume a polemic concerning the empty tomb, this Easter narrative is clear enough.[115] By the insertion of 16:7, the resurrection takes on a provisional character which shall be exceeded or, more probably, consummated by an imminent and greater event.

Finally, the προάγειν in 16:7 (and in 14:28) is to be interpreted from this point of view. Here, it was thought, the Risen Lord (on the third day) made his triumphal march to Galilee at the head of his disciples.[116] But the meaning is "purely temporal: He has set out before you toward Galilee." [117] This is supported in turn by the significance which Galilee has for Mark. Jesus is "already there." This is why there is such emphasis upon his activity in this land by the Sea. To be sure, his presence is hidden, but it will shortly be manifest. Clear also is the way in which his presence in Galilee is now experienced—in the proclamation.[118]

The interpretation proposed above can be supported from yet another angle. We shall take up a few of the ideas advanced

[114] Lightfoot is correct (*The Gospel Message of St. Mark*, p. 93) : ". . . to the fact of the resurrection St. Mark has given full expression in 16:1-8 —a point, which is sometimes overlooked." Cf. also *Locality and Doctrine in the Gospels*, p. 58.

[115] Rengstorf, *op. cit.*, p. 40, shows that in other respects the Easter event had to be defended at a very early date.

[116] Thus J. Weiss, *Die Schriften des Neuen Testaments*, I, on 14:28; Albert Schweitzer, *The Quest of the Historical Jesus*, trans. W. Montgomery (New York: The Macmillan Company, 1948) , p. 386, n. 1; Klostermann, *Das Markusevangelium, ad loc.* (16:7) .

[117] Lohmeyer, *Das Evangelium des Markus, ad loc.;* W. Bauer, *A Greek-English Lexicon of the New Testament and Other Early Christian Literature,* trans. and ed. W. G. Arndt and F. W. Gingrich (Chicago: University of Chicago Press, 1957) , pp. 708-9. Whether the idea of discipleship in suffering is also connected with this verb (Kittel, *op. cit.*, I, 130) , does not appear certain enough for us to be able to decide here (but cf. below, study four) .

[118] On this topic, cf. study three. From entirely different observations I have tried to show that this idea is actually present in Mark. Cf. Marxsen, *op. cit.*, p. 271.

by W. Michaelis in his debate with E. Hirsch.[119] Michaelis begins his studies on Mark 14:28 and 16:7 with the former passage. He regards this verse as a logion of Jesus. What is striking is that this verse contains a reference to time ("after I am raised up") which—viewed from Jesus—points to an event removed from the resurrection and thus later in time. This verse can only refer to the Parousia.[120]

Michaelis, of course, encounters a few difficulties. First, it would have to be stated that such a Parousia in Galilee simply did not occur. But this poses no problem for the exegesis of Mark 14:28. It does, however, imply another interpretation for 16:7. Michaelis assigns this next-to-last verse in the Gospel a status below that of the prediction in 14:28. Citing Matt. 28:7 where "there you will see him" must undoubtedly be joined to the appearance subsequently reported, he assumes the same meaning for Mark 16:7. In that case, Mark would have already altered the sense. We could only assert that an *ancient* tradition (14:28) referred to an awaiting of the Parousia in Galilee. But this tradition was (because it was not fulfilled, or due to the evangelist's misunderstanding?) converted to an appearance (or appearances). This occurred via the addition "there you will see him" in 16:7.

And what if 16:7 is *not* secondary? Michaelis also weighs this possibility.[121] On the one hand, he supposes that even then a connection with the Parousia could not be retained for Mark 16:7. "For such a Parousia in Galilee simply did not occur. It would be harder to explain an 'error' in the angel's message in the situation *following* the resurrection than an 'error' on Jesus' part in the announcement of 14:28." On the other hand,

---

[119] *Op. cit.,* pp. 61-65.
[120] Actually, this reference also appears in 16:7 *following* 16:6. Cf. Lightfoot, *Locality and Doctrine in the Gospels,* p. 60.
[121] *Op. cit.,* p. 139, n. 68.

Michaelis correctly sees that it is impossible to assume a discrepancy between the two verses to the effect that

Jesus really did mean the Parousia in 14:28, but that this saying was corrected in the angel's message of 16:7 and made to conform to his appearances. Still, the difficulties here shall not be pursued. To the extent they can be solved at all, their solution will correspond with the fact that the angel's message as such cannot claim the same historical value as a saying of Jesus (and that a saying of the Risen Lord). Rather, it will necessarily be influenced by the views and ideas of the community handing down the tradition.

A few questions emerge here. First of all, we have grave doubts about interpreting the phrase in Mark 16:7 ("there you will see him") from Matthew's point of view, and then concluding for appearances (in Galilee). Were this in fact correct, to conclude with 16:8, as Michaelis intends, would still pose considerable difficulties.

Next, we must call attention to the phrase "as he told you" in 16:7. This phrase clearly refers the utterances of the verse back to 14:28. The disputed "there you will see him" immediately precedes. This can only mean that even if 14:28 does not explicitly refer to a seeing, the idea should be supplied. This is *not* true of Mark's sources! But it is true of the Markan context. This should be quite clear since both verses are redactional.[122] Now, if Michaelis' assumption is correct, viz., that the "seeing" was inserted in 16:7, then it seems simplest to assume a doublet. In that case, 14:28 and 16:7 stem from *one* saying whose original form would be better preserved in 14:28. But for the Markan context it is of lesser importance whether (with Lohmeyer) we interpret 14:28 by 16:7, or (with Michaelis) 16:7 by 14:28.

In any event it is important to distinguish sharply an exegesis which is possible in isolation from an exegesis in

---

[122] Michaelis disputes this (*ibid.*, p. 138, n. 59); cf. also Lightfoot, *Locality and Doctrine in the Gospels*, pp. 60-61. But this ignores the redactional work, as we will show.

context. Just at this point Michaelis does not appear entirely consistent. In one instance he focuses on the "views and ideas of the community handing down the tradition," and in the next inquires after "historical value." Redaction is thus contrasted with tradition. But if I intend to exegete the evangelist's utterance, I must set aside the question of the historical value of the individual logia.[123]

We may not inquire *here* whether or not 14:28 is a Jesus logion. But aside from this, the time reference still points to a signal event which is removed from the resurrection. Surprisingly enough, nothing is said here of an appearance. And we may not read it into the text because we know of it from other traditions. The Risen Lord is to stand at the heart of an event in Galilee. Can anything but the Parousia be intended? The mutual interpretation of 14:28 and 16:7 ought to establish this hypothesis.

We can refer to another feature. It can scarcely be accidental that Mark inserted 14:28 at just this point. Theoretically it would have been possible to set the logion, circulating in isolation, at another spot and with the same effect, viz., as an anticipation of 16:7. Why then does the verse appear here?

We will demonstrate more than once that insertions into an existing context are for the purpose of interpreting this context, particularly the preceding verse or clause.[124] But this means that 14:28 interprets 14:27. Jesus will gather his scat-

[123] This is not an objection to the fundamental propriety of such an inquiry. But it is an impossible alternative to assert, as does Wendling (*op. cit.*, p. 170), that in 14:28 "it is not Jesus but the redactor" who is speaking. Even if Wendling's subsequent observations were correct, such a contrast may not be drawn. Redactional insertions of verses can contain very old traditional material and in context can still be credited to the evangelist.

[124] Cf. the remarks on 8:35; 10:29; 13:10 in the two studies which follow. But also the passage just discussed (16:7) is to be cited here if the phrase "there you will see him" is the evangelist's insertion. This phrase then interprets the "going before" in 16:7 *and* 14:28. Finally, we can also refer to Mark 1:4 where the ἐν τῇ ἐρήμῳ characterizes the Baptist.

tered flock in Galilee.[125] Formulated from the perspective of redaction history, Galilee is the meeting place of the scattered communities. This coincides exactly with the Parousia. So the insertion of 14:28 immediately after 14:27 proves that in our examination of the Galilee passages we have viewed Mark's plan correctly.

If we inquire from a strictly redaction-historical point of view, all the doubts arising in light of the Parousia's delay are finally put to rest. Michaelis stated "it would be harder to explain an 'error' in the angel's message in the situation *following* the resurrection than an 'error' on Jesus' part in the announcement of 14:28." [126] This is true, however, only if the evangelist *looked back* to the Parousia, or could already have established its nonoccurrence. The situation is quite different if he awaited it as imminent. *Today* we can see that this was an error, just as Matthew and Luke saw it and accordingly made alterations. At the same time, we must now state that all our observations of the oldest Gospel lead to the conclusion that Mark shared such an expectation. Once this is recognized, all the problems raised by Michaelis here are solved. We can also gain from Mark's plan a clue as to why

---

[125] Cf. Schlatter, *Der Evangelist Matthäus*, on 26:23 and also *Markus, der Evangelist für die Griechen*, on 14:28; Schniewind follows Schlatter (though with reservations) in *Das Evangelium nach Markus*, on 14:28. Michaelis has doubts (*op. cit.*, p. 139, n. 65), but his objections are unsound. The difficulties he sees here are again due to the fact that he (as Schlatter) is too insistent on 14:28 as a logion of Jesus. Under certain circumstances this view can be defended. But doubts naturally arise when we see that the connection between 14:27 and 14:28 is "not so strong" (a fact to which Michaelis correctly refers). *Originally*, therefore, the concepts "Parousia" and "gathering of the community in Galilee" *cannot have formed a unity*. But the *evangelist unites them*. Michaelis further states that the idea (i.e., gathering of the communities in Galilee), if actually intended, "would have had to be more clearly expressed." This is true only to the extent we intend to find this idea in its *original form* here. Mark's method and point of view seem to indicate as clearly as we might wish that he intends to say just this.

[126] *Op. cit.*, p. 139, n. 68.

a "conclusion" dealing with appearances was later appended to 16:8, and why Matthew and Luke have a similar conclusion. Might this correspond with the delayed Parousia? We will return to this question. Such a conclusion, however, extinguishes the hope which still informs Mark's ending, an ending in itself contradictory.

We must now come to grips with this problem. First of all, we contend that this "contradiction" between 16:7 and 16:8 was created by the redaction. But we note at once its similarity with that other "contradiction," between the injunctions to silence and their transgression. There is redaction there also.[127] In both instances there is a tension between speech and silence, though at times in the reverse.[128] The injunctions to silence actually stimulate transgression, spreading of the news. In the Markan ending, the command to spread the news is inhibited by the women's fright and dread. Back of this common tension lurks an inner compulsion to spread the news which is also inhibited and restrained. We are dealing here with a literary expression of that tension between disclosure and concealment which marks the "messianic secret," a typically Markan phenomenon. We can establish a "contradiction" only if we inquire behind the redaction in historical or historicizing fashion.[129]

It is most typical of Mark to conclude his Gospel in this peculiar way. He characterizes his work as proclamation, just as with the term εὐαγγέλιον in 1:1.[130] The Messiahship is still

---

[127] Thus among others, Dibelius, *From Tradition to Gospel*, pp. 73-74; Bultmann, *Theology of the New Testament*, I, 32; H. J. Ebeling, *op. cit.*, pp. 114 ff., is of another opinion.

[128] This has to do with the fact that the tradition at times contains the opposite feature. In the injunctions to silence, the tradition generally reported the recital of the event; Mark prefixes this with the injunction. Here (16:8) the silence motif was of a piece with the tradition; Mark prefixes this with the command to speak.

[129] Elsewhere, I have tried to show that the so-called parable theory is also to be explained in this fashion. Cf. Marxsen, *op. cit.*, pp. 270-71.

[130] Cf. below, study three.

hidden but presses toward its disclosure—in the Parousia. The proclamation of the hidden Messiah occurs in the preaching. And wherever this proclamation is carried on, the "secret epiphany" takes place, the Parousia is anticipated in hiddenness.

Thus, in essence, the Parousia again stands behind this tension at the Gospel's end. Finally, when we consider that for Mark the messianic secret is tied to Galilee,[131] the picture is complete.[132]

4. Summary

Before we consider developments beyond Mark, let us take another backward look. The impression gained can be formulated as follows: Mark writes a "Galilean Gospel." The tendency to "consolidate," already established in the first study, shows up here again. It takes literary expression in the arrangement of isolated, disparate pieces via the redactional device "Galilee." For Mark, however, Galilee is not primarily of historical but rather of theological significance as the locale of the imminent Parousia.

We might inquire how this came about. Three stages can be detected. The first is that of *the historical Jesus*. To the best of our knowledge, he worked in Galilean (and neighboring) regions. The tradition refers to specific cities and towns. Whether we are dealing here with reliable data or with local traditions formed later on will vary with the particular instance and can hardly be decided with certainty (except for

---

[131] Cf. Lohmeyer, *Galiläa und Jerusalem*, p. 33.

[132] We have yet to deal with Mark 15:41 within the context of the passion narrative. The hand of the evangelist cannot be clearly seen here. Bultmann (*History*, p. 274) thinks vss. 40-41 are an isolated piece of tradition, which leaves unanswered the question as to whether Mark first inserted it into this context, as Sundwall supposes (*op. cit.*, p. 83). We ought scarcely make a decision here, since the names are fraught with considerable difficulties. Still, we should note that the Galilee motif later elaborated by Luke is already anticipated here. Cf. further below.

Jerusalem). Locales furnished by the tradition are more or less accidental. For this reason, we ought not conclude from the absence of certain place-names (e.g., Tarichea, Sepphoris, etc.) that Jesus "at least never devoted the chief part of his public ministry in Galilee to one of these places." [133] But considering the geographical data in the tradition, it is natural to compile a "Palestinian Gospel" out of them. Though a considerable number of Galilean sites appears, it is surprising that Galilee itself is not anchored in the tradition. On the other hand, it is quite clear that this area by implication has a slight advantage which—also by implication—is heightened by the traditional name "Nazareth."

The second stage is that of *the primitive community,* which in all probability attached itself to Jerusalem. Paul is the chief witness here. We know nothing of a "primitive" community in Galilee (which Lohmeyer took for granted). But it is undeniable that the community did not restrict itself to Jerusalem. Later on it moves toward Galilee (just as the first community in Jerusalem also abandons the city). This shift in concentration evidently coincides with the Parousia awaited in Galilee. We might ask, Why in Galilee? It is natural to suppose that the Second Coming was awaited where the first coming occurred. Galilee thus becomes the new center.

The third stage is that of *Mark.* The orientation to Galilee is already a present fact for him—he at least stands in midst of it. And when the evangelist's work concentrates Jesus' activity in Galilee, this is of geographical significance only to the degree this area is important to Mark's own time. Mark's Galilean Gospel reflects no "historical-geographical" interest. His concern might rather be termed "eschatological-geographical." To overstate the case, Mark does not intend to say: Jesus worked in Galilee, but rather: Where Jesus worked, there is

[133] Contra A. Alt, *Where Jesus Worked,* trans. K. Grayston (London: Epworth Press, 1961), p. 24.

Galilee. In any event, he steers the tradition handed down to him in this direction.

We must look still further. Jesus has already gone on ahead to Galilee. There he is hidden; there he will be seen at the Parousia. Galilee is thus Jesus' "home" in a far deeper sense than the merely historical. It is the place where he worked, where—hidden in the proclamation—he is now working, and will work at his Parousia.

We have gained an important perspective for interpreting the evangelist. If form history indicated the kerygmatic rather than the biographical character of the individual tradition, the same applies to the work of the oldest evangelist. By consolidating he has not simply heaped up isolated pieces of the tradition but has united them into a proclamation. The kerygmatic character of the individual traditions has been transferred to his work. For this reason, the geographical data of the tradition are of no interest to him. Where he finds them he incorporates them; where they are lacking, he adds none. He is concerned only with Galilee. The consolidation uniting the disparate material into *one* "sermon" is all-important to him.[134] In this way he achieves identification of the earthly Jesus with the Exalted Lord. The material deals with the earthly Jesus. But as proclamation it represents the Exalted Lord whose Parousia is at the door.

But all this is oriented to Galilee. It is possible that ideas are

---

[134] The concept "sermon" is intended merely to express the unity and character of the proclamation, and does not imply (as in G. Hartmann, *Der Aufbau des Markusevangeliums* [Münster i. W.: Aschendorff, 1936], esp. pp. 120 ff.) that this sermon was delivered orally in this way. By comparing Mark's Gospel with Peter's speeches in Acts as well as with I and II Peter, Hartmann believes he can recognize Peter as author of this sermon. To establish agreement between the two types requires considerable examination of the Gospel's style; therefore, Hartmann now concludes, these types must originate with Peter and the evangelist's share in his work is quite minimal. There is a vicious circle in this argument. Moreover, this hypothesis runs aground on form history which Hartmann does not take into account.

involved here which were prepared for in Jewish tradition and to which Lohmeyer refers when he speaks of the "so-called churchly concept, Galilee." [135] We may leave open the question of direct literary dependence. In any case, the kinship of ideas is unmistakable. Though we can locate on the map the Galilee which is or will be the heart of the community, what is crucial for that community can only be believed, just as a man may "hear" the proclamation in Galilee "but not understand" (Mark 4:11-12) because he has no "ears to hear."

This unique quality of Mark's Gospel can perhaps come clearly to the fore when we compare it with the major Gospels. At this point, then, we take a brief look at the subsequent development. In the context of our discussion, we can only give clues and not detailed descriptions, since this would require separate studies. For Luke, we can refer to Conzelmann's work. There is still no corresponding monograph on Matthew.[136]

B. Alterations in the Major Gospels

1. Matthew

We turn now to the beginning and conclusion of Matthew's Gospel. Matthew 3:13, but even more clearly 4:12 ff., indicate

[135] *Galiläa und Jerusalem*, p. 26.

[136] Some clues are given in Lightfoot, *Locality and Doctrine in the Gospels*, pp. 126 ff. But a question as to method should be raised here. Lightfoot begins with Burkitt's evaluation, to which he assents and which he appropriates. Matthew presents "a fresh, revised and enriched edition" of Mark's Gospel. Agreement of the Galilee data is at the forefront. There is in fact such agreement, but there are also deviations, some of which are minimal, as Lightfoot asserts. But if Matthew's ideas are to be stressed, then these changes must be taken as the point of departure for any investigation. For it is at this point that the evangelist himself speaks, and his intention is most clearly recognized. The agreement, on the other hand, is simply appropriated. Acceptance of Mark's Galilee data does not *eo ipso* imply an appropriation of his point of view [cf. the translators' note 61].

how the evangelist breaks up what Mark consolidates. Now the locales have definitely geographical significance. If Jesus begins his ministry in Galilee, what would be more natural than to mention his native city? K. L. Schmidt points out that there is no transition from 4:12 to 4:13.[137] The withdrawal toward Capernaum directly follows. Here Matthew's view really becomes clear. His references do indeed have a theological basis, but it is entirely different from Mark's. Jesus' ministry begins in the north, in "Galilee of the Gentiles," because it is predicted in Scripture. Of course, this is a formula quotation. Matthew chose it in dependence on his sources. But this quotation now requires geographical data which are really to be construed geographically. Otherwise Scripture would not be fulfilled. Viewed from Mark, Jesus' decisive activity occurs in Galilee, since Galilee is the land of the imminent Parousia and thus belongs to the expectation of faith. In Matthew it is quite the reverse. "Galilee of the Gentiles" is, as it were, ennobled because Jesus worked there.[138] The Old Testament prophesied his appearance in Galilee. Jesus, therefore, must really have appeared in Galilee, since this alone furnishes "proof" that Scripture is fulfilled in him. We see clearly how Matthew is beginning to historicize and is at least on the way to a *vita Jesu*. Taking the Old Testament as his starting point, the place of Jesus' *actual* appearance must claim his interest.

Here we see how widely the two evangelists' thought and work diverge. Viewed from the Risen Lord (in Galilee) the transmitted tradition becomes gospel for Mark. He sees everything in the light of his own time. Viewed from Jesus, the Old Testament prophecy becomes gospel. Viewed from his own time and the awaited Parousia, Galilee becomes the locale for the activity of the earthly Jesus. Matthew, of course, also sees prophecy in light of its fulfillment, i.e., he searches for

---

[137] *Rahmen*, p. 55.
[138] On "Galilee of the Gentiles," cf. Strack-Billerbeck, *op. cit.*, I, 153 ff., 160-61; further Bauer, *Jesus der Galiläer*, p. 18.

Old Testament passages which can be used as prophecies of the event to be related. But these elements are used and arranged in precisely reverse fashion, i.e., in terms of proof. So Matthew must focus upon the facticity of what is reported; only then can true fulfillment of prophecy be achieved.

In contrast to Mark, the conclusion of Matthew's Gospel contains something which is quite new. In 28:7, he of course appropriates the substance of Mark 16:7, just as in 26:32 he appropriates the prophecy of Mark 14:28. But in 28:7 Matthew characteristically adds: ὅτι ἠγέρθη ἀπὸ τῶν νεκρῶν, and changes καθὼς εἶπεν ὑμῖν (which in Mark 16:7 clearly refers to 14:28) to ἰδοὺ εἶπον ὑμῖν. That is, this word in the angel's mouth is merely a reflection of the command just received and no longer corresponds with Matt. 26:32. Matthew thus prepares for a reinterpretation of the Markan ending by giving his conclusion independent significance. The tension of expectation is also removed. The women's silence (Mark 16:8) is replaced by the report of (or intent to report) the angel's message to the disciples, which naturally includes obedience to the angel's command. Presently the Risen Lord also appears, removes the women's fear, and repeats the command (28:9-11).

Finally, the event is described which for Matthew is predicted in 28:7. It is immediately clear that this is not the Parousia of Mark 16:7. Viewed from Mark, we could call it a "substitution." By that term we refer only to the context, not to the piece of tradition as such, for which Matthew evidently had sources at his disposal.[139] Two elements are clearly appropriated from Mark: the location (of the mountain) in Galilee,[140] and the phrase "see him." But these features are tied to the report of an appearance which, compared to the rest of

[139] On this point, cf. Lohmeyer, " 'Mir ist gegeben alle Gewalt,' Eine Exegese von Mt. 28:16-20," in *In Memoriam Ernst Lohmeyer,* pp. 22 ff.

[140] The command in 28:7 points toward Galilee, but not toward a mountain, which in 28:16 is the place to which Jesus directed his disciples. The redaction fuses the two data.

97

the Easter tradition, is "most radically simplified and condensed." [141]

We will not be able to say for sure what it was that motivated Matthew to transform and reshape Mark's ending. Was he the first to feel Mark's ending was only a torso? Did he then construe Mark 16:7 as a prediction of appearances? Or did he understand the passage correctly but—because of the Parousia's delay—feel the necessity of creating a "conclusion"? If Mark lived during the imminent expectation of the Parousia, for Matthew time is beginning to draw out. He then offers a kind of "interim solution" by inserting the period of missionizing.[142] We shall see later (on Mark 13:10) that this motif is definitely present also in Mark. But it is not yet an epoch with independent significance. In Matthew, on the other hand, this interval takes on significance with the task of making πάντα τὰ ἔθνη disciples.

Matthew's conclusion has another special quality which again is typical of his reconstruction. His "Life of Jesus" is, as it were, concluded with 28:16-20. The period of missionizing follows the time of Jesus. It extends from Easter until at least the time of Matthew. It can extend still further, in fact, to our own time. The Matthaean ending is thus all but timeless, since after concluding one epoch he allows another to begin which continues till the end of the world.

The beginning, to which the conclusion of the time of Jesus corresponds, is preceded by still another epoch—the time of the Old Testament. From this vantage point we can understand how the evangelist joins both epochs via his own peculiar "scriptural proof." Since the time of Jesus is one epoch between two others, it becomes a *vita,* or at least develops in this direction. As we will try to indicate in the next study, we must distinguish the Gospel framework from the speech complexes. The historicizing of Mark's outline results in the framework

---

[141] Cf. von Campenhausen, *op. cit.,* p. 15.
[142] Cf. Lohmeyer, "Mir ist gegeben alle Gewalt," p. 43.

which now becomes a course of events, aims at giving a sequence and is thus concerned with the facticity of the report. But into this framework speech complexes are built which reflect Matthew's own time, but which still—in historicizing fashion—are speeches of the *earthly* Jesus.

An illustration can perhaps clarify this. The Gospel of Mark is a large "knot," a sermon, a uniform complex. The entire disparate tradition is tied up in it. Matthew, however, unties the knot. A "red thread" hence emerges, viz., the course of Jesus' life as portrayed in the framework. What is of interest here is that in this life Jesus reveals himself to be Messiah. But from time to time the thread displays a "knot," i.e., a speech complex.

In other words, most of Mark's consolidation is to be found at the beginning. Matthew breaks up this consolidation. The same is true, though with variations, of the third evangelist.

2. Luke

Here also we confine ourselves to a few remarks, and for the total picture as offered by Luke refer the reader once more to Conzelmann. Again, at the very beginning of Luke's Gospel an entirely new aspect appears.[143] In Luke 3:1 Galilee is a political region. Verse 4:14 then makes Jesus begin in Galilee, a characteristic interruption of Mark 1:14b. The eschatological significance of Galilee is deleted. The historicizing element turns up again in Luke's allowing Jesus to deliver an "inaugural sermon" in Nazareth. He achieves this by anticipating Mark 6:1 ff. and inserting it after Luke 4:15.

This displacement has given rise to all kinds of reflection.[144] If the phenomenon were "typical," the difficulties would not be so great. This is not the case, however. Its significance lies

---

[143] It was pointed out above that in Luke the Baptist does not belong to the gospel but is distanced from Jesus.

[144] Special source? Proto-Luke hypothesis? On this point, cf. Conzelmann, *op. cit.*, pp. 31-32.

precisely in its uniqueness.[145] In light of this observation we must inquire into the meaning of Luke's rearrangement. Conzelmann most appropriately describes it thus:

> [Luke] is not aware of the distinction between the chronological and soteriological. For him, historical sequence as such is *fundamentally* important. Yet he is not a modern, "secular" historian; he is a believer. That is, when the meaning of an event for salvation history has been disclosed to him, he can deduce from it the "correct" chronology, e.g., can exercise criticism of Mark. In contrast to Mark, there is no "historical probability" per se in Luke, but a logically coherent christological conception consistently set forth as the chronological sequence of events of the life of Jesus.[146]

Despite the differences, this again indicates the proximity of Luke's to Matthew's method. If for Luke the sequence of events is theologically significant and if he "correctly" deduces this sequence from his point of view, then what is essential to Matthew is the facticity of the recorded event in Jesus' life. This event, particularly in its details, must be shown to be a fulfillment in accordance with Old Testament prophecies. This is of course another kind of historicizing, but historicizing nonetheless.

Characteristic of Luke is his reshaping of the Markan Galilee concept. He achieves this in a twofold way. Galilee becomes an "epoch" in Jesus' life alongside two others. This epoch is marked by the gathering of those who go up with him to Jerusalem.

Both alterations are expositions of Markan beginnings. But in Mark they were without this special significance. Mark 15:41 tells of the women who followed Jesus when he was in Galilee. Luke appropriates this feature. The Galileans take on significance as "witnesses." Galilee thus loses its theological significance. It does not even denote an area (as in Matthew),

---

[145] Conzelmann, *ibid.,* p. 33.
[146] *Ibid.,* pp. 33-34. [Translators' translation.]

but is included only "on account of the 'Galileans.' It is Judaea
that has a significance of its own as a locality, especially Jerusalem as the place of the Temple." [147]

Toward that point—and not back toward Galilee—Luke's
Gospel is oriented. Luke pretends to know nothing of a
journey *toward* Galilee. He deletes Mark 14:28. By means of
a little artifice which indicates how extremely deft he is as a
redactor, he alters Mark 16:7 (Luke 24:6). The prediction of
a journey toward Galilee is changed to a Galilean prophecy
referring to Jerusalem.[148] In the historicizing, the eschatological expectation becomes past event. The witnesses who were
there "in the beginning" (23:5) have positive significance.
They have gone with Jesus from Galilee to the capital (23:
49, 55); but they are to remain there, as expressly commanded
(24:49).

Jesus' "beginning" was thus in Galilee. By breaking up the
unity in Mark, Luke expands Jesus' career into three periods:
Galilee/Journey/Jerusalem. Conzelmann indicates that these
sections "are meant to be roughly equivalent in time." [149] This
breaks up the consolidation Mark created by his introduction
of the concept "Galilee." Simultaneity in Mark's proclamation
becomes sequence in Luke's description.

The real motive for this reconstruction can again be seen at
the conclusion of Luke's Gospel. Measured against Mark,
Luke's conclusion, like Matthew's, can be described as a "substitute" for the awaited Parousia. The time of Jesus is concluded; the time of the church begins with Ascension and
Pentecost.

[147] *Ibid.,* p. 41; cf. also Lohmeyer, *Galiläa und Jerusalem,* pp. 41 ff.

[148] Cf. Conzelmann, *op. cit.,* pp. 93, 202; Lohmeyer, *Galiläa und Jerusalem,* p. 44.

[149] Conzelmann, *op. cit.,* p. 65. Conzelmann's statements regarding
Luke's geographical notions are of interest here. He says that Luke is
"not familiar with the country," that he describes Galilee and Judea as
immediately adjacent and in such a way that he views the country from
abroad. He connects Judea to the coast, situates Galilee inland, and supposes Samaria to be north of Judea (*ibid.,* pp. 68-69).

But this means that time begins to draw out with the Parousia's delay. More exactly, one is conscious of an extension of time. It is this totally new *experience of time* felt in his own day which Luke aims to master theologically. Luke makes the attempt by means of the *Heilsgeschichte,* whose structured continuity results in his dual work.

We will let the matter rest with these few clues. We will add to them at various points as we attempt now to formulate our results.

C. Results

We turn first of all to the problem posed by Lohmeyer's investigation which, as we shall see shortly, still confronts us.

1. Galilee or Jerusalem?

As is well known, Lohmeyer proposed that the earliest Christian community had a twofold origin—Galilee and Jerusalem.[150] But when we survey what we have established till now and take into account Luke's point of view, how much of this thesis is to be retained? Conzelmann thinks Lohmeyer's thesis needs correcting—and from Luke's point of view.[151] But his statements at this point are very terse and somewhat unclear.

The term "Galileans" in the Lukan traditions at least does not refer to a community in Galilee, but to the primitive community

[150] Lohmeyer also wants to show that the two primitive communities transmit different Christologies. But this is doubtful. On this question, cf. Bultmann, *Theology of the New Testament,* I, 52, whose objections *at this point* are quite appropriate. (For Bultmann's further objections, cf. footnote 158.) In reply to Lohmeyer, Conzelmann states that the significance of "Jerusalem" is not to be understood from the angle of Christology but of eschatology (*op. cit.,* p. 74, n. 1). In our context, we can avoid discussing the christological problem.

[151] *Op. cit.,* p. 38, n. 1.

in Jerusalem. The heart of the Galilean idea is that the Galileans know they have been led to Jerusalem by Jesus and that now they are to stay there. Luke makes no mention of Galileans in Galilee.

We must ask whether this can really be called "correcting." Lohmeyer also asserted that Luke's Gospel reflects the primitive community at Jerusalem. True, Conzelmann describes this primitive community more exactly when he indicates that its nucleus consists of Galileans who made the journey together. So his arguments amount to a modification of one half of Lohmeyer's thesis.

But questions still arise, and precisely where Conzelmann is concerned. He is unclear as to whether his data should be played off against a "primitive Galilean community" in Mark. The qualification "in the Lukan traditions at least" opens the possibility for such an understanding, though he makes no formal assertion.[152] The statement that the Galileans "now" are to stay in Jerusalem points in the same direction. Finally, when Conzelmann says that Luke "makes no mention of Galileans in Galilee," the question is whether such existed or could have existed *prior* to Luke. Does this mean that the primitive Galilean community (represented by Mark) is older than the Jerusalem community (affirmed by Luke)? What idea should we have of it? Or does this mean that there is a primitive Galilean community, but that Luke is not aware of it?

These questions should be followed up. And we must begin with the insight that we are dealing with a conception of the evangelist, as Conzelmann clearly shows. We must also state that this "Galilean idea" had already begun to emerge in Mark's tradition, but that Luke was the first to carry it through

[152] That would in fact be a correction of Lohmeyer. I arrive at this conjecture not only on the basis of Conzelmann's published work, but also from a knowledge of his (mimeographed) dissertation which makes this quite clear. "There is a group which is distinctly Galilean; but it is situated in Jerusalem and steadfastly lays claim to this city. Since the journey, it is no longer situated in Galilee" (Dissertation, p. 147).

consistently by altering his materials. This means—we must now proceed in strictly redaction-historical fashion—that the notion of Galileans in Jerusalem is *one* main idea in Luke. Whether the third evangelist's ideas on this score are appropriate can be left open for the moment. To begin with, we only affirm the *possibility* that Luke is aware of Galileans in Jerusalem who appear with this claim.

But if we note Luke's systematic transformation of his Markan exemplar, another possibility at once emerges. Is there a polemic here? Must the Galileans in Jerusalem strive to enforce their claim? In that case, their journey with Jesus would be a polemical device intended to give historical support to their claims. But this would argue for the existence of a Galilean community in that same period. Tensions would then have existed between the two communities. Luke's work would then have to be interpreted as expressing these tensions, the third evangelist clearly siding with the Jerusalem community. Be that as it may, one thing must be maintained in any event—a "refutation" of Mark's from Luke's point of view is impossible.[153]

Before we approach a solution to the problem we must extend the scope of our inquiry. Conzelmann emphasizes that Luke is not really familiar with the country.[154] That seems to be correct. But does not the Lukan view, oriented as it is to Jerusalem, really presuppose the evangelist arranges his Gospel with Jerusalem in mind? Can it really have its origin anywhere else than among Galileans in Jerusalem? If the journey of the Galileans is Luke's idea, are not the Galileans in Jerusalem his idea also—from a distance? Such a fiction is conceivable, given the considerable lapse of time. Yet we must

[153] Put in another way: Lohmeyer's view cannot be "corrected" solely on the basis of an examination of Luke. We will hold in abeyance the question as to whether Conzelmann really (still) intends to oppose the hypothesis of a primitive Galilean community. If he does not, then our concern is to carry his insights further.

[154] *Op. cit.*, pp. 68-69.

now inquire into the background, keeping in mind the concern of a later age and another area to attribute special significance to Jerusalem by taking up the Galilee motif (and on the part of Galileans!).

This requires a comparison with Mark, whom Luke alters. It is important to see that Luke's geographical data cannot be compared with Mark's right off, since in each these data serve a different function. This is true, first of all, of the redactional materials. We can evaluate them correctly only when we take into account the history of the redaction. The peculiarities of each Gospel *for its own sake* must be brought out before comparisons can be fruitful. We must at least gain some sort of clarity as to the evangelists' ideas, tendencies, and varying points of view resulting from them. The situation out of which they wrote must also be explained as clearly as possible.

It is a fallacy to believe that merely because each of the Synoptists wrote a Gospel we can compare them side by side. It is an age-old fallacy implied in the term "Synoptists," a term requiring correction today. After what we have observed to this point, it ought to be clear that Mark is no more to be compared with Matthew and Luke than with John. We ought not be deluded by the great similarity of material. There is no Gospel "genre," at any rate, in no more than a superficial sense. And here there are still so many open questions, scarcely taken up till now, that it could be years before a problem such as "Galilee (and/or) Jerusalem" can be furnished with a generally accepted solution.

But the attempt should at least be made. We will begin with our findings in Mark so far, and at the same time refer to Luke's point of view as elucidated by Conzelmann.

An elementary description of the leading motif of the two evangelists would be that for Mark location, for Luke time is all-important. The unity in Mark results from an orientation to place. Time is not yet taken into account, at least not to the degree we could speak of an experience of time as a sequence

105

of events. Such is true of Luke, however, who breaks up the Markan consolidation. Sequence is all-important; epochs emerge with the time of Jesus at the center. Geography serves this reconstruction regulated by the experience of time. Time is thus the motivating factor in this historicizing description. It actually requires the Lukan outline. The references to place are a means to carrying out this point of view.

No doubt, Mark and Luke intend to make theological statements by means of their points of view; or, conversely, the separate problem each is to master leads to a separate redaction expressive of his point of view. When we inquire back of the two evangelists, we may not level out this difference. If we want to know what the facts are behind the two presentations, what picture we can glean from their Gospels of the primitive community at the time of each evangelist, or what picture we can glean of the evangelist himself, then we must face the fact that inquiry behind Mark leads to a place as a geographical factor and inquiry behind Luke to a time, a date. This date denotes the dawning of a consciousness of history as a sequence of events, the beginning of an experience of time. *Only by proceeding further back* can we on occasion draw inferences from Mark regarding time or draw inferences from Luke regarding place.[155]

If these observations are correct, the results gained to this point allow us to draw a few conclusions and yield a quite graphic picture. Here we get an insight into the very early history of the church, for the most part still shrouded in darkness. We get it from the sources of that period itself, and thus can measure them against later witnesses, and vice versa.

Mark's use of the term "Galilee" compels us to ask whether or not it implies a community in Galilee, or whether a move-

---

[155] Conzelmann has not always paid strict enough attention to Luke's distinction between time and geography. The locale of Luke's primitive community is much harder to determine than the time in which he wrote. Lohmeyer never quite saw the problem of time in this sense.

ment *toward* Galilee was in the offing. Even the passion narrative with its Jerusalem locale takes on this new orientation. We believe that the reason for the communities' sojourn in Galilee, or the reason for their journey to Galilee might be seen in the fact that the Parousia was expected there. This makes clear the problem of locale.

We now take up the question of time. Is there, at any period known to us, a situation in the primitive community to which these observations might correspond? The scope is quite limited, and our knowledge of the time is very scanty. But we are at once reminded of the period after A.D. 66, of the primitive community's flight from Jerusalem to Pella. This exodus would not only have been related to the political events, but to a heightened expectation of the Parousia as well. We still do not know how the two are related. There are also questions where Pella is concerned. To begin with, we can only say that Mark does not define Galilee narrowly. Does he consciously regard the boundaries as fluid? Still, there is a real point of comparison in the fact that the community was forced to move. It is yet to be decided whether the reference to Pella has any source value and if so, what kind. We will deal with these questions presently.[156] In any event, it is clear to this point that the Gospel of Mark assumes a community for Galilee which is already in existence[157] or which is about to emerge.[158]

---

[156] Cf. the next section and study four.

[157] A community could have existed in Galilee even earlier. But now for the first time it takes on real significance.

[158] This disposes of the criticism Bultmann leveled at Lohmeyer's thesis (*Theology of the New Testament*, I, 5). Bultmann concedes the existence of a primitive Galilean community, "though it scarcely had the importance that Lohmeyer attributes to it. Paul at any rate takes only the Jerusalem Church into account. . . ." It was Lohmeyer's error to extract a Galilean community *as such* from Mark (Matthew). In any case, Matthew does not come in for discussion; and as to Mark, we must inquire into the time when he assumes the existence of this community. Redaction history deals with the evangelist's *own* time. This primitive community (with precisely the significance Lohmeyer assigns it!) exists only in the late sixties. But then it is clear Paul was not aware of it.

Perhaps we can go a bit further. There is a passage in Mark which refers to Galileans (14:70). Peter is "one of them" *because* he is a Galilean; his speech betrays him. Does this not mean that to the popular mind any Galilean belongs to Jesus? [159] From this Lohmeyer[160] concluded that according to popular opinion and, more significantly, in Christian tradition "the Galileans" are regarded as "a kind of *populus christianus* and Galilee the *terra christiana.*" [161] He thinks that this is "really an error." But must we limit our terms so strictly? The community in Galilee which awaits the Parousia and the community which journeys toward Galilee for the Parousia make of the land a *terra christiana.* So it is with Mark.

Luke must be approached differently. In his case, it is not possible to draw direct inferences in the matter of locale. This must be stated in opposition to Lohmeyer (and perhaps also in opposition to Conzelmann). The "community in Jerusalem" is Luke's fiction. This does not mean, of course, that there never was a community in Jerusalem. There is no doubt about that. But there is no evidence in Luke's Gospel that such a community existed *in the evangelist's time.* This statement requires further qualification. Such a community could have existed in Luke's day, but it is in no way identical with the Jerusalem community of Galileans (originating with Luke's redaction) who made the journey with Jesus and now make their appeal to it. How could we possibly conceive of it? We need only inquire when the third Gospel arose, we need only recall the events of A.D. 66-70 so as to heap doubt after

[159] On the language, cf. Strack-Billerbeck, I, 156-57.

[160] *Galiläa und Jerusalem,* p. 28; cf. Lohmeyer, *Das Evangelium des Markus, ad loc.*

[161] We must add the qualification that it cannot be definitely proved whether and to what extent Mark shaped this passage. So we must be content to assert that 14:70 is to be interpreted in this fashion *in the context of Mark's Gospel.* Matthew interprets by deleting the term "Galilean" (26:73).

doubt upon such a hypothesis. It must be a problem of Luke's own time which gave rise to his redactional work.

The third evangelist, then, must be approached differently. His intention—precisely as elucidated by Conzelmann—is not to defend a locale, but to handle the problem of the experience of time gained in the interim. This is done, of course, with the aid of geography, but not exclusively. Luke thus reflects a community which must come to terms with the delayed Parousia as well as the newly emergent problems of the second and third generation.

Now only can we inquire into the location of this community. But the answer is very doubtful. One place, at least, is absolutely to be eliminated—Jerusalem. If Luke were there, he would be familiar with the country. To the objection, Why does the third evangelist orient his work to Jerusalem? we must answer that there is no such orientation, at any rate not in the form most often assumed. Jerusalem is only a point of intersection. It has preeminence as the center. Toward this place, the place of the temple, salvation history at the "center of time" is moving. This is also the point at which the third epoch begins. If thus far the entire event is confined to Palestine, and if Luke scrupulously omits any activity of Jesus outside the country, now the bounds are burst. *Return to Galilee would denote not merely a spatial but, to the evangelist's mind, an actual regression.* Thus Easter follows Good Friday, and Pentecost, the time of mission, follows the Ascension. The gospel makes its way into the world.

Luke lives in this *epoch*. But his community lies at some extreme point of the lines of mission. The community knows full well that Jerusalem is its center. Jesus' way from Galilee led toward Jerusalem; from Jerusalem the gospel came to Luke's community. But the gospel does not penetrate the missionary communities from Jerusalem by way of Galilee; it makes direct entry. It is not at all necessary to assume a connection between Luke's community and Jerusalem. It is

109

not even necessary to assume that when Luke wrote his Gospel there was still a Jerusalem community of considerable importance. What is important for him, the believing historian, is merely that the good news once went out from Jerusalem into the land of the Gentiles.

More can be said. As already suggested, Luke might reflect a polemic, and in fact against a stress on the gospel's ancient habitat, a polemic against the "Holy Land's" claim to priority, a defense and assertion of equal rights on behalf of the missionary communities.[162] For those who were there from the beginning did *not* subsequently remain in Jerusalem; they became missionaries. We could actually put it this way: the Galileans are not in Galilee, nor even in Jerusalem; they are now in Gentile territory, much to the amazement of the Jews (cf. Acts 10:45 together with 10:37).

Thus a redaction-historical investigation of the Gospels can shed much light on a period so remote from us. First of all, we must view each Gospel more strictly as a unity. Then the development which the primitive community (communities) underwent becomes clear. Precisely because each Gospel is altogether a "child of its time," it is a source of extraordinary significance for just this time. It is only secondarily a source for the event it records.

Once we set out upon this method, we will abandon the desire to harmonize the Synoptics simply because they (we might almost say accidentally) present much the same material. We will no longer attempt to eliminate Galilee as an "error" of Mark, since the Gospel of Luke and Acts would otherwise be unintelligible. Further, we will no longer come with the rash idea of searching for Galilee in the neighborhood

---

[162] Possibly Pella's claim to have become Jerusalem's legitimate successor is being disputed. If Paul, in spite of many difficulties, preserved his connection with Jerusalem, Luke now breaks that connection by historicizing. The result of this is that no longer can any claims be raised in Luke's own time.

of Jerusalem, or anything of that sort.[163] And we will no longer consider John so exclusively as the only independent theologian among the evangelists. We will then understand why the Gospels differ, take seriously their variety, and on that basis attain a better understanding of the isolated pieces, within the framework of the whole. Finally, we turn to Mark once again, taking up questions which emerged with our proposed interpretation of the last verse.

2. Mark 16:7

If, as we supposed, this verse really deals with the Parousia, then we have hit upon an oft-discussed problem whose solutions till now are open to serious question. The problem has to do with the relation in time between the resurrection and Parousia. As is well known, advocates of the so-called "thorough-going eschatology," [164] but others as well,[165] have proposed that Jesus was not aware of an interval between the resurrection and Parousia, a view which Kümmel describes as "in every respect untenable." [166] How does our exegesis of 16:7 (and 14:28) relate to this disputed question?

It should first be stated that our exegesis cannot be used in support of either of the two opinions, at least not directly. We are not inquiring into Jesus' own idea but into the evangelist's interpretation. In any case, what Jesus thought, if it can be detected at all, can only be detected with a degree of prob-

---

[163] Cf. the evidence in Lohmeyer, *Galiläa und Jerusalem*, p. 8, n. 1.

[164] Thus Martin Werner (*The Formation of Christian Dogma*, trans. S. G. F. Brandon [New York: Harper & Bros., 1957]) in dependence on Albert Schweitzer. Cf. Schweitzer, *op. cit.*, p. 365: "Therefore Paul also makes one and the same event of the metamorphosis, resurrection, and translation."

[165] Cf. Kümmel, *Promise and Fulfilment, The Eschatological Message of Jesus*, trans. Dorothea M. Barton (London: SCM Press, 1957), pp. 64 ff. Other literature is referred to there.

[166] *Promise and Fulfilment*, pp. 82-83.

ability when the evangelist's view has first been brought to light.[167]

For Mark the situation seems to be self-evident. He cannot construe the resurrection and Parousia as successive or even as simultaneous events for the mere reason that he writes his Gospel between them. But the way he sets to arranging them is all the more clear. The angel who announces the resurrection also announces the imminent Parousia. The aim is not to equate the two events, though Mark relates them directly to each other. We shall not deal with the question as to whether primitive Christian faith (generally) viewed the resurrection as a "transition." [168] Mark at any rate understands it

[167] Thus, e.g., it is questionable when Kümmel (*Promise and Fulfilment*, p. 66) assigns Lohmeyer to the group which supports an immediate connection between the resurrection and the Parousia. It is true that Lohmeyer interprets Mark 14:28 and 16:7 as a "transition from the resurrection to the Parousia" (*Galiläa und Jerusalem*, p. 13); but on the next page he speaks of a later journey of the disciples and reflects on the type of experience which held them to Jerusalem. Still, we must agree with Kümmel that Lohmeyer is not quite clear here. This is probably due to the fact that he did not consistently think through his preliminary statement. There are long sections in which he is unclear as to whether we are dealing with the words of Jesus, with the conception of the community, or with the evangelist's own composition. Accordingly, his critique is always in danger of beginning at the wrong place. On the other hand, we cannot overlook Kümmel's attempt to control the isolated pieces as quickly as possible, and to use them to discuss the question of "authenticity." On Mark 13 he states (p. 98): "Busch's demand to abstain from separating Jesus' sayings from the tradition of the church takes no account of the historical fact." But is not that "historical fact" located first of all in the coherent chapter before us, or in the entire work? Its situation-in-life should be learned. When that has been done, then light is shed from there on the individual pericopes. Both types of investigation have their place. But their results may not be set against each other—without keeping these distinctions in mind. Our historical investigation of the whole *cannot* lead to a life of Jesus, but only to the history and theology of the evangelist. On the other hand, *all* reports of the life of "Jesus" have been transmitted solely within the totality of the individual Gospels; and in their arrangement, but to a degree also in their (trans-) formation, they have been inserted into this totality.

[168] Lohmeyer, *Galiläa und Jerusalem*, p. 13.

as such. But the very expression he gives to his idea is typical for him. He all but eliminates the interval between the two events. The resurrection is behind him. Thus an "epoch" has actually begun, the "epoch of the resurrection" in which Christ rules as Risen Lord,[169] an epoch to be concluded with the imminent Parousia. The redaction (insertion of 16:7) does not describe this "epoch" as a time sequence, but actually reduces it to a transition connecting resurrection and Parousia. It now appears as if the Parousia were directly linked with the resurrection. But it appears so only to the one who makes historical inquiry, who thus bypasses Mark and, instead of focusing first upon the narrator, desires immediate and direct control of what is narrated. This type of inquiry is false since it is oriented to time, a factor which Mark did not yet consciously experience as a sequence of events, as did Luke later on.

Here too we must consistently maintain that the work of the earliest evangelist is proclamation, that what is narrated is subordinate to it. In the next study we will show that in this very proclamation, representation (of the resurrection, of the Risen Lord) and anticipation (of the Parousia) coincide. Here again there is a "consolidation."

Once we recognize this, we can go back a step further to raise a second question. "From the standpoint of church history," the events took another shape than Mark's point of view allows them. The resurrection has occurred; the Parousia is viewed as imminent. Between the two lies "time," even decades. But the "history of the church" lies outside the evangelist's horizon. He proclaims.[170]

[169] An analysis of this epoch (Resurrection/Ascension/Pentecost) has not yet been made. Hence we cannot speak of the "Exalted Lord" as the term was *later* used; but the Risen Lord is already the Exalted Lord whose exaltation will be manifest at the Parousia.

[170] Hence it is not quite correct to speak of the "elimination" of time. That is, of course, an idea which appeals to our way of thinking. But it does so because *our* experience of time can no longer be made retroactive. We cannot penetrate behind an imminent expectation which was later

If it is also correct that the delay of the Parousia is related to the events between A.D. 66-70, then Mark 16:7 may shed light on a passage in Eusebius. In connection with the community's exodus, Eusebius (Ecclesiastical History, III, 5) tells of a χρησμός received by its leaders δι᾽ ἀποκαλύψεως. Epiphanius of Constance (de mensuribus et ponderibus, 15) adds to this the note that an angel gave the oracle.[171] The sources of these data are uncertain. Harnack perhaps assumes a common source.[172] Zahn already indicated that the more colorless description of Eusebius can hardly have been Epiphanius' source.[173] He assumes rather that Epiphanius is dependent upon Hegesippus. But this must be left open. The question is still whether or not Mark 16:7 is closely linked to this oracle.

At first glance we might suppose that the evangelist's work furnishes something like a "theological foundation" for this revelation, possibly an interpretation of the χρησμός. If the

---

abandoned. But probably, where Mark is concerned, still another factor must be taken into account. The interchangeability of perfect and imperfect is peculiar to the Jewish conception of time. The past can be actualized in the cultus and in proclamation. Time is thus eliminated (to our way of thinking; cf. M. Noth, "Die Vergegenwärtigung des Alten Testaments in der Verkündigung," Evangelische Theologie, 102-103. Jahrgang (1952-53), pp. 6 ff.). It is just this element which seems to be reflected in Mark's Gospel. It is reasonable to suppose Mark was a Jew, The locale we furnished the Gospel fits this assumption—just as this locale in turn suggests a Jewish concept of time. Luke's reconstruction has to do not only with the delayed Parousia, but also with the peculiar structure of his concept of time. And if Matthew assumes a uniquely interim position, this is due to the fact that he not only experiences "time" following the delayed Parousia, but also as a Jew recognizes contemporaneity in the proclamation. On this question, cf. the next study's remarks on the "tension" between framework and speech complexes.

[171] Adolf von Harnack, Mission und Ausbreitung des Christentums in den ersten drei Jahrhunderten, 4te Auflage (Leipzig: J. C. Hinrichs'sche Buchhandlung, 1924), pp. 634-35.

[172] Op. cit., II (first ed., 1906), 81.

[173] Theodor Zahn, Forschungen zur Geschichte des neutestamentlichen Kanons und der altkirchlichen Literatur, 6te Teil (Erlangen: Andreas Deichert, 1900), p. 270.

oracle dealt merely with the μετανάστασις, Mark deals with what is to occur after the emigration—the Parousia.

But it is more logical to assume an opposite development. The oracle would then have originally contained a command to depart as well as an announcement of the imminent Parousia. This is easily conceivable. An oracle is scarcely needed for flight from a city threatened by siege. Some special content will always be assumed. And, it is easy to see why the oracle was not transmitted if it dealt with the Parousia. The non-occurrence of this event later gave rise to a separation of the proclamation from the tradition. A torso remained. The dissimilar and more meager data in Eusebius and Epiphanius can thus be explained and can at least give indirect support to our interpretation of Mark 16:7 and to the point of view we assigned the evangelist.

There is still another note which is of some importance. According to *Epiph. Haer.* 29:7, 8,[174] the departure occurs at Christ's command; according to *Epiph. de mens.* 15, an angel delivers the divine directive. Both are found in Mark, in 14:28 and 16:7.

The picture is rounded out. In Mark and in the tradition underlying Eusebius and Epiphanius, we encounter a common feature traceable to the same event. The Lord orders his community to move to Galilee[175] and repeats his command by the word of an angel.[176]

---

[174] Holl, *op. cit.,* I, 330, 7-10.

[175] Even without the express use of the imperative, 14:28 reflects a command.

[176] Of course, a certain difficulty arises in connection with the reference to Galilee as a destination. Pella is not situated in Galilee. A few things should be noted in this connection. First of all, it was already established that Galilee's borders are not only fluid (cf. also Schlatter, *Der Evangelist Matthäus,* p. 565), but that Mark evidently did not intend any clear delineation. In addition, we probably ought not follow Epiphanius and interpret the exodus to Pella strictly to mean that the Christian community was totally established there (cf. Harnack, *op. cit.,* pp. 635-36). Several references to place emerge in this context. Not all can be clearly

Mark's report of this (second) command as given the disciples "on the third day" (16:1) poses no problem for redaction history. The Gospel is the evangelist's proclamation to the community of his time. The community sets out on its journey, but since the Parousia is still in the offing, the fulfillment of 16:7 cannot be reported.

The evangelist's point of view thus requires the conclusion at 16:8.

---

located. Yet Basanitis is named—by the Galilean Sea. There are problems enough. But if it is true that Mark somehow reflects the "oracle," then the Gospel must first of all be viewed as the older source. We could then conclude that the orientation was originally toward Galilee, perhaps with the Sea as center. Later, there was a further shift eastward (after the nonoccurrence of the Parousia?). Then Pella became a new center to replace Jerusalem. Mark knows nothing of this as yet. The Parousia was detached from the oracle, and the reference to place was altered. Is the oracle now to support the legitimacy of Pella's succession, and is Luke's new geographical orientation a polemic against it? (But not on behalf of Galilee! Cf. above.) Again, the situation is different in Matthew. If he appropriated the essential traditional features of 28:16 ff., it would be reasonable to suppose that this "missionary command" (which is more than a mere "command" and also contains the "Ascension kerygma") represents a Galilean "substitute" for the delayed Parousia. Now Galilee becomes the "motherland of discipledom" (Lohmeyer, "Mir ist gegeben alle Gewalt," p. 44). Galilee is now the center of mission. Despite all the unanswered questions we can see connections between Mark and the oracle. And redaction-historical work on the Gospels can help shed a bit of light in the darkness.

Study Three | Euangelion

Mark's work is designated a "Gospel." It shares this title with a number of other writings. The title is obviously oriented to the content, but not to the genre of these writings. A comparison between the so-called Synoptists with John and, finally, with the post-canonical Gospels makes that clear at once. But can the term "Gospel" sufficiently and aptly characterize the genre of these works? Is not precisely this collective term calculated to level out important differences?

Till it came to refer to these writings, the term "evangel" already had a history behind it which continued on into later times. Hence the much-debated question as to whether Jesus Christ belongs to or brings the gospel. Another closely related question is whether the genitive in the phrase εὐαγγέλιον Ἰησοῦ Χριστοῦ is objective or subjective. At this point, we must sharply distinguish the exegetical and dogmatic aspects of the question. We will avoid the latter in our discussion.[1]

---

[1] This must be given special stress because a frequent (probably often unconscious) crossing of boundaries can be noted here. Whatever dogmatic overtones this concept may have are included in the exegetical discussion. On the development of the concept under these aspects, cf. Harnack, *The Constitution and Law of the Church in the First Two Centuries*, trans. F. L. Pogson (London: Williams and Norgate, 1910), pp. 275 ff.

It roots in the fact that the entire New Testament was later termed "Gospel" and contrasted with the "Law," or Old Testament.

On the other hand, if we examine the exegetical aspect and take inventory of Paul who most often uses the term "evangel," we can assert with Friedrich that the question should not be given the attention it most often receives.[2] We simply cannot draw such sharp distinctions. Very often no real alternative is involved. Paul intends the genitive to be taken objectively as well as subjectively.

Yet what is true of Paul is not necessarily true of the Synoptists. Here again we must differentiate total findings from findings in each of the Gospels. The total findings easily fit those in Paul. The reason for this, however, is that Paul does not always proceed uniformly but stresses now this, now the other aspect. As to the relation between the generic term "Gospel" and its application to the individual writings, the two must be kept distinct. If, according to Mark 1:14-15, Jesus proclaims the gospel, this gospel is not to be equated off-hand with the "book" itself. But the same term appears in 1:1. Are we dealing with a title here? Does it characterize the writing as a whole? A comparison with Matthew, who describes his work as a βίβλος, suggests this.

One factor clearly requires that we examine this complex within the context of the inquiry pursued here. Synoptic usage indicates considerable differences. Mark uses only the noun εὐαγγέλιον, Luke[3] only the verb εὐαγγελίζεσθαι. It is striking that Luke never uses the verb in passages where the Markan parallel uses the noun. Matthew is not consistent. He

---

[2] Kittel, *op. cit.*, II, 731-32 (and the literature cited there); further, Asting, *op. cit.*, pp. 323-24.

[3] Acts is apparently the exception. The noun occurs twice here, but in quite distinct connections. 15:7 treats of the λόγος τοῦ εὐαγγελίου which the Gentiles have heard; 20:24 of the εὐαγγέλιον τῆς χάριτος τοῦ θεοῦ.

uses the verb on only one occasion and never uses the noun absolutely but always with a supplement.[4]

Friedrich asserts that these differences have been "frequently noted but never explained."[5] Are they connected with the point of view of each evangelist? In light of the observations made till now, this does not seem impossible.[6] We shall now try to determine what Mark understands by the concept "evangel" and whether anything can be learned from this which could contribute to a total understanding of his work. We must also inquire why the two major Gospels use another terminology and whether this usage enables us to recognize their points of view. We shall exclude, however, the question of Jesus' own use of the term, which seems only proper since the differences obviously have their origin in the redaction.[7]

A. Analysis of the Synoptic Findings

First of all, we will attempt to indicate each evangelist's method by way of a synoptic comparison. To do so we must

[4] Albertz smooths over all the differences, partly because he does not sharply enough distinguish the noun from the verb, and often because he does not distinguish them at all (*op. cit.*, I, 1, 165 ff.; cf. p. 166 on Luke 3:18; p. 168 on Acts 8:12, *passim*).

[5] Kittel, *op. cit.*, II, 727. And yet, Wellhausen (*Einleitung in die drei ersten Evangelien*, pp. 108 ff.) comes very close to an explanation!

[6] At the same time, it is not our concern to elucidate the concept (or concepts), esp. with reference to its history. We give no attention to this aspect except in cases where our inquiry touches on the history of the concept. On this subject, cf. among others Schniewind, *Euangelion, Ursprung und erste Gestalt des Begriffs Evangelium*, I. Teil (Gütersloh: Gerd Mohn, 1927); II. Lieferung, 1931; Friedrich on "Εὐαγγελίζομαι" in Kittel, *op. cit.*, II, 707-37, and the literature cited there.

[7] For the most part, εὐαγγέλιον is considered an improbability in the speech of Jesus. Wellhausen, *Einleitung in die drei ersten Evangelien*, p. 19; Gustaf Dalman, *The Words of Jesus*, trans. D. M. Kay (Edinburgh: T. and T. Clark, 1909), p. 102; somewhat more cautiously Friedrich in Kittel, *op. cit.*, II, 727. Kümmel cautiously allows for the possibility of Jesus' use of the term ("Die Eschatologie der Evangelien, ihre Geschichte und ihr Sinn," cols. 229-30). But he does so by way of the verb in Matt. 11:5. Most often, however, the verb is quite differently evaluated and to a great extent regarded as (probably) "genuine."

examine Mark 8:35; 10:29; 13:10; 14:9, and parallels.[8] In connection with 8:35 and 10:29 [9] Friedrich believes εὐαγγέλιον did not appear "in the original Mark, i.e., in the earliest stratum of the tradition," [10] as a comparison with synoptic parallels shows. We will examine these two passages first of all.

A saying of Jesus in 8:35 reads that whoever loses his life ἕνεκεν ἐμοῦ καὶ τοῦ εὐαγγελίου will save it. Both parallels (Matt. 16:25 and Luke 9:24) agree almost literally with Mark,[11] but in both the καὶ τοῦ εὐαγγελίου is lacking.[12] This suggests that Mark inserted "and the gospel's sake" here.[13] Lohmeyer[14] supposes the evangelist did so in order to abstract "the speech from a single situation binding on the disciples," and give it greater force "as a rule for the community" whose battle cry, by which it suffered and triumphed, was "Christ and the gospel." [15]

The next passage to be discussed is very similar. In Mark 10:29 Jesus promises a reward to those who leave house, family, and lands ἕνεκεν ἐμοῦ καὶ ἕνεκεν τοῦ εὐαγγελίου. But when we note the parallels, the problem has shifted over against Mark 8:35. Luke 18:29 reads, εἵνεκεν τῆς βασιλείας τοῦ θεοῦ, and Matthew 19:29, ἕνεκεν τοῦ ἐμοῦ ὀνόματος. We can no longer be so

[8] In Mark the noun also appears in 1:1; 1:14, 15 (as well as in 16:15).

[9] In 1:15 as well.

[10] Kittel, op. cit., II, 727. But in contradiction (?) to this he says (p. 728) that "as formulated this verse undoubtedly derives from Mark."

[11] Matthew reads εὑρήσει instead of σώσει. 'Απόλλυμι is thereby softened (instead of "destroy" the reading now is "lose"). Cf. Lohmeyer, Das Evangelium des Markus, ad loc.

[12] In cotrast, P[45], D, the Old Latin witnesses, and Sy⁸ omit the ἐμοῦ καὶ in Mark 8:35.

[13] We leave open the question as to whether the addition was missing in Urmarkus (Bultmann, History, p. 93, evidently [?] holds this view) or—as we would prefer to suggest—in the tradition available to Mark. (More on this below.)

[14] Lohmeyer, Das Evangelium des Markus, ad loc.

[15] Also in support of a Markan addition: J. Weiss, Die Schriften des Neuen Testaments, I, ad loc. (an explanation similar to Lohmeyer's); Wohlenberg, op. cit., ad loc.; Klostermann, op. cit., ad loc.; Sundwall, op. cit., p. 56.

sure as before that we can even make an evaluation, since Mark after all uses the same formula in both passages. We should perhaps also note that this is not a fixed formula,[16] but merely denotes a topical connection between the two passages. But neither of the two co-evangelists is consistent.[17] So we must at least ask whether or not Matthew and Luke for some reason alter the phrase in Mark,[18] in one case by omitting the term εὐαγγέλιον, in the other by providing a new wording.

We can argue in reverse fashion, of course, and assert that all these formulas are expansions of an original ἐμοῦ.[19] But then why did Matthew and Luke at one time expand or restructure, and at another leave the old form intact? It is difficult to agree with Bultmann that Luke's formula is the original since it more easily explains Mark's alteration than vice versa.[20]

In any event, the question cannot be answered hastily or unequivocally; and it does no good to view the problem as solved by appealing to 8:35.[21] Next, then, we turn to the following passages.

In midst of the admonition in 13:10 appears the saying: καὶ εἰς πάντα τὰ ἔθνη πρῶτον δεῖ κηρυχθῆναι τὸ εὐαγγέλιον. What is striking here is that this word is connected to the phrase in 13:9 which brings to mind what was discussed above. The dis-

---

[16] Only in B* and a greater number also from other groups does it become such a formula by omission of the second ἕνεκεν.

[17] Here it is difficult to maintain the hypothesis of an *Urmarkus* since each co-evangelist goes his own way.

[18] E. C. Hoskyns and Noel Davey, *The Riddle of the New Testament* (London: Faber and Faber Ltd., 1958), pp. 92-93. For Matthew and Luke, Mark's use of the term "gospel" was for some reason "cumbersome."

[19] Thus (with a question mark) Klostermann, *Das Markusevangelium, ad loc.* For Mark, 13:9 could be cited (at least indirectly).

[20] *History*, pp. 110-11; cf. p. 127.

[21] Thus Lohmeyer, *Das Evangelium des Markus,* on 10:29. Whether we may construe Mark 10:29 and parallels as synonymous (in exegesis) is another question. Cf. K. L. Schmidt's article on "Βασιλεία" in Kittel, *op. cit.,* I, 587-88. But in this way we pass too lightly over the differences and bar the way to the individual evangelists.

ciples will stand before governors and kings ἔνεκεν ἐμοῦ εἰς μαρτύριον αὐτοῖς. This time, only the ἔνεκεν ἐμοῦ appears in Matt. 10:18. Luke (21:12) of course uses the phrase we previously identified in Matthew (19:21) : ἔνεκεν τοῦ ὀνόματός μου. If Mark had a tendency to expand, he did not exercise it here, at any rate—or so it appears at first glance. Can 13:10 be a substitute for such an expansion? [22] Luke furnishes no parallel. In Matthew, however, the verse reads: καὶ κηρυχθήσεται τοῦτο τὸ εὐαγγέλιον τῆς βασιλείας ἐν ὅλῃ τῇ οἰκουμένῃ (24:14). In addition we note the following differences: Matthew defines the gospel more closely by a τοῦτο and by the addition of τῆς βασιλείας.[23] Matthew uses ἐν, but Mark εἰς, when referring to the κηρύσσειν of the εὐαγγέλιον. This use of prepositions is peculiar to each evangelist. Matthew's alteration of Mark's text at this point seems to follow from his providing commentary on the πρῶτον (Mark 13:10) by way of the καὶ τότε ἥξει τὸ τέλος.[24] And yet there is every indication that Mark 13:10 is the evangelist's insertion.[25] We must keep this in mind.

Finally, 14:9 should be noted. In connection with the anointing at Bethany Jesus says that ὅπου ἐὰν κηρυχθῇ τὸ εὐαγγέλιον εἰς ὅλον τὸν κόσμον καὶ ὃ ἐποίησεν αὕτη λαληθήσεται εἰς μνημόσυνον αὐτῆς. Again, Luke lacks a parallel. The alterations in Matthew (26:13) are slight. But again, the addition of the τοῦτο is typical, and again the proclamation of the gospel takes place ἐν τῷ κόσμῳ, whereas in Mark εἰς τὸν κόσμον.

There is widespread agreement that vss. 8-9 later grew onto the story of the anointing, which in this form was attached

---

[22] We will still have to come to terms with this verse in the next study.

[23] In Luke 18:29, βασιλεία τοῦ θεοῦ appears *in lieu of* εὐαγγέλιον in Mark's parallel.

[24] Cf. Klostermann, *Das Matthäusevangelium, ad loc.*

[25] Bultmann, *History*, p. 129; Sundwall, *op. cit.*, p. 78. The argument is particularly clear in Lohmeyer, *Das Evangelium des Markus, ad loc.* (We believe the conclusions Lohmeyer draws are false. More on this in the next study.)

to the framework of the passion narrative.[26] Of course, the question is still open as to whether this was Mark's doing or whether he found the story already joined to the passion narrative.[27]

For the time being, this exhausts the passages which permit synoptic comparison. The picture we have gained of the evangelist's method is not too clear. But before we summarize, we should consider the two Matthaean εὐαγγέλιον passages which have no parallel in Mark. These are 4:23 and 9:35.

Matthew 4:23 (together with vss. 24-25) turns out to be Matthew's summary report. A more detailed examination reveals that these verses are almost totally composed of Markan material. Their arrangement corresponds exactly with Matthew's penchant for combining materials from definite points of view.[28] The term εὐαγγέλιον has after all one Markan parallel in 1:14. But Matthew has again expanded it by adding the τῆς βασιλείας. The case is much the same in 9:35.[29] We can actually speak of a doublet here. Both passages are summary reports composed by Matthew, both introduce a complex composed by the evangelist. Verse 4:23 is a prelude to the Sermon on the Mount; 9:35 is a prelude to the commissioning speech.

To begin with, this much seems certain: Matthew did not take up the term εὐαγγέλιον into his Gospel on his own, nor did he derive it from his own sources. In Q the noun might not have appeared at all.[30] Mark is his only source for this term.

[26] Bultmann, *History*, pp. 36-37; Dibelius, *From Tradition to Gospel*, pp. 178-79; Klostermann, *Das Markusevangelium, ad loc.*; Lohmeyer, *Das Evangelium des Markus, ad loc.*; likewise Wellhausen, *Das Evangelium Marci, ad loc.*

[27] Thus Sundwall, *op. cit.*, pp. 78-79. Moreover, Luke 7:36 ff. indicates that the anointing was handed down independently and with another thrust.

[28] Cf. Klostermann, *Das Matthäusevangelium, ad loc.*

[29] Cf. Harnack, *op. cit.*, p. 207; Asting, *op. cit.*, p. 325.

[30] Harnack, *op. cit.*, p. 200.

Naturally we can ask whether Matthew did not read εὐαγ-γέλιον in those other passages where Mark uses it (1:15; 8:35; 10:29). But that is highly improbable. The fact that Matthew takes over the term from Mark 1:14, that it is absent in Matt. 4:17, but then emerges at two new places (4:23; 9:35) which definitely betray their actual origin in Mark 1:14, indicates that he deals quite independently with his material. Matthew uses the term εὐαγγέλιον whenever, in his opinion, it is pertinent. But in places where, to his mind, it does not belong, he either omits it (4:17; 16:25) or replaces it with another (19: 29). We can also anticipate something else. For Matthew the "gospel" is of a piece with his speech complexes. Twice he prefixes the term to such a complex (4:23; 9:35); twice he finds it in a piece of tradition which he inserts into his speech complexes, viz., in the Parousia speech (24:14) and in the passion narrative (26:13). But in each case he characteristically adds a τοῦτο. By so doing he moves from the core of that speech toward the speech as a whole. This can only mean that *for Matthew the "gospel" is just such a speech complex*. But then in 4:17; 16:25; and 19:29 he *cannot* use the term εὐαγ-γέλιον, at any rate not in the way his exemplar gives it.

This hypothesis proves useful to the degree it can explain all three differences in Mark and Matthew. We see why Matthew alters his exemplar and inserts a τοῦτο; we see why he omits the term in a few instances or replaces it with another; we see, finally, why he inserts the term at two new places. (We should note that "new" refers to his outline, though the literary descent from Mark is clear.)

If this (indirectly, at least, and exclusive of an Ur-Mark hypothesis) covers the εὐαγγέλιον passages in Mark, we should now ask whether Mark already found the term in the tradition, or whether he himself inserted it. If we can establish that the synoptic material as a whole is not aware of the term εὐαγγέλιον (except for passages where Mark gives it or which are dependent on Mark), that at least indicates that the evangelist quite probably introduced the term into the tradition. This hypothesis can be verified. It seems immediately plausible and is quite generally recognized for 1:1 and 1:14-15. For the other passages we begin with Mark 13:9. This verse indicates that Klostermann's suggestion reviewed above contains an element of truth.[31] He assumes that Mark 8:35; 10:29, and parallels (!) reflect a common ἕνεκεν ἐμοῦ. We would have to put it more precisely, however, and say that this phrase lies back of Mark. He then expanded it. This means that he proceeded in a different way. In 8:35 and 10:29 he makes additions within the verse itself. In 13:9 he expands by a subsequent verse. Only 14:9 is obscure. But everything points to the fact that this verse also should be assigned to the evangelist.[32] What is true of six passages is probably true of the seventh. It would be strange if it were otherwise at just this point.

Mark thus introduced the noun εὐαγγέλιον into synoptic tradition. But he set the same term over his entire work. Our analysis has therefore led us to a valuable point of departure for further questions. After Mark 1:1 the Gospels are called "Gospels." But we need no longer interpret this concept on the basis of 1:1. On the contrary, from the redaction within the Gospel itself, we can try to glean the meaning the evangelist gives this concept. It will soon become clear that this is not only easier but more easily leads to results than an investigation beginning with 1:1.

Something else can also be said here. The noun εὐαγγέλιον is evidently a favorite of Mark's.[33] To it he attaches a specific idea which his successors did not take up *in the same way*. Their alterations prove that. We already noted the independence of Matthew's work. Luke avoids any use of the noun. On

[31] Klostermann, *Das Markusevangelium*, on 10:29.

[32] Whether this is true also of 14:8 depends on whether Mark inserted the pericope into the framework of the passion narrative or whether this already took place in the tradition.

[33] Verse 1:1 should be evidence enough that this is not an overstatement.

that score Harnack maintained that "we cannot possibly regard this negative factor as purely accidental." [34]

The question now is, can we find a reason for this varying usage in the meaning each Gospel gives the term? From the meaning Mark gives the term and from what we know of Luke's point of view, can we explain why the third evangelist avoids any use of the noun?

B. Mark's Point of View

First of all a preliminary comment. Investigations carried out on our problem till now were for the most part burdened with the question as to whether or not Jesus himself used the term εὐαγγέλιον and, if so, how. A beginning was made with the Synoptists (which, given this direction of the inquiry seems the only logical approach), and then turned to the significance of the term in Paul.[35] But now if it is true that Mark himself introduced εὐαγγέλιον into synoptic tradition, then Paul's understanding is *prior* to Mark's. We may not conclude from this that their understanding of the term must

[34] *Op. cit.,* p. 211, n. 1.
[35] Cf. Kittel, *op. cit.,* II, 729 ff. Asting (*op. cit.,* pp. 300 ff.) of course rules out the question, but still makes a point of indicating the development from the Synoptists through Paul to later times (cf. pp. 454-55). But the observation that after Paul there is a rapidly diminishing use of the term εὐαγγέλιον (p. 426; cf. p. 456), and that even the Synoptists seldom use it (pp. 453-54) should have compelled him to caution. Despite that fact, Paul's "extensive use" of the term is supposed to agree with the "usage of the earlier primitive Christian period" (p. 456). How then can we explain its rare occurrence in the traditional synoptic material, above all, its absence from Q? In the latter case, Asting speaks of an "enigma" (p. 336). Here especially his hypothesis breaks down, according to which εὐαγγέλιον and λόγος supposedly run in competition (pp. 334 ff.). If Asting correctly indicates the term's tendency to diminish, then this suggests we take Paul as the point of departure. (Asting's error is due in part to the fact that though he recognizes the differences between the noun and the verb, in actual practice he often smooths them out. Also, a more extensive use of literary criticism would have enabled him to see many things differently.)

be identical at this point. But in the exposition of Mark we will occasionally be able to refer to Paul and must keep in mind the question as to whether or not the evangelist alters Paul's understanding of the term.[36] This problem can be discussed only after we have tried to give an interpretation of the term solely as it appears in Mark.

It is striking that Mark always uses the noun εὐαγγέλιον in the absolute (except in 1:1; 1:14), i.e., without further modification.[37] Matthew never does. That is all the more surprising, since Matthew's additions (τῆς βασιλείας or τοῦτο) are conscious transformations of the Markan text. This fact indicates the proximity of Markan to Pauline usage. Paul is aware of both uses of the noun, but his use of the term in the absolute is striking because it is so uncommon elsewhere. On the other hand, Matthew differs from Paul to the extent that Paul never makes the βασιλεία the content of the gospel.[38]

It has often been pointed out that Mark's formulation is influenced by primitive Christian missions terminology.[39] If so, it is all the more striking that Mark should put it in the mouth of Jesus (1:14-15).

In keeping with our aim, we will not begin with this hotly disputed passage but rather with 8:35 and 10:29. Wellhausen[40] supposed that ἕνεκεν τοῦ εὐαγγελίου is almost identical to ἕνεκεν ἐμοῦ. Accordingly, the Jesus of Mark would not be the

[36] On the meaning in Paul, cf. above all Kittel, *op. cit.,* II, 729 ff.; cf. also Harnack, *op. cit.,* pp. 211 ff.

[37] The εὐαγγέλιον passage in the later conclusion (16:15) also matches this usage, as Harnack already indicated (*op. cit.,* p. 201, n. 1) .

[38] Kittel, *op. cit.,* II, 730. (The same is true of Luke, though in connection with the verb. Is this really accidental?)

[39] Cf. the relevant passages in the commentaries by Klostermann, Lohmeyer, *et al.;* in addition, Wellhausen, *Einleitung in die drei ersten Evangelien,* p. 109; Bultmann, *History,* p. 118; Martin Werner, "Der Einfluss paulinischer Theologie im Markusevangelium," *Zeitschrift für neutestamentliche Wissenschaft,* Beiheft 1, XXII (1923), 102; Sundwall, *op. cit.,* p. 8.

[40] Wellhausen, *Das Evangelium Marci,* on 8:35; likewise Asting, *op. cit.,* p. 320.

127

proclaimer but rather the content of the gospel. "The gospel is the Christ preached by the apostles." Harnack [41] retorted that this explanation has no support in the context, that the context in fact contradicts it, "for it is in the Kingdom of God that a man will save his soul and receive a hundred times more than he lost here." For that reason, says Harnack, the term "gospel" must denote the "gospel of the Kingdom." [42] It cannot be a tautology or hendiadys of the ἕνεκεν ἐμοῦ, "since the ἕνεκεν is expressly repeated in the second passage." (But that applies only to 10:29.)

It [sc. the meaning assumed by Wellhausen] can indeed be found in the ἕνεκεν ἐμοῦ. The stress clearly given it alongside the ἕνεκεν τοῦ εὐαγγελίου points in this direction. At the same time—precisely because it has this special emphasis—it preserves to the term "gospel" the meaning of "gospel of the Kingdom."

Literary-critical analysis has shown, however, that *Mark* added to the original ἕνεκεν ἐμοῦ a second phrase: καὶ (ἕνεκεν) τοῦ εὐαγγελίου. *Here* is where the emphasis lies. This is true at least of the evangelist. The addition aims to provide an interpretation. The καί is epexegetical. As it stands, the ἕνεκεν ἐμοῦ is certainly clear enough. All the same, if Mark intends an interpretation and furnishes it with a term from missionary vocabulary, this means that for him the Lord is present in the gospel. Whoever suffers today for the gospel's sake or abandons this world's goods for the gospel's sake does so for the sake of the Lord.

It is important to interpret the redaction strictly from the evangelist's own time. For Mark the gospel is that present factor which represents the Lord. We use the word "represent"

[41] *Op. cit.*, p. 204.
[42] In his exposition, Harnack begins with Mark 1:14 and (initially) has the advantage over Wellhausen to the degree he conducts a unified exegesis of all the εὐαγγέλιον passages in Mark, whereas Wellhausen assumes the term has several meanings.

in that dual sense peculiar to it. On the one hand, for Mark the gospel is the (or a) form in which Jesus is made present. For this reason, Mark inserts the term wherever Jesus is mentioned. On the other hand, the (proclaimed) gospel is Jesus' representative. It thus reflects a feature which all but eliminates historical distance, but by emphasizing and retaining the historical reference. Not only in Jesus' lifetime could a person undertake something for his sake. He can do so today as well, and in fact when he undertakes it for the gospel's sake.

Mark 13:9-10 takes precisely the same tack. The context of vss. 9 and 11 states that the disciples will bear testimony for Jesus' sake. The evangelist now interprets the ἱστάναι ἕνεκεν Ἰησοῦ εἰς μαρτύριον (vs. 9) by a parallel comment in vs. 10: κηρύσσειν τὸ εὐαγγέλιον. The same picture results. Jesus could have uttered the words of vs. 9. Verse 10 then tells how this prediction takes shape in missionary practice (in this case, in the peculiar situation resulting from the period of persecution). The content of τὸ εὐαγγέλιον corresponds with the ἕνεκεν ἐμοῦ. Wellhausen's statement that this denotes the apostles' preaching *about* Jesus[43] is inaccurate, to say the least. Here, Jesus is rather the content of the gospel in the sense that he is preached. At the same time light is again shed on this passage from vs. 11. In a real sense, it is not the persecuted who proclaim Jesus here; rather, the content of the proclamation is given them by the Holy Spirit.

Mark 14:9 is also instructive. We should first note the parallel construction. The gospel will be preached in the whole world. This will not be a report about the woman's deed, but a report of the deed itself. What this woman does is, so to speak, a part of the gospel—not in the sense that the gospel consists of a sum total of such pericopes. Rather, the two belong together, penetrate each other. The proclamation of this woman's deed is a part of the gospel proclamation.

---

[43] Wellhausen, *Einleitung in die drei ersten Evangelien,* p. 110.

Wherever her deed is proclaimed, the gospel is proclaimed.[44]
But now a further clause is added which states the goal of this
proclamation more precisely: εἰς μνημόσυνον αὐτῆς. Lohmeyer
correctly states that this does not refer, say, to the woman's
"sacred renown" which believers of all times will extol.[45] On
the other hand, contra Lohmeyer, it is not said that God re-
members her fame.

Here we encounter (and *only here* in Mark *expressis verbis*)
that motif of remembrance which is to be interpreted in terms
of a *representation*, an actualizing of the deed. Where an act
is proclaimed, the act is present; or more generally, where a
proclamation occurs, what is proclaimed becomes a reality.[46]

This rounds out the picture. The motif of representation
belongs to the gospel, for the proclamation of the gospel
renders its content contemporaneous.[47] As to Paul's use of the
noun εὐαγγέλιον, Friedrich asserted: "If we were to sum up
the content of the gospel in a single word, it would be Jesus
the Christ." [48] Reviewing the passages examined thus far, we
can state that the term has the same content in Mark. We
can test this by substituting "Jesus Christ" for εὐαγγέλιον. But
we should note that we cannot make the substitution simplisti-
cally. He is hidden in the gospel, in the proclamation—but it
is really he. So it is not a matter of speaking of or about him,
but of "speaking him," of "proclaiming him." At any rate,

[44] Cf. Lohmeyer, *Das Evangelium des Markus, ad loc.* "The proclamation has for its content the whole story of Jesus replete with all its individual scenes; it is 'the gospel' as in 1:15."

[45] Lohmeyer, *loc. cit.*

[46] At this point, cf. Marxsen, *Die Einsetzungsberichte zum Abendmahl*
(Kiel Dissertation, 1948), pp. 111 ff.; also by the same author, "Repräsen-
tation im Abendmahl?" *Monatsschrift für Pastoraltheologie*, 41. Jahrgang
(1952), 69 ff.

[47] The situation is very similar in the case of the messianic secret. Cf.
Marxsen, "Redaktionsgeschichtliche Erklärung der sogenannten Parabeltheorie des Markus," *Zeitschrift für Theologie und Kirche*, 52. Jahrgang
(1955), 270.

[48] Kittel, *op. cit.*, II, 731.

we should note the reality inherent in this speaking and which this proclamation evokes.

We turn now to the other passages, first of all to 1:1. Εὐαγγέλιον is set over the entire work as a kind of "title." But if we bear in mind the direction of Mark's composition, we must put it somewhat more precisely: the entire work is marked and qualified as εὐαγγέλιον. It is *a* gospel. From the outset that means that his work is to be read as proclamation, and as such is an address and not a "report about Jesus." From this aspect, it is almost accidental that something in the way of report *also* appears. In any case, it is only raw material. Paul can largely disregard this raw material. As we will see later, though, it is not unimportant that just *this* material was absorbed.

In this connection, we return once more to the results of our previous study. If we interpret the Gospel's origin consistently from Mark's own time, we can say that the Risen Lord is also the author of the gospel which has him for its content.[49] Through the event of this proclamation the Risen Lord actualizes himself.

This also makes clear the similarity in Mark's use of εὐαγγέλιον and "Galilee." The fact that we are dealing with *a* gospel here makes for an intensive consolidation. Sequence, chronological order—all this is certainly in the material or is at least intended there, but it is proclaimed in the present and for the present. In and by his gospel, the Risen Lord re-presents his own life on this earth. And the goal is that he himself become contemporaneous with his hearers in the proclamation. We also saw that this presence which is hidden in the proclamation shall shortly become manifest.

Εὐαγγέλιον in 1:1 is thus to be interpreted *from Mark's own time.* For that reason, the term "title" is not quite apropos.

---

[49] Schniewind (*Das Evangelium nach Markus, ad loc.*) is correct: "The gospel which is proclaimed in the Christian communities is Jesus Christ's own word." (This is true at least for Mark.)

Mark's work is constructed in the direction of this verse ("passion narrative with an extended introduction.") The title in 1:1 has become a summary of the whole. Finally, the ἀρχή in 1:1 is also to be interpreted from Mark's own time. This word has time and again obscured the understanding of the term εὐαγγέλιον. If we interpret the ἀρχή as the starting point of a sequence just now beginning, then it is very difficult to find an interpretation other than that which Harnack proposes: "Here begins the good news preached by Jesus Christ concerning the coming of the Kingdom." [50] Or we must assume with Johannes Weiss that 1:1 contained "primarily a reference to content which the author—not too adroitly—described in this way. . . ." [51] But now ἀρχή, coming as it does at the beginning of the Gospel, is not the starting point in a continuum, but rather the point toward which this event is to be traced. The Gospel harks back to this point, viz., back beyond the time of the Baptist and the time of Old Testament prophecy. But this means—and here Lohmeyer could certainly be right—the beginning is traced back to God. He is the author of this event. This is no mere historical reflection; it is the community's "article of faith," [52] just as the awaited Parousia. But both articles have at their heart the one who proclaims himself in his gospel. For this reason, the gospel—and therefore Christ—requires faith (1:15).

With this we turn to the two remaining passages: 1:14 and 1:15. As we noted, it is generally conceded that we are dealing here with a summary report formulated by the evangelist. [53] Wellhausen [54] saw here a kind of comprehensive statement of the content of Jesus' preaching. But that is put too inaccurately. We must interpret these verses as well from the situation

[50] *Op. cit.*, p. 206.

[51] J. Weiss, *Das älteste Evangelium*, p. 25 (in reference to Hosea 1:2).

[52] Lohmeyer, *Das Evangelium des Markus*, p. 10.

[53] Schmidt, *Rahmen*, p. 33; cf. Bultmann, *History*, p. 341; Kittel, *op. cit.*, II, 728, among others.

[54] Wellhausen, *Das Evangelium Marci, ad loc.*

of Mark who (as already mentioned) appropriates primitive Christian missions terminology. It is first of all the Risen Lord who speaks, summarizing his preaching in these verses. The material later reworked is then—to Mark's way of thinking—an interpretation or unfolding of this proclamation with the aid of the tradition of the earthly Jesus.

In 1:14 (against the background of all the other passages discussed, particularly 1:1) we see how Jesus himself is both subject and object of the gospel. Harnack denied that we ought to view the qualifier τοῦ θεοῦ as a christological statement.[55] Armed with his interpretation he could come to no other conclusion. And insofar as Jesus is the bringer or proclaimer of the gospel, we must agree with Harnack. From this standpoint, the qualifier merely characterizes the proclamation and points to its origin. But insofar as Jesus himself is the content of the gospel, the τοῦ θεοῦ in 1:14 is in fact a christological statement. Jesus is the gospel of God.

How is the gospel's content more closely described? The καιρός is fulfilled. When? First of all, in the proclamation occurring in Mark's own time. Now the βασιλεία τοῦ θεοῦ is immediately at the door. In the temporal sense, ἐγγίζειν designates "an event which is near, but has not yet taken place."[56] It is obvious what the evangelist means by it—the Parousia. It requires μετάνοια and also πίστις ἐν τῷ εὐαγγελίῳ.

The πεπλήρωται ὁ καιρός brings to mind Paul's ὅτε δὲ ἦλθεν τὸ πλήρωμα τοῦ χρόνου (Gal. 4:4). But the point of view in the two phrases is different. For Paul, "world time" (χρόνος !) is fulfilled in the sending of the Son which took place in the incarnation.[57] The end time begins with Christ's entering this

---

[55] *Op. cit.*, p. 202; cf. p. 235.

[56] Kümmel, *Promise and Fulfilment*, p. 19.

[57] Cf. Heinrich Schlier, *Der Brief an die Galater. Kritisch-exegetischer Kommentar über das Neue Testament*, herausgegeben von H. A. W. Meyer, 11te Auflage (Göttingen: Vandenhoeck & Ruprecht, 1951), *ad loc.*

aeon. The fulfillment has thus occurred. Paul can speak paradoxically of the passing of the old aeon and the coming of the new (II Cor. 5:17). The phrase has a different ring in Mark. In his case, we are dealing with a fixed date. This καιρός (!) whose content is "the hour of final consummation," [58] is now fulfilled because of "the great turning point in world history, of the coming of the Kingdom of God directly into the present as the miracle of God." [59] Toward this Mark directs his gaze. In our context, this idea disturbs only the one who expects Mark to give a sequence of Jesus' life and is then forced to deny Jesus could have spoken in this way. But Mark does not set this word at the beginning of the historical Jesus' preaching, but at the beginning of the proclamation of the Risen Lord. This proclamation is therefore not directed to Jesus' contemporaries, but to the communities "in Galilee." Here is where Mark stands. Here is where he is addressed.[60] Briefly put the gospel declares: I am coming soon.

[58] Lohmeyer, *Das Evangelium des Markus, ad loc.*

[59] Preisker's article on " 'Εγγύς, ἐγγίζω" in Kittel, *op. cit.*, II, 331.

[60] Not even Asting aims to determine to what degree Jesus may have used the term εὐαγγέλιον (*op. cit.*, p. 315). In contrast, he sets the evangelist's intention in the foreground (pp. 316-17). Still, he probably does not exegete strictly enough from Mark's own time. He rather works back from Mark into the time of Jesus. This is especially clear in his remarks on 1:14-15 (p. 318). God's rule is fully realized only with the suffering, death, resurrection, and Parousia of Jesus. Yet the "great turning point of the ages" occurs in "Jesus' preaching." The question here is: Does Mark describe the life of Jesus in the ideas of his own time? Or does he use the tradition as an aid to preaching in his own time? Asting states that the Gospel of Mark intends "to be a description of this realization of God's plan of salvation through Jesus" (p. 324). Or, in another place (p. 454) : "The gospel is the message of Jesus which the Scripture mediates to men." But then he states (p. 324) that the gospel certainly contains reports, yet "the reportorial element" is "not the main thing," is not what constitutes Scripture's uniqueness. This is "in the very first place directed forward." We could accept these last remarks (as well as a series of other excellent observations). But how does Asting arrive at this point despite the other line he first pursues? If we look more closely we discover an almost imperceptible leap! He detours by way of Matt. 24:14 and 26:23 and on this basis interprets 1:1 (p. 324). When Asting also cites Mark

This proclamation, however, requires faith. The phrase
πιστεύειν ἐν has long attracted attention. It appears in the LXX
but not in the New Testament.[61] Scholars have puzzled over
its meaning.[62] Still there is no reason to deviate from the translation "believe in," [63] especially when we note the content of
that which demands faith—the returning Lord. But this gives
rise to another thought. This returning Lord is present in the
gospel which is proclaimed. We can thus rewrite the phrase
to read: Believe in the gospel (=the returning Lord) because
of the gospel (=*his* proclamation of his return). Again, the
objection that "Jesus would not have said this" [64] misses the
point. We are located within the primitive community. There
πιστεύετε ἐν τῷ εὐαγγελίῳ is identical to πιστεύετε εἰς Χριστὸν
᾿Ιησοῦν. Just as Christ who will come and has come requires
faith here and now, so also the gospel which embraces both
aspects and as present address re-presents the Lord. The presence of the Lord is experienced in the proclamation.

Form history has shown that even the tradition prior to
Mark was proclamation. But it is significant that our evangelist
neither reproduces this proclamation nor makes of it a *vita
Jesu.* He does not even offer any instruction about Jesus.
Rather, his so-called "redaction" is a continuation of the ser-

---

14:9, he can do so precisely because he had previously exegeted this passage on the basis of Matt. 24:14 (pp. 321-22). There seems to be a subtle
harmonizing here (cf. also p. 454) and its result is—and this is surprising—that nothing further can be said which would be peculiar to Matthew (pp. 325-26).

[61] Lohmeyer, *Das Evangelium des Markus, ad loc.*

[62] Hofmann: "on the basis of"; Wohlenberg: "bei"; Deissmann and
Moulton: "in the sphere of" (according to Bauer, *A Greek Lexicon of the
New Testament,* p. 666). Lohmeyer vacillates. He does translate "in," but
weighs the possibility that the "means" and "basis" of faith could be
meant here, and not its object.

[63] Thus Blass-Debrunner, § 187, 6; Wellhausen, *Das Evangelium Marci;*
J. Weiss, *Die Schriften des Neuen Testaments,* I; Klostermann, *Das
Markusevangelium;* Schniewind, *Das Evangelium nach Markus, ad loc.;*
also Bauer, *A Greek Lexicon of the New Testament,* p. 666.

[64] Klostermann, *Das Markusevangelium* (2nd ed., 1926), *ad loc.*

135

mon already at his disposal in the tradition, and with his community in mind. What was once readily eliminated as a "community formulation" proves to be indispensable, for it is the necessary continuation of the tradition.

By way of summary, we will review the meaning of the term in Mark. What is decisive is our observation of the factor of re-presentation in connection with εὐαγγέλιον. This term expresses the manner in which the Lord is present in his community. Passages in the tradition which speak of Jesus can be interpreted by εὐαγγέλιον and thus adjusted to Mark's situation (8:35 and 10:29). For Mark, the dispute as to whether Jesus is the content or bringer of the gospel must be settled in such a way that both ideas apply.

This indicates great similarity with Paul's use of the term. And yet a shift can perhaps be noted which in turn sheds considerable light on Mark. As is well known, εὐαγγέλιον has a dual root. One leads back to the Old Testament, the other to the Greeks.[65] As to the verb εὐαγγελίζεσθαι, it appears quite certain that the New Testament usage originated in Judaism. This is true at least of Matt. 11:5. In Luke's case, though, it is open to debate, as we shall see shortly.

For the noun, however, this derivation can at best be only assumed.[66] We should note that in the Old Testament בשרה is used only in a secular sense.[67] And nowhere in rabbinic Judaism is there "a suggestion that the eschatological good news is called בשרה." [68] If we add that Paul was probably the first to introduce the noun into the New Testament, we will not dare overlook the "common oriental" [69] idea connecting the gospel and the Caesar cult. In this setting "gospel" is a

[65] Cf. Schniewind, *Euangelion*, Vols. I and II; Kittel, *op. cit.*, II, 721 ff.
[66] Friedrich confirms this view by way of analogy (Kittel, *op. cit.*, II, 728-29).
[67] Kittel, *op. cit.*, II, 721.
[68] *Ibid.*, II, 726. The LXX is also excluded (p. 725).
[69] Lohmeyer, *Christuskult und Kaiserkult* (Tübingen: Mohr, 1919), p. 24 (quoting Kittel, *op. cit.*, II, 725).

broader and familiar term. Paul can assume it among the readers of his epistles. It is not entirely out of the question that in dependence on the use of the verb, Paul first gave to εὐαγγέλιον its Christian connotation.[70]

We should be aware of the somewhat mythical aspect of the term εὐαγγέλιον in the Caesar cult. It is true that the myth always takes concrete shape in a particular emperor (birth, enthronement, news of victory, etc.); but waiting and hoping for a new εὐαγγέλιον follows hard after. Paul proclaims that Jesus Christ is the gospel. Here "Jesus Christ" is the subject and εὐαγγέλιον the predicate.[71] The term thus relates the myth to a person and as predicate denotes what constitutes this person. For this reason, Paul can speak at once in Christian circles of the "gospel." Everyone knows *who* is meant. In the primitive community and above all in its missionary practice, this term plays a decisive role, since it can be associated with current ideas. It is possible that it soon became a formula.[72]

Mark then arrives on the scene and makes a more detailed comment on the gospel. He states that the gospel is Jesus. The gospel is now the subject and Jesus the predicate. Mark can therefore piece together "stories about Jesus" and construe their proclamation as gospel. The tradition is used to interpret the gospel.

It would of course be wrong to say that Paul and Mark proceeded with an eye to grammar here. But the difference can reveal this much, that "gospel" means the same to both.

[70] This is vigorously disputed by Werner, "Der Einfluss der paulinischen Theologie im Markusevangelium," pp. 103-4. Though the reasons given there are not at all convincing, we must admit that we can gain no certainty here. Bultmann (*Theology of the New Testament*, I, 87-88) leaves the question open. But this does not change much of what we established. Paul introduced the term *into the New Testament*. It is only a small distance from his to Mark's understanding of the term, as we shall see shortly.

[71] The predicate, as it variously occurs in Paul, can be more precisely defined.

[72] Cf. Lohmeyer, *Das Evangelium des Markus*, on Mark 8:35.

It is only that Mark expresses what Paul has in mind, but *(Paul)* leaves unexpressed or merely implies. Put in another way, *the "gospel" which Mark writes is his commentary on the term "gospel" which Paul leaves (for the most part) unexplained.*[73] Commentary, however, does not mean "explanation." Exegesis is, rather, *the* form of primitive Christian preaching.

Just for this reason, we may not think first of the "Book" which Mark writes. Rather, we should think of the proclamation which represents that which, or better, the one who is proclaimed. Insofar as Jesus is the content of the tradition, he is also the content of the gospel. Insofar as he sets in motion this proclamation as Risen Lord, he is himself the gospel. This means that he proclaims himself. This in turn corroborates our earlier statement (to be repeated in the next study) that Mark writes *a* sermon which is gospel.

We turn now to the later development.

C. Further Development in the Major Gospels

We shall consider *Matthew* first. We already established that in Matthew the term εὐαγγέλιον displays a connection with the speech complexes. There is, besides, another change over against Mark. The first evangelist never uses the expression without modifiers. In two passages he adds the genitive τῆς βασιλείας (4:23 and 9:35); in one passage he adds a τοῦτο (26:13); in another both additions appear: τοῦτο τὸ εὐαγγέλιον τῆς βασιλείας (24:14). But we must also note those passages in which Matthew avoids the noun though Mark contains it (16:25; 19:29).[74]

---

[73] So it seems incorrect to say that Mark affixed the term εὐαγγέλιον to the name of Jesus in his introduction (1:1). Precisely the reverse is true: In his introduction, Mark affixed the name of Jesus Christ to the term εὐαγγέλιον (contra Lohmeyer, *Das Evangelium des Markus*, p. 7).

[74] Perhaps we should cite 4:17, though the term was taken up from Mark 1:14-15 into 4:23 and 9:35. Later on, we will return to this point.

What do these changes mean? It is clear that εὐαγγέλιον and Christ are no longer identical for Matthew as they are for Mark (and prior to Mark for Paul). Jesus is no longer as before the content of the gospel. He is rather its bearer, its proclaimer.

When we consider that previous studies largely fall under the stated or tacit rubric of the synoptic use of εὐαγγέλιον we see how perilous such harmonizing is. Exegesis of Matthaean passages is carried over into Mark.

The modifier τῆς βασιλείας is proof of the fact that we are viewing Matthew correctly when we assume he conceives Jesus as bearer of the gospel. Here we have the content of the gospel stated *expressis verbis*.

This coincides with the character of the "Gospels" according to Mark and Matthew. Disregarding the evangelist's point of view and considering merely the material which he reworked and presented as well as the effect produced, it is chiefly the *acting* Jesus who is emphasized in Mark, whereas in Matthew the emphasis is on Jesus' *preaching*. Mark, of course, takes note of Jesus' role as teacher, but seldom mentions any teaching. Contrariwise, for Matthew it is chiefly Jesus' teaching or teachings which are to the fore, and it is this "teaching" which is identical with the gospel.

In the second study we identified a certain tension in Matthew's Gospel. In contrast to his Markan exemplar, Matthew historicizes the sections belonging to the itinerary,[75] while in the speech complexes the preaching of the primitive community is identified with the preaching of Jesus. It is clear that Matthew invented the speech complexes. But he sets them into his historicized framework, so as to convey the idea that Jesus delivered these speeches.

This corresponds with Matthew's further definition of their

[75] The eschatological significance of the geographical references is eliminated for the sake of scriptural proof (cf., e.g., Mark 1:14 with Matt. 4:12 ff.).

content. They contain the message of the Kingdom; give the law of the Kingdom (Sermon on the Mount); instruct the messengers of the Kingdom (the Commissioning Speech) and teach concerning the future of the Kingdom (Parousia discourse), etc. It is characteristic that all these speeches clearly reflect Matthew's own situation, but that he also historicizes his situation by allowing Jesus to give this instruction, these teachings, etc.

Jesus is thus the point of departure for the proclamation. He has significance as the first to preach with prime and unique authority. We may already have here *in nuce* (more or less unconsciously) an idea which was to have towering significance in later church history, viz., the ideal period of the beginning as criterion for the subsequent church.

The discourses of Jesus are thus "gospels." Like Mark, Matthew appropriates primitive Christian missions terminology. But the two also differ. Whereas in Mark the Risen Lord *now* proclaims his gospel—and thus himself—for Matthew the preaching of the primitive community is identical with the preaching of the earthly Jesus. Hence, it is not he who is proclaimed; rather, the proclamation is about him and his instructions to the disciples which have paradigmatic significance for the community.

In such a way then, "*this* gospel of the Kingdom" must be proclaimed throughout the whole world [76] before the end

[76] Something should be said about the prepositions ἐν and εἰς. The common tendency is to replace the dative with the accusative (Blass-Debrunner, *op. cit.*, §§ 205-6). The substitution of ἐν for εἰς is less frequent (*ibid.*, § 218). We should not place too much stress on the different usage. But it is still striking that for Mark the proclamation of the gospel always occurs εἰς, whereas in Matthew it occurs ἐν. This would reverse the trend of the development which can usually be seen. So we should at least inquire whether this reflects a difference in interpretation. If so, Mark would see more clearly the inherent power of the gospel to grip the hearer. Contrariwise, in Matthew, for whom the gospel is not proclaimed towards or with a view to but rather *in* the world, we can detect a preponderance of the static element—we might almost say of the

comes (24:14; likewise 26:13). It has been suggested that the τοῦτο is intended to set up a connection between the gospel as such and the book of Matthew.[77] This could hardly be so. Yet there is a kernel of truth in this hypothesis. Matthew does not call his entire book a gospel (measured against Mark, it is no longer a gospel; against later usage, not yet such). Rather, Matthew presents gospels *in* his book (1:1).[78] True, parts of the book are used or are intended to be used in proclamation. But what is distinctive is that the proclamation has taken on a framework which is arranged historically, more, which is concerned with the factual details of the story of Jesus. The dual character of the entire work is due to this insertion of proclamations (sermons, or gospels) into the story of Jesus. On the one hand, it is clear that we have before us here the preaching of the community in Matthew's time. On the other, these proclamations now have their etiology in the story of Jesus which substantiates them. Jesus already preached in such fashion.

Vis-à-vis Mark, this is a total reconstruction. The consolidation has been broken up, not, however, because Matthew removes the connecting devices which make for the consolidation. Rather, Matthew clearly construes his material in a different way. We venture to think that in his time "gospel" meant something else than it meant to Mark. Gospel is the proclamation which the community carries on because (and for Matthew, just as) Jesus carried it on.

"institutional" ("doctrine"). But obviously the various dialects also play a role in the use of prepositions (*ibid.*, p. 1, n. 2), so that all conclusions are open to considerable debate.

[77] Schniewind, *Das Evangelium nach Matthäus. Das Neue Testament Deutsch*, herausgegeben von Paul Althaus und Johannes Behm, 5te Auflage (Göttingen: Vandenhoeck & Ruprecht, 1950), on 24:14.

[78] Similarly (but inaccurately) Dibelius (*From Tradition to Gospel*, p. 264, n. 1), speaks of *the* gospel which Matthew presents in his book. His note on Mark also requires a correction here. In connection with this problem, cf. also Friedrich in Kittel, *op. cit.*, II, 729; Asting, *op. cit.*, pp. 321-22 and 335.

It is this idea which Matthew introduces into the Markan framework. Wherever the earliest evangelist uses εὐαγγέλιον in a sense which neither agrees with his interpretation nor can be bent by him in that direction, Matthew replaces the term with another (1:1; 19:29) or omits it (4:17; 16:25). Wherever he can take over the term, he modifies it so as to agree with his own interpretation (24:14; 26:13; in addition, 4:23; 9:35).

Dibelius[79] stated that "The word 'evangel' is the name given to the preaching of salvation, and the earliest Christians made no difference between the preaching of Jesus and the preaching about Jesus. . . ."[80] That is correct. But *we* must make a distinction and recognize the development from Mark to Matthew.

When we own up to this development, we see why *Luke's* "Gospel" consistently avoids the noun εὐαγγέλιον.[81] He actually distinguishes Jesus' preaching from apostolic preaching. Hence, his work is neither a "gospel" in the Markan sense, nor a βίβλος with gospels in the Matthaean sense but, rather, a "life of Jesus." The time of Jesus has paradigmatic value as the "center of time." It plays a special role and is unique precisely in this role. Of course, the preaching Jesus carried on has something to say to the community of Luke's day, but

---

[79] *From Tradition to Gospel*, p. 264.

[80] But what follows in Dibelius must be improved upon. The book of Matthew does not contain *the* gospel, but gospels. For Mark, the gospel is not an entity "outside" his work; his work is (a) gospel. But we must see how the content of the gospel changes from Mark to Matthew. (Thus Bultmann's criticism of Dibelius is not quite appropriate; cf. *History*, p. 347.) And when Dibelius in conclusion states that it "is really true only with the appearance of John's Gospel," viz., that it contains "The gospel," this is also inaccurate, for again the term is to be construed in a different sense there. It would be more to the point to state that the Gospel of John is a "gospel" (but analogous to Mark; yet, to interpret a written work as a gospel, however Markan, would be—for John—post-Johannine. Cf. further below).

[81] Conzelmann also assumes a deliberate avoidance of the noun (*op. cit.*, p. 221).

it cannot be described as gospel and thus not as an element embracing past *and* present. The two are kept distinct. The time of the church is to be distinguished from the time of Jesus, though both are related and touch each other.

If our comments on εὐαγγέλιον thus far are valid, and if this description of Luke's point of view is correct, then we can conclude, as it were, theoretically, that Luke cannot use the term εὐαγγέλιον in the first part of his dual work, though indeed in the second. Our findings confirm this hypothesis.

However, the Gospel of Luke does use the verb εὐαγγελίζεσ-θαι. For this reason a few remarks are required here, since it might very well be that the same idea is expressed by the verb as by the noun in the other two Gospels. Yet it will shortly be clear that the verb as such is not qualified at all but requires a modifier for such a purpose. Luke's use of the verb is in clear contrast to its interpretation elsewhere in the New Testament, particularly in Paul. Friedrich's[82] statement that Jesus' "manifestation, not merely His preaching but His whole work, is described in terms of εὐαγγελίζεσθαι" is hardly true of the third evangelist.[83]

In Luke 1:19 and 2:10 the εὐαγγελίζεσθαι occurs via an angel; in 3:18 it describes the activity of the Baptist. This is surprising in light of Luke's usual tendency to dissociate the Baptist from Jesus. But we come nearer to a solution when we observe that it is only *after the Baptist's death* (16:16) that the content of the εὐαγγελίζεσθαι is described as the βασιλεία τοῦ θεοῦ. This suggests that for Luke the verb has a quite general connotation, viz., that of "preaching." [84]

Passages in which Markan materials are to be found are instructive. Here, κηρύσσειν at times has been replaced with

[82] Kittel, *op. cit.*, II, 718.

[83] Friedrich comes to this conclusion after discussing the Lukan passages, and Eph. 2:16-17. A sharp distinction here leads to another result.

[84] Cf. Harnack, *op. cit.*, p. 209. Εὐαγγελίζεσθαι is not "in the strictest sense" a technical term.

143

εὐαγγελίζεσθαι.[85] It is also striking that the reference to the content of the εὐαγγελίζεσθαι as the βασιλεία τοῦ θεοῦ appears only in the words of Jesus, not in the words of angels (1:19; 2:10), nor of the Baptist (3:18), nor of the disciples (9:6).[86] At the same time, we can state that where this reference most often appears as a word of Jesus Luke is the originator of the formula (4:43 and 8:1; but not in 20:1). But where the verb already appeared in his sources, Luke does not add to it (4:18 and 7:22).[87] We may therefore not associate the εὐαγγελίζεσθαι with Jesus' deeds, etc. Only his preaching is involved. In fact, in 7:22 the preaching of the good news is clearly contrasted with Jesus' ministry through deeds.[88] Also in 20:1 Jesus' διδάσκειν τὸν λαὸν καὶ εὐαγγελίζεσθαι in the temple is to be construed in terms of preaching.

Hence, Luke's understanding of the verb is altogether uniform. It does not have the broad range which we can find, say, in Paul's use of the term, but it is the oral proclamation which a designation of its content (βασιλεία τοῦ θεοῦ) more closely describes.[89]

[85] In Mark 1:38 the κηρύσσειν equals the εὐαγγελίζεσθαι τὴν βασιλείαν τοῦ θεοῦ in Luke 4:43. In Mark 6:12 the κηρύσσειν (used of the disciples) equals the εὐαγγελίζεσθαι in Luke 9:6.

[86] But cf. 9:2. The disciples by Jesus' commission can proclaim the βασιλεία.

[87] Verse 16:16 is unclear because it is uncertain whether this word uttered by Jesus refers to his own or his disciples' preaching.

[88] Accordingly, in Luke 9:6 the disciples' preaching (εὐαγγελίζεσθαι) is contrasted with their healing. This is in turn confirmed by 9:2, in which the κηρύσσειν τὴν βασιλείαν τοῦ θεοῦ corresponds to the εὐαγγελίζεσθαι (vs. 6). Such a juxtaposition clearly indicates the intimate relationship but also the difference between the two functions.

[89] In these passages Luke's literary work can also be clearly seen. Only 7:22 can be assumed clearly to originate in Q (in the parallel, 11:5, occurs Matthew's single use of the verb). Verse 16:16 (originally also from Q?) is reshaped by Luke, as a comparison with Matt. 11:12 indicates. Verses 3:18 and 4:18 derive from Lukan special material (in the second passage the verb is a quotation from the LXX version of Isa. 61:1), as

We can add to these observations a few passages from Acts.[90] In Acts 5:42; 8:35; 11:20; 13:32, and 17:18,[91] εὐαγγελίζεσθαι is modified by τὸν ᾿Ιησοῦν, or τὸν κύριον ᾿Ιησοῦν, or the like). From this Harnack concludes:

How carefully and accurately Luke again has gone to work here! He knows and scrupulously reports that Jesus preached the Kingdom of God as good news, but that the apostles preached the Lord Jesus Christ!

But this is just the wrong conclusion! Luke is not historically accurate. Rather, he historicizes.[92] What we proved to be true of Matthew is not true of Luke, viz., that the preaching in his Gospel takes its shape from the way in which the primitive community does its preaching. For this reason Matthew can still use the noun, at least to an extent. Measured against the historicizing features which can be observed also in his Gospel, such usage is "inconsistent." Luke, on the other hand, is thoroughly consistent.[93]

---

also the substance, at least, of 8:1-3 (8:1 probably originates in a formation by Luke, as a comparison with Matt. 4:23 and 9:35 shows; Luke replaces the noun with the verb). Verses 4:43, 9:6, and 20:1 stem from the Markan source (in the first two cases κηρύσσειν is replaced, in the third Luke has given the introduction entirely new shape).

[90] On the following, cf. Harnack, op. cit., pp. 209-10.

[91] In Acts 8:12 (the only passage in Acts) βασιλεία τοῦ θεοῦ also appears as a modifier.

[92] It is a quite different question whether Luke attains historical accuracy in this fashion. Friedrich (Kittel, op. cit., II, 728) thinks that Luke renders his sources more exactly, since in Jesus' case the verb would have been "the more common." This is not only possible; everything speaks for it. But the reason for this "more faithful" transmission (despite the noun in his Markan source) is not due to the evangelist's historical research, but to his historicizing.

[93] From this standpoint, the two occurrences of the noun in Acts offer no further difficulties. The evangelist had no occasion to strike them from his sources. We might ask whether it was he who modified εὐαγγέλιον in 20:24 (cf. Dibelius, Studies in the Acts of the Apostles, p. 199). But in 15:7, a more "dogmatic" understanding of εὐαγγέλιον shines through.

One more passage should make this clear.[94] We turn to Luke 4:14-15. After 4:14a, the evangelist breaks off his summary of Jesus' preaching.[95] But then he immediately notes its effect, though Jesus (even according to his description!) still has given no occasion for spreading a rumor. We must simply be aware that Luke 4:14b may not be interpreted on the basis of Mark 1:14b and 1:15. Luke's Gospel, too, is first of all to be interpreted chiefly from out of its own context. Any exposition, however, which begins with the discrepancy noted above (the "call" prior to the actual ministry) commits this error.[96] In vs. 14, Luke marks off the first (Galilean) epoch of Jesus' ministry.[97] A geographical (and exclusively geographical) reference provides the introduction. Harking back to 4:1 and paving the way for 4:18,[98] he formulates 4:14a and in 4:14b-15 marks off the first frame. The entire eschatological thrust of Mark 1:14-15 is eliminated. We note how a life of Jesus is emerging here. It is important to see *how* it emerges, viz., by a historicizing dismantling of Mark's consolidation.

D. Summary

The result of our literary investigation is that Mark introduced the term εὐαγγέλιον into the material of synoptic tradi-

[94] In our context it is not possible to develop the entire range of Luke's point of view. But on this subject, refer again to Conzelmann, *op. cit.*

[95] We already established that Luke removed from 4:14a any connection with the Baptist. Hence he consciously reworks his source.

[96] Such an explanation proceeds as follows: Mark 1:14-15 is read first, *then* Luke 4:14-15. In this way it is ascertained that the subject matter of Luke 4:14b would have to follow Mark 1:14b, 15. But if the Markan source is not taken over, Luke lacks a real basis for the statement of vs. 14b. But we should not use this passage "to illustrate the carelessness of the editorial work in the Synoptics" (thus correctly Conzelmann, *op. cit.*, p. 30). Concerning the exegetes' guesswork on this passage, cf. Schmidt, *Rahmen,* p. 37, n. 1.

[97] Cf. Conzelmann, *op. cit.*, p. 30 (we are not merely dealing with a preview of the following pericopes; contra Schmidt, *Rahmen,* p. 37). Cf. also the similar introduction in Luke 9:51 ff. and 19:28.

[98] Bultmann, *History,* p. 336.

tion. Its frequent occurrence in Paul indicates that the earliest evangelist did not give it its specifically Christian character. Paul's understanding is the presupposition for Mark's, though we need not assume direct dependence. And yet, decidedly Pauline ideas recur.[99]

Yet, in contrast to the apostle's usage, the term has a special nuance in Mark. He offers a kind of commentary on Paul's understanding of the term. If we note that Paul's usage is theological, we can say of Mark's that it replaces this theological content with material from the tradition. Mark thus arrives at the same expression, though by an entirely different route. He connects theology and tradition. This connection in turn constitutes an enormous process of consolidation. The outward impression conveyed is of the Gospel's more graphic character. But we must recognize that this vividness serves a theological statement which aims at proclamation.

Mark's Gospel is the confluence of two streams coursing through primitive Christian preaching. One is conceptual-theological, represented, e.g., by Paul. The other is kerygmatic-visual, using the so-called material of synoptic tradition. Mark brings the two streams together. The term εὐαγγέλιον gives evidence of this, a term which Schniewind asserted [100] allows

---

[99] Cf. above all the characteristics which Friedrich compiles under "C" in Kittel, *op. cit.*, II, 731-33. The gospel is "living power"; it "does not merely bear witness to salvation history; it is itself salvation history. It breaks into the life of man . . . "; it "demands decision and imposes obedience," etc. All this is true of Mark's Gospel as well. For the rest, the following possibility must be kept in mind: In primitive Christianity, the term did not have the significance, or at least the breadth which today is most often tacitly assumed for it. We must keep in mind that the scripture which has come down to us offers only a very limited insight into the language. Further, we must by no means overlook the fact that it is really only Paul who uses the term with any frequency. But when we recognize that Mark introduces this term, then that strongly suggests that he is at least indirectly dependent upon the apostle. On this, cf. also the concluding remarks.

[100] Schniewind, "Zur Synoptiker-Exegese," p. 152, thinks this is also true of the term λόγος. But that is much less clear, to say the least.

us to see the evangelist's "real intention." But this fusion is Mark's achievement and cannot be too higly prized. He is certainly a redactor, he works as an "author," and yet completely in the service of his theological point of view, of proclamation.

For Mark Jesus is the subject and object of the gospel. He achieves this declaration by viewing the earthly Jesus and the Exalted Lord as one. Paul does the same. For him also the Risen or Exalted Lord is always the Crucified One, and vice versa. What is unique in Mark, however, is that he describes the "Crucified One" of Paul's theology not by appropriating the term, but by using the tradition of the earthly Jesus which is now proclaimed by the Exalted Lord.

This gives the Gospel its peculiar concept of re-presentation. Christ himself is the gospel. At the same time the gospel makes contemporary the one who has come and the one who will come. In this way the term "gospel" becomes a connective device which Mark presses into the service of his consolidation and by which he summarizes his entire work.[101]

But Mark's Gospel (if we have described it correctly so far), by its very origin and intent, is most intimately related to the concrete situation of its author and his community. After only a few years this point of view can no longer be assigned to other situations and communities *in just this way*.[102] Later on, there *must* be reconstruction. And, as we have seen, this reconstruction begins with the framework.

But the term εὐαγγέλιον has a history which induces later hands to alter the sources.[103] It is also possible that they read their materials differently because they approached them from an altered understanding of the term. By "gospel" the primi-

---

[101] That 1:1 "speaks in . . . Pauline terms" can by no means be cited against its originality (contra Wendling, *op. cit.*, p. 2).

[102] This fact also proves it is a typical "sermon" which, if really a sermon, is anything but timeless but rather addresses the concrete community of its time.

[103] See the reinterpretation of Mark 1:1.

tive community understands the preaching of salvation as
carried on in the community. Paul has this idea (I Cor. 15:
1 ff.). It then appears in Mark, but with a unique stamp. The
material as a whole becomes a gospel which Christ, the Risen
Lord, proclaims *and* which proclaims Christ, the Risen Lord.

Matthew also construes the term in quite similar fashion.
He is aware of such preaching of salvation; he collects such
gospels or composes them himself, and combines them in a
book. By historicizing the Markan framework, he takes from
it its character as *a* gospel. But by inserting his gospels into this
framework, he makes Jesus proclaim them. So, despite the
difference, the great similarity to Mark is unmistakable. Jesus
is subject of the gospel insofar as *Matthew* makes him proclaimer of the gospels. And this very portrait is achieved
through his style of composition. No special stress is laid on
this fact (as in Mark's case). The re-presentational character
of the term εὐαγγέλιον in Mark is absorbed by the historicizing
process underlying Matthew's framework. But the substance of
the Markan idea is still there and is arrived at (from one
aspect, at least) in the evangelist's identification of the primitive community's preaching with the preaching of Jesus. The
object now is emphatically the βασιλεία, at times viewed from
various aspects. Luke also seeks to understand the gospel as
the preaching of salvation carried on in the community. But
this makes use of the noun impossible, since he writes a life
of Jesus in historicizing fashion. He thus omits it and uses only
the verb which, however, does not mean the same to him as
it does, say, to Paul. It rather expresses the act of preaching
as such, and, to be qualified, requires a modifier.

We can now draw a clear picture of the later development
of the term. The point of departure is Mark 1:1, to be construed as the final statement of the evangelist's backward directed composition. This alone explains that here too "Christ"
is both objective and subjective genitive. But after the verse
had originated in this way, it took its place at the very begin-

149

ning. J. Weiss[104] might then be correct in assuming "that
even if Mark intended it otherwise (!), his first readers construed the genitive as objective." [105] In conjunction with
Mark 1:1, but interpreting by way of Matthew and Luke,
"Gospel" becomes the designation of a book. These "Gospels
according to Mark, Matthew, and Luke" now contain the
"story of Jesus." This is a complete revision of what Mark
understood by (his) Gospel. That which plainly distinguishes
his work—proclamation with a view to the concrete situation
—was lost. Applying the same term to entirely different works
results in leveling out the differences.[106] It is but a short step
to applying this title also to John's work, and logical development presses for a Gospel harmony.[107] This gives rise to a
new tendency by which the entire New Testament is finally
designated as "Gospel." [108] Lastly, the dogmatic Law-Gospel
distinction is taken up into the development.

Paul furnishes the point of departure for this history of the
term. The development is, of course, sequential, but earlier
stages are at times retained. It is just this which has produced
confusion. A history of this development with a view to the
peculiarity of each "evangelist" can clarify matters. As it
turned out, Mark provides an important key to such a history.
He, in any event, is truly an evangelist in the full sense of
the term.[109]

[104] *Das älteste Evangelium*, p. 27.

[105] However, J. Weiss doubts that Mark *did* intend otherwise.

[106] Briefly, the difference is this: Mark really writes a Gospel; in his
book, Matthew offers a collection of gospels which are etiologically joined
to the life of Jesus; Luke writes a *vita Jesu*.

[107] Cf. Cullmann, "Die Pluralität der Evangelien als theologisches
Problem im Altertum," *Theologische Zeitschrift*, I (1945), 23 ff.

[108] Cf. Harnack, *op. cit.*, pp. 222 ff.; Friedrich in Kittel, *op. cit.*, II, 736.

[109] It is idle to ask what would have happened if. . . . But we may
still ask what name those writings we today call Gospels would have had
without Mark 1:1. Merely this reflection may well characterize the peculiarity (and autonomy) of the oldest evangelist, but also warn us against
harmonizing these writings. It is highly problematic whether we may
speak of a Gospel "genre."

Study Four | Mark 13

The results submitted thus far are hypotheses. The accuracy of hypotheses can almost never be proved conclusively. What is decisive, however, is the question of their usefulness, the question as to whether one can work with them. Hence this study in the final analysis leads toward a reinterpretation of the entire Gospel.

But has the time already come for such a reinterpretation? At the moment, redaction-historical investigations are being widely discussed. They will perhaps furnish many additions and surely some corrections. And again we must note that Mark's situation is infinitely more complicated than Matthew's or Luke's, since it is much harder to achieve consensus as to the oldest evangelist's sources. But much depends on singling them out as clearly as possible.

Still, we will make the attempt with at least one passage to test the validity of our hypotheses. Clearly, there is no section more suited to our purpose than chap. 13 of Mark,[1] the chapter most often titled "The Markan Apocalypse." For now, we will defer the question as to whether this title is apropos. This

---

[1] In "Religionsgeschichtliche Erklärung der sogenannten Parabeltheorie des Markus," pp. 255-71, I have ventured an exposition of the parable chapter in the context of Mark's Gospel.

much is clear in any event—the "end" is spoken of here, however interpreted. If it is true that the evangelist writes with a view to the *imminent* Parousia, we must be able to recognize the fact. There is still another problem. A brief glance at Introductions to the New Testament indicates that Mark 13 is continually hailed as chief witness for the fixing of the Gospel's time of composition.[2]

But we must inquire whether the arguments cited are tenable. Strictly speaking, we do not return to Mark himself, but rather to the pieces of tradition which he reworked. But these pieces can be used as evidence only to the extent we grasp the degree to which they were reworked. Is the temple considered destroyed as, e.g., in Luke, or do the traditional pieces imply that it is still intact? Even if the latter be true—as is assumed for Mark—this still need not prove the factuality of the report. Hence we must keep much more clearly in mind the evangelist's redactional work so as to draw conclusions from it for his own time.

Opinions on Mark 13 "even today . . . diverge widely." [3] In asking why this is so, we select various views and examine them, not so much for the fact that but for the way or method by which they were reached.

A. Questions on the Methods of Previous Studies

After several generations of scholars had tried to ferret out the individual components in Mark 13, first by literary-critical means, then by historical-critical and later form-historical studies and evaluations, Friedrich Busch, in the last significant work to appear on the problem, strongly emphasizes the chap-

---

[2] This also applies to Roman Catholic Introductions to the New Testament. There, of course, Luke's Gospel plays a special role in fixing the *terminus ad quem*. Cf. A. Wikenhauser, *op. cit.*, pp. 171, 220-21. But there again Mark 13 is decisive.

[3] Kümmel, *Promise and Fulfilment*, p. 95.

ter's unity.[4] He demands that exegesis "at least make the attempt to understand these (individual) components first of all in the context of the *total* kerygma offered by the evangelist. . . ." [5] "What the evangelist lifts out of the fluid tradition must be understood from within *his* work." [6] Busch even states all but programmatically that "the further task is apparently simple and yet sufficiently important: to understand the evangelist by temporarily deferring every critical question concerning authenticity and the 'historical Jesus.' " [7]

We will have to admit that Busch has seen the task correctly.[8] Mark's Gospel is to be construed as a unity, and it is altogether legitimate to interpret the individual pieces from out of this unity and within its framework.

But now Busch commits a grave error. With the one-sided emphasis of his method, he does not achieve a proper evaluation of the methods of literary criticism and form history. Rather than simply noting their dissimilarities, he sets up a contrast. Then, armed with his own point of view he polemicizes against the results attained by other methods. The result is that almost everything he says in opposition to literary criticism and form history appears false.

Busch believes that in view of the "minimal and uncertain results," he must reject as an "impossible undertaking" any distinction between the sayings of Jesus and community formulations.[9] But this is no argument! He himself agrees that

[4] Friedrich Busch, *Zum Verständnis der synoptischen Eschatologie, Markus 13 neu untersucht* (Gütersloh: Bertelsmann, 1938).

[5] *Op. cit.*, p. 8. Busch gives a more detailed description of the kerygma as the "message of suffering"; he later adds the "message of the Kingdom and Messiah" (p. 35). For now, we will defer the question as to whether this is an appropriate or sufficient characterization and limit ourselves to the question of method.

[6] *Ibid.*, p. 46.

[7] *Ibid.*, p. 37.

[8] It is unfortunate that Kümmel's critique of Busch (*Promise and Fulfilment*, pp. 96 ff.) does not sufficiently evaluate this positive aspect.

[9] *Op. cit.*, p. 30.

"the isolated individual sayings, though clear in their context, can convey a meaning which contradicts the kerygma of the entire chapter," and therefore does not want to "ignore clearly existing structure and framework." [10]

If we look closely, we see that basically Busch is not hostile to literary criticism and form history, but rather to the "verdict on authenticity" they both hand down or can at any time hand down. So he stresses the evangelist and his work in contrast to historical inquiry. But he overlooks the fact that there are no real contradictions here, for however the verdict turns out in the individual instance, in Mark's Gospel those isolated pieces are "genuine" in any case. Busch could thus have confidently accepted the labors of literary criticism and form history without being disturbed by a verdict on authenticity. Instead, he "refutes" the verdict with a synoptic comparison, but without considering the totally different method of investigation.[11] Finally, he is untrue to his original aim, since he carelessly assigns Luke's intention to Mark.[12]

Yet with all his polemic against literary criticism, Busch is not at all in a position to do without it. How, e.g., can we ferret out special material and Q if not by means of literary criticism?

[10] *Ibid.*, pp. 36-37.

[11] "The examination of its connection with Luke 17:22-37 teaches substantially more about the 'genuineness' of Mark 13 than many literary-critical investigations or the compiling of 'possibly genuine Dominical sayings' in terms of their originality" (*op. cit.*, p. 42). By comparing Mark 13:2-3 with Luke, Busch aims to give "the original connection of the two verses the highest degree of probability" (p. 45). Yet he again maintains that "the history of the synoptic tradition cannot be retraced" (p. 46). But the loss of the "seam" (K. L. Schmidt) between Mark 13:2 and 3 in Luke's Gospel is a gloss which cannot be used in historical argument. Busch's criticism of K. L. Schmidt (pp. 45 ff.) totally misses Schmidt's intention. Schmidt undertakes a historical inquiry, and his result is negative, but he says so himself.

[12] "A verse such as Luke (21) vs. 12 proves that the evangelist cannot have a chronological sequence in mind . . ." (*op. cit.*, p. 51). Where Luke is concerned, we will leave the question open; in Mark's case the verse proves nothing.

And so all of a sudden, literary criticism must support the results of Busch's theses on Mark.[13]

It is really quite difficult to determine exactly what method Busch is pursuing and exactly what he is opposing. Time and again he *covertly* abandons his intent and shifts his interest back of Mark—in the direction of the historical Jesus.[14] For, "reference to contemporary events is for the most part unnecessary since the images stem from the traditional eschatological scheme. Everything has its roots in the Old Testament and in the core of the Jesus tradition." [15]

But what is meant by the "core of the Jesus tradition"? On one occasion Busch describes Mark 13 as "Jesus' farewell discourse," not to be construed historically or biographically but in relation to the "material structure" of the Gospel.[16] Here the evangelist supplied "sayings on the meaning of the cross for the disciples who remain behind, sayings on the confession and suffering of the community. . . ." Should we interpret this "core of the Jesus tradition" to mean the kerygma? Then it is hard to understand why Busch rejects as "unnecessary" any reference to contemporary events. It is just at this point that the evangelist's purpose could be grasped.[17]

The expression "core of the Jesus tradition" is extremely

[13] "The parallels to Mark 13 in Q and in the special material of Matthew-Luke prove that the connections indicated do not originate in the random work of Mark, but are anchored, materially established, in the words of the text" (*op. cit.*, p. 41).

[14] Cf. the quote from Luther on p. 49, n. 3. Also pp. 13-14. "Prior to critical inquiry into the historical connection between Jesus' teaching and the teaching of the Synoptists, attempt must at least be made to view the relationship between the most significant motifs in the synoptics . . . as a unity (!) and to test whether or not this synoptic message can in its essential content be regarded as the message of Jesus."

[15] *Op. cit.*, p. 62.

[16] *Ibid.*, p. 44.

[17] It is quite another question whether such references are possible. Still, Busch cites a whole series of them (*op. cit.*, p. 62) —unfortunately without evaluating them.

liable to misunderstanding, and we cannot help feeling he is secretly concerned to refute the literary-critical opinions on authenticity or, better, inauthenticity.[18] He does not realize that when he excludes the questions of authenticity, which his method demands, he also excludes refutation.[19] It is not possible to keep in mind both the unity of Mark 13 *and* the historical Jesus. We must rather be clear about the situation-in-life against whose background we intend to exegete. Thus, despite its valuable beginnings, Busch's investigation remains largely unfruitful. Only in individual instances can it be of any use.

What we have said of Busch applies in part to his teacher, Julius Schniewind.[20] Schniewind, of course, sets great store by exegeting the individual, isolated pieces and sees this as the ultimate task of exposition. His intention is every bit the same as that of form history, though he carries it a bit further by sharply and persistently exposing the christological factor which unites the pieces. He acknowledges the genuineness of the disparate material in the kerygma. On this basis he interprets the individual traditions.

The Gospels' tradition takes for granted the great wealth of Jewish expectation, but from Jesus that expectation is given new determination. The ensuing problem as to whether Jesus himself or his community is speaking here, cannot be solved in any other way than it was solved previously : Every single word has a quality which

[18] The persistent feature in his argumentation is that he does not direct his literary-critical inquiry backward, but rather forward, i.e., in a synoptic comparison, *from which, however, he draws historical conclusions.*

[19] For the sake of comparison, a word from M. Kähler may be cited here, which—in altered form, of course—furnishes a criticism of Busch's method: "By accepting the burden of proof [*scil.* for the quality of the Bible's transmissions], however, the *necessity* of proof was thereby conceded and the legitimacy of negative criticism was in principle acknowledged wherever the counterproof was shown to be untenable." (Kähler, *op. cit.,* p. 109.)

[20] In his commentary on Mark (5th ed.) , Schniewind refers repeatedly to Busch.

only the reality "Jesus" can give it. Thus the question of authenticity is of lesser importance.[21]

There is something obscure about this statement. When contrasted with his community, "Jesus himself" must certainly denote the "historical Jesus." Conversely, the "reality 'Jesus' " clearly denotes the kerygma. But it is not clear what that new determination "from Jesus" is supposed to mean. We might assume that it refers to the kerygma. Here, as throughout his commentary, Schniewind follows Kähler's well-known approach. But is it really legitimate to dismiss the question of authenticity as "of lesser importance"? Should we not rather say, this question is dismissed out of hand? A clearer distinction should be made here, because the question of authenticity is not settled.[22] Lack of clarity in formulation ought not waken the impression that the question no longer exists.

Schniewind, of course, sees the "ultimate task" as the "investigation of each single saying by itself." He then can say it is incorrect to view the discourse "as a programme of single, future events in their logical sequence." [23] But he also asserts that "the structure of our chapter as we have it now" shows "a decided progression." [24] The question automatically arises whether or not Mark at least understood the discourse in terms of a programme. But Schniewind does not get hold of the evangelist and hence the unity of the chapter.

Which situation-in-life does Schniewind have in mind? It cannot be that of the historical Jesus, for then he could not avoid putting the question of authenticity. Nor can it be that of the evangelist, for then he would have to view the composition in an entirely different way and so abandon his *emphasis* on examining each single saying.

[21] Schniewind, *Das Evangelium nach Markus*, p. 166.
[22] Cf. Kümmel's criticism of Schniewind ("Die Eschatologie der Evangelien, ihre Geschichte und ihr Sinn," col. 228).
[23] Schniewind, *Das Evangelium nach Markus*, p. 166.
[24] *Ibid.*, p. 171.

Schniewind hence remains within the bounds of form history, the bounds of the "second situation-in-life," though he continually oversteps them on both sides. Thus much of what he does remains uncertain.[25] Schniewind and Busch never come to grips with Mark 13 itself. This is possible only when we regard the unity of this chapter strictly as the evangelist's own work. Redaction can then be an expression of the kerygma. When we find sufficient evidence of this, say, in Mark 8:34, then we can assert that "Mark 13 . . . is an explication of Mark 8:34." [26] Proof must then be given. It will not do a priori to assume the kerygmatic motif is the evangelist's (only) leading motif. We would obstruct our view to other features which may have been present and allow us to draw inferences regarding the community, the time, the author, etc.

We get a quite different impression than the one just noted when we turn to the scholars who make their way to the isolated pieces via critical analysis. As one example, we will single out Werner Georg Kümmel, the last to work in this fashion.[27] Kümmel would like to demonstrate that Jesus' eschatological preaching is "in complete contrast to the apocalyptic world view; that for this reason the significance of his preaching the imminence of God's Kingdom cannot lie in the announcement of the mere *fact* that the end of the world is near. . . ." [28] Accordingly, he distinguishes three groups of speeches in Mark 13. The first reflects the experiences of the Christian community (13:6, 9, 10, 11, 13, 21-23); the second contains the "strictly eschatological saying of Jesus, 13:2, which . . . is con-

---

[25] Cf. H. J. Ebeling's criticism of the method of Schniewind, who arrives at the same conclusions from the study of a totally different complex (*op. cit.*, pp. 88 ff.).

[26] Busch, *op. cit.*, p. 48.

[27] *Promise and Fulfilment*, above all pp. 95 ff. (Cf. also "Die Eschatologie der Evangelien, ihre Geschichte und ihr Sinn," cols. 225 ff.)

[28] Translators' translation of Kümmel, *Verheissung und Erfüllung*, 3. Auflage (Zürich: Zwingli-Verlag, 1956), p. 97.

tinued in 13:28-37"; the third includes the Jewish-apocalyptic portions (13:7, 8, 12, 14-20, 24-27). There is little difference between Kümmel's literary-critical analysis and that of other scholars.[29]

What is gained by this singling out of sorces? First of all, it gives a most interesting glimpse into the history of synoptic tradition. That is its enduring service which is worth utilizing fully. But immediately more problems than solutions arise. Jewish-apocalyptic elements must be separated from community formulations. We must insist, however, that *both* elements circulate within the community. Kümmel's statement that the apocalyptic portions at "no point" reveal "the particular circumstances of Jesus or primitive Christianity" [30] is open to serious question. For how the evangelist came to take those portions up into his Gospel then remains an enigma. For him at least no tensions can have existed here.

But if Kümmel's assertion were really valid; if Jesus' eschatological preaching were in contrast to the apocalyptic and thus to the Markan preaching (in this chapter, at least) what would be the consequence for the oldest Gospel? Would we not have to conclude that the evangelist radically misunderstood Jesus' preaching? Or that in his time, at least, the community's preaching underwent such a change that we would have to say of even the oldest extant source that eschatology was surrendered to apocalyptic? Actually, we could turn the question right around. By what right does Kümmel analyze and—what is more important—interpret chap. 13 on the basis of the remainder of the Gospel, i.e., on the basis of the remaining eschatological *portions?* Why are these not interpreted on the basis of chap. 13? Of course, it could be objected that these diverse eschatological pieces are present at every level of the tradition, but that nearly all the apocalyptic portions are to be found here. But is proof by majority valid here?

[29] Cf. the next section.
[30] *Op. cit.*, p. 102.

Assuming for the moment that it is, would it not at least be more discreet exegetically to assume that *Mark* understood the eschatological portions of the tradition *also* on the basis of chap. 13, or at least in conjunction with it? [31] But that would mean that Mark's eschatology was apocalyptic. What then should be said of the evangelist and his work?

An analysis of sources is absolutely essential. But when it is widened to a *separation* of sources, the entire enterprise is thrown in doubt, since a literary judgment easily becomes a theological value judgment.

Of course, we dare not ignore Kümmel's concern to emphasize Jesus' eschatology. So he puts the historical question and does not inquire after the composition. But we must be aware that the documents which give information about Jesus unfortunately appear in a later context. Kümmel's analysis should be supplemented by constructive investigation. Once more we are faced with the demand for an exegesis in the context of the whole which gives attention to the redaction.

One thing more should be noted. The results of Busch and Kümmel are astonishingly similar at one point. Both eliminate the apocalyptic factor. For Busch this involves the entire chapter. He achieves his goal by interpreting away, on the basis of a piece outside the chapter (8:34), everything in the "discourse" which smacks of apocalyptic. Kümmel arrives at the same goal by eliminating—again, on the basis of pieces of the tradition outside the chapter—the apocalyptic sections via a critical analysis.

But the message of Mark 13 is not approached in such fashion. We will now try to bring this message to light. We will begin with an analysis of the chapter so as to recognize as clearly as possible Mark's work and hence his point of view.

[31] Yet Kümmel himself says that the evangelist intended to describe "a succession in time of eschatological happenings" (*Promise and Fulfilment*, p. 97), and correctly emphasizes that "it is incontestable that Mark 13 as a whole is intended to be a prediction of the events immediately preceding the end, and of the end itself" (*ibid.*, p. 98).

B. Analysis of the Chapter

We can summarize here. Our concern is merely to give a glimpse into the evangelist's work. We can refer to much which has already been said. The chief thing is the total impression. It is generally conceded that Mark 13 is the evangelist's own composition. Two groups of material separate almost automatically, though we must avoid any precise definition— apocalyptic portions and materials from the synoptic tradition in the narrower sense.[32]

The apocalyptic sections are located in vss. 7, 8, 12, 14-22, 24-27.[33] Possibly vs. 13b can be included in this group,[34] whereas vss. 21-22 cannot.[35] It is a moot question whether an originally Jewish apocalypse can[36] or cannot[37] be reconstructed more or less intact from these verses. This raises the further question as to whether we still can recognize the conclusion to such an apocalyptic leaflet. Bultmann[38] thinks he sees it in vs. 30; Klostermann[39] thinks it may also be present in vss. 31, 32a.

At the same time, though with appropriate variations, there are the "Christian sections" which may include vss. 5-6, 9-11,

[32] We can hardly give them an entirely appropriate label. Bultmann, *History*, p. 122, speaks of "Christian additions" to the Jewish apocalypse. But by the same token we could speak of apocalyptic additions to the Christian material (thus, e.g., Sundwall, *op. cit.*, p. 77). The term "addition" involves at least a literary judgment which is best avoided.

[33] According to Bultmann, *History*, p. 122.

[34] Klostermann, *Das Markusevangelium* (2te Auflage), p. 147. In his fourth edition, Klostermann revised this opinion (p. 132).

[35] Kümmel, *Promise and Fulfilment*, p. 102.

[36] Bultmann, *History*, p. 122.

[37] Kümmel, *Promise and Fulfilment*, p. 98. According to him, arrangement of the pieces yields too colorless a picture to enable us to assemble the alleged apocalyptic leaflet. It would also have been too short. Thus Kümmel rejects an originally literary connection (similarly in "Die Eschatologie der Evangelien, ihre Geschichte und ihr Sinn," col. 228).

[38] *History*, p. 122.

[39] *Op. cit.* Of the unit 28-37, Sundwall regards only vs. 32a as apocalyptic (*op. cit.*, p. 78).

13*a*, 23, 28-37.[40] Here too the question is whether or not an original coherence can be detected. From his study of stylistic features (repetition of words) Sundwall [41] thinks he can detect such a coherence in vss. 5-6, 9, 13*a*, 11, 23, 30-31 (in that order). But again, any precise definition is open to question. One hypothesis tending in this direction seems worth noting, for the reason at least that it would explain the unusually broad introduction (vss. 1-5*a*) which is doubtless the evangelist's work.[42] Verse 3 would then have introduced this section which, of course, was not appropriated *in toto*, but was either supplemented or replaced by vs. 4. Verse 4*a* harks back to vss. 1-2 (prefixed by Mark), and thus forms the conclusion to what precedes. Verse 4*b* forms the connection to what follows by using the ὅταν μέλλη ταῦτα συντελεῖσθαι πάντα to provide a transition to the subsequent "apocalypse." [43]

In this way, the evangelist's literary work *can* be made clear, at least to a degree. Mark would then have connected the following parts:

1. A "Christian" piece which he already found connected (vs. 3—one verse is lacking[44]—vss. 5-6, 9, 13*a*, 11, 23, 30-31). To this he prefixed:

2. An individual saying (vs. 2), to which he prefixed the geographical and temporal frame of vs. 1, which now relates to the entire chapter. With this he connected:

3. The apocalyptic leaflet or apocalyptic material. With this arrangement, he finally inserted into the context:

4. Further individual sayings from the tradition (vss. 10, 13*b*, 28-29, 32? 33-37).

[40] Thus Bultmann, *History*, pp. 122-23. Kümmel naturally includes vss. 21-22 and all of vs. 13. Klostermann again puts a question mark behind 30-31, 32*a*.

[41] *Op. cit.*, p. 77.

[42] After many others, finally Lohmeyer, *Das Evangelium des Markus*, ad loc.

[43] Cf. Wendling, *op. cit.*, pp. 162-63.

[44] He would have reshaped vs. 4 in the manner described above.

The case appears more complicated than it really is, for it is scarcely different from Mark's other compositional work. The existence of another source (apocalyptic material) does not alter the literary task. In either case disparate material is connected.[45] Various passages show even more clearly how the material scatters when divided into separate pieces. We will refer at least to a few.

An oft-treated phrase is the unusual ὁ ἀναγινώσκων νοείτω (vs. 14), which clearly contradicts 13:3, the situation of the discourse. Actually, a ὁ ἀκούων νοείτω would be called for here.[46] *What* should be read? Either the book of Daniel, echoed in the phrase τὸ βδέλυγμα τῆς ἐρημώσεως, or the apocalyptic leaflet from which Mark took this verse. But in the former case, would it not have to read "ὁ ἀκούων ἀναγινωσκέτω —that is, the book of Daniel?"[47] Busch denies this, unfortunately without giving a reason.[48] Yet he could have referred to Matt. 24:15 where the reference is certainly to Daniel— the book is directly cited there. Matthew's version is a simplification, an early exegesis of this passage.[49] This does not mean it is correct, for if Mark copied this phrase from a leaflet, the meaning must not have been clear to Matthew.

If we reject the idea that Mark made an insertion here,[50]

[45] If the existence of two sources be disputed, then it is sufficient to assume an apocalyptic source enriched by traditional material. This is not too decisive for the composition. We may not ask here what the sources once *intended* to relate, but only what Mark *wants* to say by using them. It will become clear that the two questions are not always identical.

[46] Klostermann, *Das Markusevangelium, ad loc.*

[47] *Ibid.*

[48] *Op. cit.*, p. 93.

[49] Wellhausen's assumption that this phrase penetrated Mark from Matthew is most improbable (*Das Evangelium Marci, ad loc.*). If this were true, the reference to Daniel would hardly have been broken off. Schlatter advances a similar hypothesis, viz., an abridgement of Matthew's text by Mark (*Markus, der Evangelist für die Griechen, ad loc.*).

[50] This is probably (?) what Schniewind means (*Das Evangelium nach Markus, ad loc.*) when he assumes the evangelist deliberately used veiled

then we should probably look to his sources.[51] Apart from the linguistic difficulties, even the idea of a "literary reference"—without further mention of the source—seems too complicated. Why then did not Mark delete these words when he appropriated his material? He did not cling so slavishly to his sources as to avoid alterations. This question once more forces us to an interpretation of the whole, for whatever the origin of this expression, it must have some meaning in Mark's Gospel.

If the inconsistency just discussed amounts to a tension between one verse and the entire chapter as discourse, there are also certain contradictions within the discourse itself. They border rather closely on passages which stem from various sources. But it is also striking that sayings of the same origin do not always harmonize.

Verses 30-31 state that "all this" will occur within the lifetime of the present generation; but in vs. 32, no one, not even the Son, knows the day or the hour. Verse 9 describes the communities of the Diaspora; the events indicated do not take place on Jewish soil.[52] Verse 14 addresses the people of Judea and probably refers particularly to Jerusalemites[53] who witness the abomination in the temple precincts. Contrari-

---

language here. The reference to Mark 4:9, 23 is appropriate only as regards subject matter, since the words there suit the discourse. Whether the phrase in 13:14 has this meaning in the *Gospel* is another question. D and a few old Latin texts evidently understood it in this way. They add: τι ἀναγινώσκει. But cf. further below.

[51] The phrase has most often been interpreted in this way; e.g., by Klostermann, *Das Markusevangelium, ad loc.*; Lohmeyer, *Das Evangelium des Markus, ad loc.*; Kümmel, *Promise and Fulfilment*, p. 96. In his article on " 'Αναγινώσκω," Kittel, *op. cit.*, I, 343-44, Bultmann leaves the question open. Hölscher differs to the extent he assumes that another hand added a marginal note to the manuscript containing the original (for him, Hebrew) copy of Mark ("Der Ursprung der Apokalypse Mk 13," *Theologische Blätter*, XII [1933], col. 196; cf. also cols. 193 ff.) .

[52] Lohmeyer, *Das Evangelium des Markus, ad loc.*

[53] Klostermann, *Das Markusevangelium, ad loc.*, is of another opinion. The notion that the inhabitants of the countryside are commanded not to flee to Jerusalem would be absurd—no one flees toward an "abomination."

wise, vss. 15-16 assume rural conditions[54] and are out of place here.[55] Finally, we should note that we can locate contradictions between the discourse itself and the redactional introduction to the degree we interpret each part in isolation. But these contradictions can actually aid us to an understanding of the whole.

It can be argued, of course, that disparate elements have been juxtaposed and mechanically connected here.[56] If we stop at the individual sections, it is difficult to avoid this verdict. But we dare anyone to believe that Mark composed or reproduced [57] such a welter of different views for the sole purpose of furnishing an apocalypse.

[54] Lohmeyer, *Das Evangelium des Markus, ad loc.*

[55] Thus J. Weiss, *Die Schriften des Neuen Testaments,* I, *ad loc.;* Loisy (according to Klostermann, *Das Markusevangelium, ad loc.*). They are much more suited to the situation of Luke 17:20 ff., where they reappear in vs. 31. Naturally, they may have entered there from Mark 13:15-16. But we must allow for the possibility that they were in Q. But did they *also* belong to the apocalypse? We must emphasize clearly here that the analysis of the text leads first of all to this assumption. The next section will indicate that vs. 14b should probably be interpreted differently. Verses 15-16 are then no longer out of place.

[56] "In Mark (13:9 ff.) the erratic development of ideas is the necessary consequence of the mechanical (!) blending of two sources" (Wendling, *op. cit.,* p. 156). In contrast, Sundwall at least inquires into the motives for joining the apocalypse to the Christian portions, and suggests that Mark was "lured by slogans or by a topical arrangement" (*op. cit.,* p. 77). Busch is correct (*op. cit.,* p. 39, n. 1) : ". . . the widespread opinion that Mark 13 is a 'self-contradiction' (H. Weinel in E. Hennecke, *Neutestamentliche Apokryphen,* 2te Auflage, Tübingen: J. C. B. Mohr, 1924, p. 384) is a bias which requires distinct correction."

[57] It has been suggested that Mark came upon the "discourse" as a unified whole, i.e., as an "apocalyptic leaflet" (E. Meyer, *Ursprung und Anfänge des Christentums* [Berlin: J. G. Cotta, 1921], I, 129-30; more recently by Albertz, *Die Botschaft des Neuen Testaments,* I, 1, 180-81). The reasons given for this view hardly suffice. The rhythm alone (a scheme of sevens according to apocalyptic usage in contrast to Mark's usual scheme of twelve) yields no proof (Albertz), when the text is not also taken into account. But remarks on the text (Meyer) are merely oriented to the sources and ignore the alterations made by the evangelist.

We hold that despite the divergent material and despite contradictions in the particular instance, the whole—for Mark —must have had a meaning. But this meaning may *not* be gleaned from a piecemeal exegesis which pursues the historical development of the tradition and focuses upon the original sense. It must rather be sought within the context of Mark's point of view as gleaned from his scenic framework and programme. On this basis the whole is to be interpreted. It is not merely possible but certain that individual passages have undergone considerable reinterpretation. It is further possible that some pieces were taken up into the context for the sake of one single feature (the *scopus* which Mark saw or had in mind), and without consideration for various details. But if we intend to expound the discourse in true historical fashion, we must interpret it uniformly from out of Mark's situation. At times, the discourse in turn can shed some light on this situation.

C. Mark's Point of View

A few external observations indicate that the evangelist understood the chapter as a unity. Several connecting devices can be seen. In vs. 4 the first ταῦτα refers back to vs. 2; the second ταῦτα arches over to vss. 29, 30,[58] after the evangelist inserted it at vs. 8c. The βλέπετε in vs. 5 may refer back to vs. 2,[59] and is taken up again in vss. 9, 33.[60] Further, references to time appear throughout the chapter: . . . ἀλλ᾽ οὔπω τὸ τέλος (vs. 7) ; ἀρχὴ ὠδίνων ταῦτα (vs. 8) ; πρῶτον δεῖ κηρυχθῆναι τὸ εὐαγγέλιον (vs. 10) ; τότε . . . φευγέτωσαν (vs. 14) ; καὶ τότε

Meyer is thus not in a position to interpret or give a date for the leaflet in light of *one* specific situation (he vacillates between the fifties and A.D. 62). We shall see directly that a separation of sources can yield more definite dates.

[58] Cf. Busch, *op. cit.*, p. 44.

[59] In that case, vs. 2 may have been shaped according to vs. 5.

[60] Cf. Sundwall, *op. cit.*, p. 77.

ἐάν τις . . . εἴπη (vs. 21); μετὰ τὴν θλῖψιν ἐκείνην (vs. 24); καὶ τότε ὄψονται (vs. 26), and καὶ τότε ἀποστελεῖ (vs. 27).[61] However we treat the problem of delineating the sources, these connecting devices appear in the "apocalyptic" as well as in the "Christian" material. A literary analysis thus indicates that *Mark intends to present a coherence throughout.* In order to get at its subject matter, it is best to begin with the "seam" [62] between vss. 2 and 3.[63] We stated above that it is nonsense to interpret away this seam in the interest of coherence by appealing to Luke 21:5-6, and thus render the "original (!) unity of the two verses most probable." [64] Verses 21:5-6 are Luke's own harmonization. But it is clear that Mark aims at connecting isolated pieces which were originally unconnected. From this standpoint, Wendling's assertion that vss. 1-2 are "without significance" for the eschatological discourse[65] is quite correct, insofar as it applies to the sources.

This is indicated simply by the fact that the word of the temple's destruction also circulated in isolation. Mark (13:2) may already have it in "fragmented" form.[66] Still more can be gleaned here. A comparison with Mark 14:58; 15:29 (John

[61] According to Kümmel, *Promise and Fulfilment*, p. 97. Kümmel claims to see "quite unambiguously" the intention of the evangelist to set up a sequence of eschatological events. We will test whether this is so. Here we should at least inquire whether each of these time references must always introduce a new section which temporally precedes what follows.

[62] Schmidt, *Rahmen*, p. 290.

[63] Hölscher (*op. cit.*, col. 194) locates the seam between vss. 3 and 4, and thus confuses literary criticism with exegesis, for he himself must admit that vss. 1-2 are an isolated logion.

[64] Thus Busch, *op. cit.*, p. 45. As to method, his debate with Wendling ("Of course, this change of scenes is not original," *op. cit.*, p. 162) and Bussmann (*Synoptische Studien* [Halle (Saale): Buchhandlung des Waisenhauses, 1925], I, 109, 184) begins improperly. A literary- or historical-critical evaluation cannot damage an interpretation within the Markan *context*. On the contrary, just such evaluations at times allow the evangelist's intention to stand out more clearly. (We are not passing judgment here on their propriety.)

[65] Wendling, *op. cit.*, p. 162.

[66] Lohmeyer, *Das Evangelium des Markus, ad loc.*

2:19; Acts 6:14) shows that the original idea was not at all the destruction of the temple, i.e., of the building. Mention of the three days or of the customs Moses delivered indicates that this logion expresses the primitive community's new self-understanding. The people of the new covenant is contrasted with the people of the old; the Risen Lord is contrasted with the temple. Mark is the first to speak of an actual destruction.

Everything points to the fact that Mark altered this logion himself. We will find a similar situation in vs. 14. There, the source referred to an abomination. But Mark chooses to speak of a destruction.

The evangelist is dealing with the "last things." He weaves into the discourse which he composed the—reinterpreted—saying on the temple's destruction. For him, this destruction is thus a part of the end event. That seam which is still visible between vss. 2 and 3, which betrays Mark's adaptation of his sources, makes clear that *he* sees a connection here.[67] He looks toward the imminent destruction of the temple. Is this not a clue to the time of composition?[68]

Verse 4 at once confirms that we see the connections properly here. In this verse, both motifs (destruction of the temple and the end) are joined to form a question. The first part of this question points backward, toward the time of the temple's destruction. But in the same breath the disciples ask what the sign will be, ὅταν μέλλη ταῦτα συντελεῖσθαι πάντα. There can be no doubt that the second part of the question is not a repetition of the first. Lohmeyer[69] indicates that "accomplish" is almost a technical term for the final happening. In addition, the ταῦτα πάντα points beyond the mere temple ruin and refers to the future in general.

[67] Cf. Kümmel, *Promise and Fulfilment,* p. 99. "*Mark* unquestionably understood this destruction of the temple as part of the final happenings."
[68] We might ask whether this is not also a clue to the place of composition. Can the imminent temple ruin be traced from Rome?
[69] Lohmeyer, *Das Evangelium des Markus, ad loc.*

It can, of course, be shown that the disciples' question is put in "totally unhistorical fashion," [70] since the question refers to what is only later learned from the answer. But this in turn reveals the work of the evangelist who uses this stylistic means in vs. 4 topically to connect vss. 1-2 and 5 ff.[71]

Hence, from whatever aspect we approach these introductory verses, the skillful hand of the evangelist is always visible. But he never carries out his rearrangement in such a way as to obscure his own work on the sources. Only the other Synoptists whose task is no longer "encumbered" by Mark's sources connect their materials in such a way that the seams disappear.[72]

[70] Wendling, *op. cit.*, p. 163.

[71] It is not quite clear why Busch always attacks these assertions. He himself (*op. cit.*, p. 47) must admit "that in putting the question, the evangelist surely considered the answer." This is not only correct, but from Busch's point of view all-decisive. For the exegesis of the whole is totally independent of historical- or literary-critical evaluations of the isolated pieces. Busch obviously fears these evaluations could prejudice his exegesis. He would like to prove that the time and the sign are not given. Naturally this is much more difficult to do if the question was actually shaped by the answer and not the other way around. For if Busch were correct (this is for exegesis to decide), an extraordinary difficulty would result. The second question would surely be phrased in such a way that the answer is actually a refusal to answer. For such a brief question that is highly unlikely. Busch's last resort is a reference to the Matthaean parallel (p. 48). But Matt. 24:3*b* furnishes as little evidence here as Luke 21:5-6 furnished on Mark 13:2-3. Again, it is clearly a matter of a "gloss." Conversely, this gives at best indirect indication that we are dealing with Mark's own arrangement.

[72] For this reason it is totally useless to ask whether or not the division of pericopes in Huck's *Synopsis* is correct. Schmidt (*Rahmen*, p. 290, n. 1) regrets that the scene of the "Olivet Discourse" does not stand out clearly enough, since its introduction in vss. 3-4 is separated from the pericope by the division following vs. 4. Busch, in contrast, holds that vss. 2 and 4 belong together and thus supports Huck's division (*op. cit.*, p. 45). Why this dispute? If we begin with Luke's division, Busch is correct; if we begin with Mark's, much can be said for Schmidt's position, that is, if we take up only the literary arguments. (We will note below that for Matthew, the caesura should lie between 24:2 and 24:3.) If, on the other hand, we take Mark 13 seriously as the evangelist's own arrangement, and take seriously the unity of the chapter, we hardly dare to divide one pericope.

Verses 1-4 have thus shown that Mark intends to speak of the last things. Among them *he* sees the temple's destruction. So he connects the two complexes. In vs. 5 the actual "discourse" begins.

We should still inquire whether vs. 2 is a *vaticinium ex eventu*.[73] It cannot be, if we date Mark's Gospel before A.D. 70. The factor of Mark's arrangement (temple destruction/ end) also militates against it, for the events of the end would already have had to unfold. We shall see shortly that this is just what Mark does not intend to say, that he rather corrects this opinion (probably current in the community due to apocalyptic expectation). Above all, the evangelist's point of view militates against it. Here as elsewhere, Mark does not give thought to utterances of the historical Jesus. It is rather the Risen Lord who speaks—through the evangelist. That is, for Mark the gospel is the proclamation of the Risen Lord to the present. To this end he uses material offered him by the tradition.[74]

We may, however, speak of a *vaticinium* in quite another way. The very arrangement of the chapter implies it—precisely because it is a proclamation, i.e., uttered from the present for the present. If this proclamation is read from a historical point of view, then it appears as a *vaticinium*. But in that case,

---

At most, we could ask whether the heading in Huck's *Synopsis* might better be placed in front of pericope 213. In that case, we would once again have to take into the bargain the further discrepancy over against Matthew (cf. below, section 4*b*).

[73] Thus Hölscher, *op. cit.*, col. 193. Bultmann leaves the question open (*History*, p. 125) but leans toward a denial (pp. 120 ff., 128). Among others, it is rejected by Klostermann, Schniewind, Lohmeyer, and by E. Meyer, *op. cit.*, p. 125, n. 1.

[74] From Mark's point of view, a *vaticinium ex eventu* is an impossibility. In the Gospels, it occurs only where we can point to chronological sequence, as, e.g., in Luke. We shall see that the third evangelist actually works with such *vaticinia*. We should distinguish this from the other question as to whether isolated pieces originated *ex eventu* in the church tradition *prior to* Mark.

Mark's point of view is ignored, and the inquiry carried out on his Gospel is false.

Within the context of the Gospel, the situation can be described as follows: The Risen Lord "repeats" the word used against him at his trial (14:58). But he also reinterprets it, making it an announcement of the beginning of the end.

It is interesting to note in this connection that the scene of Mark 13 is Jerusalem. But the chapter also gives another bearing—away from Jerusalem (vs. 14). Here again, though in a quite different context, we encounter what we established in the second study—the Gospel's geographical orientation away from Jerusalem. Again we ask whether this reflects the flight of the primitive community. We can all the more readily assume this since we know of this flight and its connection with the temple ruin or with the threat to the temple. Again we can ask whether the Gospel of Mark (perhaps this thirteenth chapter in particular) is the "oracle" referred to in the tradition.

In any event, vss. 5-13 clearly enough depict a situation reflected by the experiences and circumstances of the primitive community in light of the turbulent events in the years A.D. 66-70. Everything hinges on refusing to be misled (vss. 5-6), refusing to be deceived by someone who claims to be "He." It is common knowledge that many messianic pretenders appeared in that era, and that "the Jewish rebellion of the year 70 is due to the imminent expectation of the appearance of Messiah who will crush the ungodly Roman empire." [75] Perhaps even names can be mentioned—John of Gischala, or even Josephus.[76] Particulars can no longer be ascertained, of

---

[75] Schniewind, *Das Evangelium nach Markus*, p. 156 (on 12:13 ff.).

[76] We are naturally skeptical of Josephus' account, yet cf. Schlatter, *Geschichte Israels von Alexander dem Grossen bis Hadrian*, 2te Auflage (Calw: Verlag der Vereinsbuchhandlung, 1906), p. 269; further, the novelistic treatment in E. Stauffer, *Christ and the Caesars;* historical sketches, trans. K. and R. G. Smith (Philadelphia: The Westminster Press, 1955), p. 143.

course. But I believe the difficulties are resolved if we interpret these verses against the background of Mark's situation.[77] "The first Christians continually had to decide who had the right to say 'I am He.'" [78]

As to 13:7, Lohmeyer[79] notes that the situation is not quite clear, since the reference is merely to hearing. Thus, only the wars of other nations appear to be involved. Why? The situation *is* clear: Rumors of war in Palestine penetrate to where there are Christians. These rumors spread either from Galilee toward Jerusalem (Vespasian began his attack on Galilee from Ptolemais in the spring of 67 [80]) , or from the beleaguered Jerusalem toward the Sea of Galilee, the present home of the community. The latter is more probable, since the war passed over Galilee very quickly.

Yet—it is not a matter of hearing alone: ἀλλ' οὔπω τὸ τέλος (13:7) —the war with all its consequences strikes even them.

We can point, of course, to a profusion of Old Testament parallels on these two verses which describe the end time as a time of war and horror.[81] The messianic age is born of woes.[82] But Mark characteristically adds: "the end is not yet."

This phrase is obviously intended to correct a current opinion. What can it be? Schniewind [83] thinks opposition to Jewish expectation is echoed here. "Christ does not come with war" (Schlatter). "Opposition to messianic revolution" is

[77] This obviously does not mean they took their shape from this situation. The three sayings (vss. 5-6, 7, 8) —as well as the individual pieces— are of quite different origin. Cf. Lohmeyer, *Das Evangelium des Markus, ad loc.* But the "contradictions" they contain are resolved when we interpret their arrangement from Mark's own time.

[78] Schniewind, *Das Evangelium nach Markus*, p. 167.

[79] Lohmeyer, *Das Evangelium des Markus, ad loc.*

[80] Martin Noth, *The History of Israel*, trans. Stanley Godman (New York: Harper & Row, 1958) , p. 436.

[81] Cf. Schniewind, *Das Evangelium nach Markus*, p. 168; Busch, *op. cit.*, pp. 83 ff.

[82] Strack-Billerbeck, *op. cit.*, I, 950.

[83] Schniewind, *Das Evangelium nach Markus*, p. 168; similarly Conzelmann, *op. cit.*, p. 129.

supposedly emphasized here. If so, the phrase would have to be a protest against revolts frequent in that period. They do not compel the coming of the Messiah.

And yet the war has come! Mark's report of it in this chapter proves that he connects it to the end. Opposition to messianic revolutions might be seen in vs. 6, where messianic pretenders come with their claim, inciting rebellion.

But the phrase "the end is not yet" is a correction of apocalyptic expectation. This expectation does not await the end in an insurrection (vs. 7 does not deal with this at all) but in a raging war. The war has come; the community is living through it. Due to apocalyptic instruction, it might suppose it is experiencing "the end." It is just this idea which Mark rejects.

The apocalyptic features are appropriated; the thought is retained. But a kind of pause intervenes.

This exegesis is confirmed by vs. 8. The term ὠδίν, current also in rabbinic literature, refers merely to the "woes of Messiah." [84] And Mark expressly characterizes these events as the ἀρχὴ ὠδίνων. They are the beginning. They symbolize (cf. 1:1) and are determined by what is to come, but they are also distanced from it. In view of the end, present events are seen to belong to it. But the end itself is not yet in sight.

We might ask what lies between, or what ushers in the actual end. It can scarcely be the events mentioned in vss. 8-12, since another redactional conclusion is attached to them (vs. 13b). [85] At the same time, these events are distinguished from what is reported in vs. 14.

With what events does vs. 8 deal? Klostermann[86] thinks that since the individual details were part of Old Testament prophecy, there need be "no connection with events such as the famine under Claudius (Acts 11:28); the earthquake in

[84] Strack-Billerbeck, *loc. cit.*
[85] We shall return to this directly.
[86] Klostermann, *Das Markusevangelium, ad loc.*

Phrygia in A.D. 61 or in Pompey in A.D. 63." This is correct—
there is no necessary connection. We are not only free to assume these details had another origin; the truth is that they
did have another origin. But the fact that these events can be
identified in Mark's time gives us the right to conclude that
this old prophecy can be regarded as fulfilled. Men now know
that they live in the ἀρχὴ ὠδίνων, but it is not yet the end.[87]
So the warning is sounded: βλέπετε δὲ ὑμεῖς ἑαυτούς (vs. 9).
As noted earlier, this verse does not have its setting in Jewish
territory, but in the Diaspora.[88] Earlier association with the
Jews is dissolved. After their trial before synagogal courts the
Christians are not turned over to the Sanhedrin but to the
Gentiles.[89] In Mark's context this would mean that the Christians are drawn into the tensions which existed and were bit-
terly staged between, say, the Zealots and the moderates (between John of Gischala and Josephus). In such situations,
denunciations before the "army of occupation" are more than
probable.[90]

At the same time, quite positive use is made of this suffering. In hearings before the Gentiles, Christians will "bear
testimony." The meaning of the εἰς μαρτύριον αὐτοῖς is
disputed. In light of vs. 10, this is not surprising. Still, with
just the help of vs. 10 this phrase can be explained.

First of all, we must insist with Strathmann[91] that "unlike
μαρτυρία, μαρτύριον does not mean the process of giving
testimony." The phrase εἰς μαρτύριον with the dative of person

---

[87] Precisely when we recognize the use of old material here, we will
have to resist the temptation to trace *every* single feature to Mark's own
situation. But it is important to see that the whole "tenor" of the sayings
suits the evangelist's own time.

[88] Lohmeyer, *Das Evangelium des Markus*, ad loc.

[89] Bauer thinks that prior to A.D. 70 Galilee withdrew from Jerusalem's
political and religious influence (*Jesus der Galiläer*, p. 25). This refers
vs. 9 once more to the Diaspora—to Galilee.

[90] Cf. Noth, *op. cit.*, p. 436.

[91] Article on "Μάρτυς," in Kittel, *op. cit.*, IV, 502.

refers rather to an objective testimony which incriminates the person involved. Thus in Mark 13:9 "the μαρτύριον cannot be the evangelistic witness of missionary preaching, which offers the chance of conversion. The goal of this witness is to make opponents guilty." [92] Not until vs. 11 do we hear what the Christians are to say. God will give it to them.[93] We must observe, however, that speaking here is not preaching but is for purposes of defense.

The continuation in vs. 11 is interesting since the promise that the Holy Spirit, not the Christians, will speak, does not quite suit the prior statement that God will give the faithful what they must say. The second clause clearly interprets the first. In God's stead now appears the Holy Spirit, representing the historical aspect of the divine activity. He is, so to speak, the connector or link identifying the speech of God and man.

This interpretation, then, is no doubt an addition. But we must leave open the question as to whether it stems from Mark or already appeared in his sources. The latter might be the more probable, since elsewhere in Mark the Holy Spirit plays no special role.[94] Yet the phenomenon as such is reflected throughout the entire Gospel, since it is the voice of the Risen Lord.

There is thus a direct connection between vss. 9 and 11. Then it really appears that Mark inserted vs. 10 into this context.[95] Lohmeyer[96] quite correctly observes that this verse is in the nature of an interpretation. It "clearly" interprets "the final phrase in vs. 9: εἰς μαρτύριον αὐτοῖς. In this verse,

[92] *Ibid.*, p. 503.
[93] The passive δοθῇ is another way of saying that God "gives" this speaking.
[94] Cf. Lightfoot, *Locality and Doctrine in the Gospels*, p. 65, n. 1.
[95] Wohlenberg, Klostermann, and Lohmeyer on this passage. Schniewind (*Das Evangelium nach Markus, ad loc.*) thinks all three verses (vss. 9, 10, 11) were originally independent pieces. But then we can explain Mark's sequence only by maintaining that *he* already found vss. 9 and 11 connected.
[96] Lohmeyer, *Das Evangelium des Markus*, p. 272.

to lay down a witness means to proclaim the gospel and 'αὐτοῖς' is synonymous with 'to all people.'" But since "this identification . . .does not do full justice to the dual content of the term," Lohmeyer concludes that vs. 10 is an insertion.

This tension between vss. 9 and 10 is an essential aid to understanding Mark. For if the evangelist inserts an interpretation, then vs. 9 is to be exegeted with the aid of vs. 10. The original meaning of vs. 9 as brought out by Strathmann and which applies *to that verse alone,* is altered in Mark's context. It does not at all indicate, as Lohmeyer thinks, that Mark "clearly" has in mind "only the type of gospel preaching which consists of μαρτυρεῖν before a tribunal." Precisely the reverse is true. Mark knows that μαρτυρεῖν before a tribunal is also a preaching of the gospel and, since it occurs before Gentiles, is a proclamation to them.

In Mark's time the community undergoes these persecutions, appears for judgment. This is what the evangelist interprets in a positive way. Hence what could appear meaningless has very great significance. *The proclamation displaces the defence to which the source referred.*

When we note the πρῶτον in vs. 10, something else comes to light. Till now, we have seen that by making redactional insertions (vss. 7, 8, and also 13*b*) Mark aims to disengage the present from the end time, but also to describe it as related to the end. A "pause" thus intervenes which now is being filled. Verse 10 echoes a motif from Rom. 11:25. There, the subject is a μυστήριον, a word which discloses the eschatological meaning of the event reported.[97] The end which is to bring about Israel's conversion is joined to the "coming in" of the Gentiles which has already occurred. In other words, the period leading up to the Parousia is given an eschatological interpretation; it is the time of preaching to the Gentiles.

Whether Mark formulated vs. 10 himself or whether he took

[97] Cf. Bornkamm's article on "Μυστήριον," in Kittel, *op. cit.,* IV, 822.

it over from the tradition, reworked and inserted it, in its context it is still his interpretation. Since such preaching occurs in Mark's time, and since the haling of Christians before Gentile courts occurs in order to proclaim the gospel to these Gentiles, persecution and defence are taken into the end event. More precisely, they are taken into the event which must precede the end.

Indeed, this proclamation helps to hasten the coming of the Parousia.[98] It shares in the preconditions, in the fulfilling of the preconditions set for the coming of the Parousia.[99]

This again confirms our view of Mark thus far. He interprets his time. This time is the time before the end. The end gives it its character; but it is still "history"; there is still a pause, though it cannot last much longer.

Verse 12 then widens the circle of persecutors and persecuted. The horror of it is that families are affected. Early Christians obviously learned that faith in Christ brought family division. Of course, we can point once more to the fact that "since Micah 7 . . . this feature is a commonplace in Jewish apocalyptic and in the description of the messianic woes." [100] This explains the origin of the saying. But again, Mark's use of it has to do with the community's present experience.

Verse 13 makes this especially clear. This verse is clearly a summary[101] in which the evangelist depicts his own time.

[98] So we cannot conclude from vs. 10 that "a certain postponement of the Parousia" is traceable to Mark (contra Conzelmann, op. cit., p. 126; cf. p. 120). It is another question whether pieces of tradition loosed from their context permit us to see that prior to Mark the imminent expectation had already begun to diminish (on this, cf. Bornkamm, "Die Verzögerung der Parusie," In Memoriam E. Lohmeyer, pp. 116 ff.).

[99] We can also refer to Col. 1:24. The relationship of ideas is characteristic. Suffering completes what is still lacking to the fulfillment. Mark, however, does not emphasize this particular feature.

[100] Wellhausen, Das Evangelium Marci, ad loc., cf. Busch, op. cit., p. 91.

[101] This does not exclude the possibility that Mark had materials at his disposal here. Cf. IV Esdras 6:25.

Characteristically, earlier specific utterances are now changed to generalities. Now every hatred endured for Jesus' sake can be included in the event not far from the end.

This leads to the exhortation: Persevere, for perseverance alone brings salvation. This exhortation is also quite general in the wake of a few concrete instructions (vss. 5, 10).

We can still recognize the sequence of perseverance in tribulation and salvation at the end.

What is still lacking is that identification of struggle and victory, patience and deliverance known to the Fourth Gospel. Faithfulness still leads to salvation and defeat to conquest, but both are connected in the idea of the end, so that the one guarantees the other.[102]

We glance once more at the previous section. We were not as concerned to investigate the isolated material as we were to glean from the redaction the evangelist's own point of view. We could quite briefly describe his work as an "exegesis," for we were continually struck by the fact that traditional material was taken up but adapted to the evangelist's own time. Precisely this kind of exegesis is proclamation.

So far, neither the first nor the second part of the question in vs. 4 has been answered. Or should we with Schniewind [103] regard the appearance of false Messiahs as the "first sign," or with Klostermann[104] take the ὅταν δὲ ἀκούσητε (vs. 7), at the latest, as introducing the first part of the answer? It is correct that the intention behind the question aims at the last things in general.[105] In that case, we can construe vss. 5-13 as replying to this intention. But we must also keep in mind that all this is still removed from the end.

Strictly speaking, the answer must begin with a saying on the temple and then deal with the final events. But this again in-

---

[102] Lohmeyer, *Das Evangelium des Markus,* p. 274.
[103] Schniewind, *Das Evangelium nach Markus,* p. 167.
[104] Klostermann, *Das Markusevangelium,* on 13:7.
[105] The wording, however, is disjunctive.

dicates that vss. 5-13 still deal with the evangelist's own time. Sayings on the "future" begin only at vs. 14.[106] The chapter can then be organized. The question in vs. 4 is a kind of title which is developed in a threefold way. First, the intent of the question, then the problems relating to the end, are taken up. The answer is given in vss. 5-13 which qualify the present moment as the ἀρχή of this end.[107] Next, a concrete event at the temple is the subject, and finally, the end event in the narrower sense.

The second part of the answer includes only vs. 14. The meaning of βδέλυγμα τῆς ἐρημώσεως is disputed. Yet, something can be established from the history of the term.[108] It is oriented to Daniel (9:27; 11:31; 12:11). This suggests the altar of Zeus which Antiochus erected in the temple in 168 B.C. (cf. I Macc. 1:54). Rabbinic tradition, later on, of course, refers to an idol set up in the temple.[109] Does this shift in meaning have something to do with the events around A.D. 40? At that time P. Petronius was ordered to erect Caesar's image in the temple. After a long delay, Caligula's murder (A.D. 41) finally prevented the execution of the plan.[110] If we assume our saying took shape (as a leaflet?) during the accompanying disquiet and during the nation's extreme agitation in light of the imminent temple desecration, then the source's meaning is disclosed.[111] In Mark's source the βδέλυγμα τῆς ἐρημώσεως referred to the image of Caesar.

But what can this phrase mean in the context of Mark's

[106] Wellhausen had already pointed this out.

[107] For vss. 5-13 at least, we must oppose Kümmel's assertion that the time references intend to yield a *sequence* of eschatological events. The previous "signs" are of course portrayed in sequence; but from the evangelist's viewpoint, they all belong to the present.

[108] For βδέλυγμα alone and in other combinations, cf. the article by Foerster in Kittel, *op. cit.*, I, 598 ff.

[109] Strack-Billerbeck, *op. cit.*, I, 951.

[110] Cf. Noth, *op. cit.*, pp. 423-24; Hölscher, *op. cit.*, cols. 200-201.

[111] Hölscher also dates the source at about A.D. 40 (*op. cit.*, col. 197).

179

Gospel? Bernard Weiss[112] refers the passage to the Roman armies as cause of the desolation. Schlatter[113] asks, only rhetorically, of course,[114] whether we ought "to think of the wild events about to occur when the temple becomes the arena of party strife." [115]

Word for word, the reference is to a "desolation." The temple certainly continues to exist, but due to the outrage it is desecrated and thereby desolated. Not only this is regulative for Mark, however. Verse 4 contained the question as to the time of the temple's *destruction* predicted in vs. 2. But *only* in vs. 14 is the temple spoken of; that is, this verse must somehow be an answer to the question. We should note that the redaction is interpretative. Now redaction first appears in vs. 4, then in vs. 2. Mark interprets the saying of the reduction or conquest of the temple in terms of its destruction. If the earlier Christian community flatly denied the witness of people who maintained that Jesus predicted the temple's actual destruction, Mark now takes this witness at face value. If the tradition still spoke of a temple made with hands which should be *replaced* by one not made with hands, Mark (in this context) omits this important restriction. This is clearly the case in vs. 2; it is certainly also true of vs. 14, coupled as it is with vs. 4.

Mark, to be sure, preserves the old term (ἐρήμωσις) intact; yet his redactional work leaves no doubt that he intends to speak of destruction. In his opinion, precisely this destruction is connected with the end, or conversely, the end is joined to the imminent destruction of the temple.

If Mark's material consisted of an apocalyptic leaflet, then he

---

[112] *Op. cit.*, p. 201.

[113] *Der Evangelist Matthäus*, p. 703.

[114] Schlatter (*ibid.*) refuses any further explanation since the question assumes "Jesus appropriated the idea from a type of prophecy, current in Rabbinism and among apocalyptists, which views the prophet as equipped with God's omniscience."

[115] Cf. also Holtzmann, *Die Synoptiker*, p. 168.

took from it one basic idea. In that leaflet, the temple's desecration marked the prelude to the end. In Mark it is the destruction which marks the prelude. The saying remains as obscure as before. The reference is to "one" who will stand ὅπου οὐ δεῖ. The masculine ἑστηκότα is an *ad sensum* construction.[116] The term βδέλυγμα has become a kind of cipher whose history we can no longer uncover, but which is to be interpreted on the basis of the verb. We may assume that the masculine form derives from the evangelist who altered still more of his source in this verse.[117] Mark thus views the βδέλυγμα τῆς ἐρημώσεως as a person. This thought fits the context well when compared, e.g., with vss. 21-22. The antichrist is the subject (cf. II Thess. 2:3 ff.).[118] He is mysteriously referred to,[119] and the temple is not even mentioned.

Lohmeyer[120] is of the opinion that no chronological datum can be gleaned from this verse, since an apocalyptic and not political event is involved. But must the two contradict each other? Are not apocalyptic events always considered in their relation to political turmoil? From Mark's situation—to the degree we have understood it till now—it is reasonable to suppose that *he himself* at least is thinking of an imminent event. The end is at the door. The messianic woes have already begun—Jerusalem is beleaguered!

By connecting vs. 2 to this "discourse," the evangelist clearly indicates that he reckons with the city's capture and the

---

[116] Cf. Blass-Debrunner, § 134, 3.

[117] We shall return to this shortly.

[118] Likewise or similarly J. Weiss, Klostermann, Wohlenberg, Schniewind, and Lohmeyer, *Das Evangelium des Markus*, on this passage; Holtzmann, *Die Synoptiker*, p. 168; B. W. Bacon, *The Gospel of Mark* (New Haven: Yale University Press, 1925), pp. 55 ff., quoted by Hölscher, *op. cit.*, col. 198); Busch, *op. cit.*, p. 93; Foerster in Kittel, *op. cit.*, I, 600.

[119] Evidently Matthew no longer understood this. Vis-à-vis Mark, the ἑστός (Matt. 24:15) could be a gloss. Schlatter however (*Markus, der Evangelist für die Griechen, ad loc.*) holds the masculine form to be secondary.

[120] Lohmeyer, *Das Evangelium des Markus, ad loc.*

temple's destruction. What he thinks this word means will then come to pass—the antichrist will assume the place which Christ deserves. The world catastrophe will then begin from the temple.

In vs. 14*b* the evangelist might well have altered his source. Originally it probably read: Then flee to the mountains! [121] This flight motif is known not only of the Maccabaean era[122] but is present throughout Old Testament tradition.[123] The evangelist now addresses this imperative to "those who are in Judea," but who already live in mountain territory! The contradiction in this passage is removed when we construe it as one last summons to those who *read* Mark's Gospel. It sounds almost banal, but it must be said once—Mark wrote his work to be read. The phrase ὁ ἀναγινώσκων νοείτω thus fits well into the context of the whole. Whatever the source and whatever its meaning there, Mark thinks of the readers of his book.[124] They should discern (in Jerusalem's siege?) the signs of the times and set out at once.

But it is also possible to see a "Markan" *vaticinium* here, i.e., a *vaticinium* inherent in the arrangement. The imperative of 14*b* then refers to the μετανάστασις (already occurred). This need not contradict the previous explanation. Whoever has already taken flight finds justification for it in this word. Whoever is still in Judea[125] should know it is high time for him to flee. But in either case, vs. 14*b* proves to be a parenthesis

[121] *Ibid., ad loc.* (and the supplementary fascicle, p. 17).

[122] II Macc. 5:27; I Macc. 2:28 (cited in Lohmeyer, *Das Evangelium des Markus*, p. 276, n. 1).

[123] Busch, *op. cit.*, pp. 94-95.

[124] On this, cf. Schlatter, *Markus, der Evangelist für die Griechen, ad loc.* He entertains the possibility the evangelist is thinking of his readers and for this reason alters his source (indeed, for Schlatter, Matthew's Gospel!).

[125] Jerusalem is beleaguered. The inhabitants are not directly addressed, but of course implied. The "mountains" (in Mark's context) would hardly be the Judean chain. Is the reference to Galilee?

which topically and chronologically *precedes* the end. The βδέλυγμα τῆς ἐρημώσεως (neuter or masculine) awaited in the near future, threateningly casts its shadow before it. Whoever has a "feel" for it, whoever discerns the signs of the times knows that now is the time to act! [126]

In this verse we encounter the "most direct" address of the entire Gospel. In no other passage are the readers spoken to so directly—"let the reader understand!" The reference to flight immediately follows—away from Jerusalem! This not only marks a literary caesura, but also a break in the life of the reader who is led, as it were, from present to future.

These sayings which follow predict still greater tribulation. Verse 14 is thus the hinge upon which the sayings of chap. 13 turn. The threat to the temple marks the point of division. The interval between threat and destruction, coupled with the

[126] What is obscure and indefinite in vs. 14a may actually be intended or at least deliberately retained. If so, then more must be intuited here than could be clearly stated. In any event, better too early than too late! In this connection, Schniewind's exegetical comments are worth noting. "Did this warning result in the Christian community's flight to Pella before Jerusalem's destruction? But this is not *à propos* of our passage which awaits the flight and end of the world simultaneously" (*Das Evangelium nach Markus*, p. 171). If we see Mark's hand more clearly in these verses and keep in mind his own imminent expectation, then this suggestion is "*à propos*"! "The flight motif as such belongs to the discussion of the last things, and we ought not to think of some historical event" (*op. cit.*, p. 172). Why not? These need not be contradictory! We must keep clearly in focus the history of Mark who lives in an era in which ancient predictions are about to be fulfilled. Even Schniewind is forced to add that "the community had to prepare itself for flight as soon as the persecution began, . . . it knew this was only a prelude to the severest tribulation. It appropriated all the details of the Jewish expectation of woes because in Jesus himself the way of the cross had become the mark of his own followers, cf. 8:31, 34. In any case, these words are an unrealized expectation, whether shaped by the earliest community or by Jesus himself; for in fact, the return of Christ was not joined to the destruction of Jerusalem." This is doubtless correct from a historical point of view, but it is an observation after the fact. If we make this later experience (which Matthew and Luke shared and which induced them to make alterations) the presupposition for Mark, then we inhibit the evangelist's interpretation.

coming of antichrist—this is the period of the last greatest distress.

The prologue to this time reads: Flight! If the goal "to the mountains" is taken from Mark's source, then, in light of all we were able to establish till now, we must ask whether by these "mountains" *Mark* has Galilee in mind.

The community is on the move. What is in store for it up to the end? We turn to the section in vss. 14b-27. These verses report events yet to occur but expected shortly. We will hardly dare force them into the scheme of a rigid sequence. We have already seen that—for the Gospel as a whole—it is false to inquire after a historical sequence of events. We have also seen that there is no such sequence in vss. 5-13 which treat of Mark's own time. It is just this that makes us hesitate about straying from our course at vss. 14b-27.

Still, we must reckon with the possibility that the material the evangelist used had some sequence in mind: vss. 14-16, the beginning of troubles; vss. 17-20, their duration; vss. 21-23, false Christs and false prophets; vss. 24-27, the coming of the Son of man.[127] But we cannot claim even that with certainty, since it is difficult to single out the source from the present text.[128]

Verses 15-16 make the flight urgent. Verses 17-20 warn of false hopes, for the flight will not lead to deliverance, but to a tribulation far in excess of everything experienced till now (vs. 19). But this last greatest distress is "shortened" for the sake of the elect (vs. 20). Nothing is said of its duration. The

---

[127] Cf. Lohmeyer, *Das Evangelium des Markus*, p. 275. Wellhausen speaks of a period with a sign at its beginning and end (*Einleitung in die drei ersten Evangelien*, p. 96). But this can only be said of Mark's source.

[128] Lohmeyer, *Das Evangelium des Markus*, points out that quite diverse material has been reworked here. Of course, this may already have occurred in the production of the "apocalyptic leaflet." But this further complicates the problem of sources, and again we must limit ourselves to what we can establish for the text of *Mark*.

reworked motifs in turn originate in Jewish-apocalyptic ideas.[129]

Is the tribulation "in those days" [130] thought of as very brief? Verse 18 gives that impression—it will be more bearable in summer than in winter.[131] Thus the event toward which the community moves is a perilous one—though the end is announced as near at hand.

But it is perilous in yet another sense, for false prophets will appear, intent on leading the elect astray (vss. 21-22).[132] In midst of the unbearable tribulation, Christians might well defect to revolutionary messiahs in the hope of attaining their goal more speedily. On the other hand, the danger is especially great because the community—if we are reading Mark correctly—is awaiting Jesus the Messiah, his Parousia. Schniewind [133] correctly states that these false messiahs are shown to be such because it can (more exactly, perhaps, must) be said of them, "Look, here is the Christ!" . . . "Look, there he is!" The Messiah comes like lightning; then there will be no more doubt as to his person.

From this point we should turn again to vs. 14. If we have read it correctly, the antichrist is to stand in the temple at the end time. The verse evidently treats of an adversary raised to titanic proportions, in contrast to which the false messiahs

---

[129] Cf. the individual references in Klostermann, *Das Markusevangelium, ad loc.;* cf. Busch, *op. cit.,* pp. 96-97. Schlatter emphasizes that "the description of the Parousia consists almost exclusively of scriptural quotations" (*Der Evangelist Matthäus,* p. 710).

[130] This phrase occurs four times in our section: vss. 17, 19, 20, and 24.

[131] On the motif, cf. Strack-Billerbeck, I, 952.

[132] Neither verse 21, in light of vs. 6, is superfluous, nor is the reverse true when we realize that in one instance the present and in another the future is referred to (contra Klostermann, *Das Markusevangelium,* p. 133). We may well be dealing with the same saying in two different forms (Schniewind, *Das Evangelium nach Markus,* p. 167). But in Mark's context there is no doublet here.

[133] Schniewind, *Das Evangelium nach Markus, ad loc.*

(vss. 21-22) are, so to speak, but "forerunners." This suggests that the event in 14a must be divided into the threat to the temple giving rise to the flight, and the destruction resulting in the appearance of the antichrist.

Naturally, a concrete event at the temple could be taken as a final signal. This would mean, however, that in spite of the antichrist who already appeared there, further pseudo-messiahs are awaited. The problem cannot be solved with absolute certainty, though the direction of the whole is clear enough. In any case, a "Judean" who reads this prediction and sees the armies approaching will not wait until the city is captured.

Verse 23 marks another insertion. The warning is given; the reader knows what is in store for him. This then concludes the prediction of events. The tribulation will cease only when the end comes, an end now described in altogether traditional features and motifs. The Danielic picture of the coming of the Son of man provides the scenic framework. Then all will see him; then what is promised in Mark 16:7 will be fulfilled.

Another feature is inserted here. Lohmeyer[134] says, "It appears as if the elect were to be united at the 'earth's summit,' i.e., at the sacred and lofty center of the earth, and from there led to the highest summit of heaven where God is enthroned." After all we have encountered in Mark till now, we can only ask: Does *Mark* (!) think of Galilee as the center of the earth? Do heaven and earth meet at Galilee?[135]

But now, after the conclusion of the actual "apocalypse," comes the question as to when all this will be. Strictly speaking, no answer has yet been given. We expected it after vs. 4. And apocalyptic is interested in precisely such things. But

[134] Lohmeyer, *Das Evangelium des Markus,* p. 279.

[135] We recall the significance of the "mountain" for Mark, particularly the Mount of Transfiguration which is to be sought in "Galilee" (without being localized!).

there is no reference to time here, not even the hidden possibility of a rough estimate.[136] A *mašal* (vs. 28) follows together with an interpretation directed solely to the inquirers (vs. 4) and thus (in the redaction) to the community reading the Gospel. The ταῦτα (vs. 29) of course does not refer to the Parousia, for when it comes there is no longer anything "near, at the very gates." It refers to the entire previous discourse, to the question in vs. 4, and to the event at the temple (vs. 14a). When something occurs there, "it" is ἐγγύς. "The reference is not merely to a coming which cannot be delayed, but to a drawing nigh which sends its unmistakable signs in advance." [137]

The first answer to the question of time, then, reads: Imminently—look at the sign! But more can be said. This generation will experience it (vs. 30).[138] Here, of course, the ταῦτα refers to the fulfillment of vss. 24-27.[139]

But the exact date is known only to the Father (vs. 32).[140] Wellhausen's[141] opinion that this principle obviates all eschatological prophecy is incorrect, since his statement really applies to *apocalyptic* prophecy. He is right on that score. But we must still ask whether we are really dealing with apocalyptic here.

What remains to be said is hortatory (vss. 33-37). The imperative is: Watch! The community does not know the καιρός (vs. 33).

From this point a great arc can be described toward 1:14-15. Jesus comes to Galilee and preaches the nearness of the βασιλεία. As a consequence: μετανοεῖτε καὶ πιστεύετε ἐν τῷ εὐαγγελίῳ. Jesus proclaims the nearness of the Parousia. As a

---

[136] Cf. Dan. 12:7.
[137] Lohmeyer, *Das Evangelium des Markus,* p. 281.
[138] We shall return to ἡ γενεὰ αὕτη in the next section.
[139] Lohmeyer, *Das Evangelium des Markus,* p. 281.
[140] Verse 31 might already have been connected with vs. 30 before Mark's time. In the context the reliability of the prediction is stressed.
[141] Wellhausen, *Das Evangelium Marci, ad loc.*

result (not only for the community, but for all) : γρηγορεῖτε. Just as Mark 1:14-15 is, after a fashion, timeless (this preaching always takes place in Galilee), so, by the very nature of the case, this "discourse" of Jesus in Mark has "a kind of timeless and spaceless note," as Lohmeyer[142] maintains. Lohmeyer then describes the chapter by stating that the Lord himself is speaking of things "which penetrate the community's life here and now" and that "the gulf of the past no longer separates the living Lord from the listening community."

But now we must add that there is no longer any gulf in the future as well. The end time has begun its course. Men stand right at the beginning of the end. And he who is with the community is the same who was and is to come.

Mark awaits the Coming One, portraying him as the one who came, because the one who is present has revealed it to him. This proposition can also be reversed: Mark portrays the one who came as the Coming One; and finally, Mark witnesses to the one who is present by awaiting his Parousia and by using for his description such means as originate in the one who came. This is no mere play on words. It only makes clear that the evangelist's description offers no real sequence of events in terms of a chronology.

From this point we can refer again to Busch. In his opinion[143] the θλῖψις is indicative of Mark's kerygma. On this basis he interprets the chapter as a unity. This observation may be entirely correct, in essence, at least. Mark himself stands in the midst of this θλῖψις. Present and future stand under its sign. Inasmuch as chap. 13 immediately precedes the passion narrative, this line is extended into the past as well. The recurring idea of the θλῖψις would then be a device Mark uses for purposes of consolidating, especially since it is not θλῖψις per se, but with theological and eschatological con-

---

[142] Lohmeyer, *Das Evangelium des Markus,* p. 287.

[143] Busch, *op. cit.,* p. 44, *passim;* similarly Schniewind, cf. above, p. 183, n. 126.

tent. The community endures the θλῖψις of its Lord; through
it leads the way to glory at the Parousia. The "way of Jesus"
becomes a kind of paradigm for the Christians.
Despite this consolidation Mark took over the apocalyptic
utterances. These utterances *can,* of course, be interpreted
apocalyptically, especially since their features and motifs shine
through almost the entire structure. And yet such an interpretation would miss just what the evangelist intends to say.
Perhaps we can put it in this way: Mark transforms apocalyptic into eschatology.[144] In *this* sense we can again agree with
Busch[145] that the "eschatological drama of apocalyptic with
its several acts" is eliminated, and that "in the picture of the
future" there is "only *one* last act." But this assertion is correct
only when we realize that for Mark this act has already begun
and that only the finale remains.

D. Further Development in the Major Gospels

Again, since we are not concerned with Mark's co-evangelists
as such, but with inferring from them the oldest evangelist's
concern and peculiarity, we limit ourselves to citing a few
distinctive passages.[146] A series of changes has already been
observed and noted.[147]

[144] This statement closely approximates the findings of Kümmel and
Busch. But in contrast to Kümmel, we need not eliminate (nor do we
arrive at Jesus' preaching—in this respect, Kümmel has a different goal
than we). In contrast to Busch, we require no polemic against literary
criticism, etc., and yet we gain what he was after: a contextual interpretation of Mark.

[145] *Op. cit.,* p. 80.

[146] We shall not debate other interpretations of the reshaping in Matthew and Luke. On this subject, cf. among others Klostermann, *Das
Lukasevangelium, Handbuch zum Neuen Testament,* herausgegeben von
Hans Lietzmann, *et al.,* 2te Auflage (Tübingen: J. C. B. Mohr, 1929),
pp. 197 ff.; recently also Conzelmann, *op. cit.,* pp. 125-26.

[147] Cf. primarily Bultmann, *History,* esp. p. 122, as well as the commentaries, particularly those by Wellhausen and Klostermann.

MARK THE EVANGELIST

1. Luke

We begin with the "caesura" in Luke, located between 21: 24 and 25. In this passage the third evangelist changes the past to future. The new "epoch" is introduced and prepared for by vs. 24 (conclusion): ἄχρι οὗ πληρωθῶσιν καιροὶ ἐθνῶν. But this means that the epoch of the Gentile mission precedes the end. This is Luke's own time! We saw above that Mark also connects this idea with the end (and we will encounter it again in Matthew). Mark 13:9-10 refers to the mission, but in an entirely different way. The oldest evangelist is not concerned with an "epoch" as such which separates Jerusalem's destruction from the Parousia, but with giving eschatological content to the present. Luke cannot put it in that way. For this reason he omits Mark 13:10.[148] If in Mark the μαρτυρεῖν before the tribunal lessens the time to be endured before the end, Luke de-eschatologizes the witness. The time of mission is now, and it continues (cf. Acts) until the καιροὶ ἐθνῶν are fulfilled.

Mark's discourse had a quite similar caesura, viz., before 13: 14. There the preceding (half) verse concludes (as in Luke 21:24) the previous section and in a sense forms a transition to what follows. But in Mark, 13:13*b connects* the disparate parts; Luke 21:24*b*, on the other hand, divides them.

The other "connecting devices" by which Mark relates present and future are absent or reshaped in Luke. The third evangelist deletes the reference to the present distress as the

[148] Luke 21:13 is also characteristic: ἀποβήσεται εἰς μαρτύριον. According to J. Weiss (*Die Schriften des Neuen Testaments*, I, *ad loc.*) the verse means, "it will end for you in martyrdom." Klostermann (*Das Lukasevangelium, ad loc.*) maintains that the οὖν in vs. 14 forbids this exegesis. Vs. 13 is then to be interpreted as follows: "It will end for you in a witness . . . to the gospel." We should note, however, that "gospel" is not a Lukan term, but that by deleting Mark 13:10 Luke took into this verse what he understood to be the idea behind the term. "As always in Luke, the alteration is a thoughtful one" (Strathmann in Kittel, *op. cit.*, IV, 504). This in turn makes clear that Luke focuses on the epoch of the Gentile mission.

190

ἀρχὴ ὠδίνων (Mark 13:8). To be sure, he also reports of wars and tumults (21:9), but men should neither fear nor be led astray for the τέλος will not be εὐθέως! By a very slight change of Mark's οὔπω τὸ τέλος (13:7), a totally different meaning results. In Mark the phrase leads to a climax and is thus the beginning of what is still to occur. Luke alters the idea in such a way as to separate past and future. The end is set off from historical events.

The same feature is even clearer in Luke 21:8. Here Luke inserts into his exemplar the *tempters'* speech: ὁ καιρὸς ἤγγικεν. Those who claim something of this sort should in no wise be followed. He can scarcely express more pointedly the degree to which he knows he is removed from the καιρός.

These are not scattered observations. From the very outset, Luke has consistently arranged and reshaped in this fashion. We already stated that the scenic framework has been smoothed out vis-à-vis Mark 13:1-4. But Luke goes still further. He eliminates the second half of the question (Mark 13:4) referring to the time of the temple's destruction and the end of the world. But the *formal* duplication of the question in 21:7 allows his source still to be clearly seen. "When will this be, and what will be the sign when this is about to take place?" [149] This severs the topical connection in which Mark viewed both events. For Luke, one of these events is a part of the past. But the end did not come with it. From this standpoint, must we not actually refer all the events up to 21:24 to Luke's own past?

We glance first of all at the sign which is sought. The city is beleaguered by armies (21:20). This is, of course, described *ex eventu.*[150] But it seems even more important to observe that *this change—measured against the Markan source—is*

---

[149] Instead of ὅταν μέλλη ταῦτα συντελεῖσθαι πάντα (Mark 13:4), it is now ὅταν μέλλη ταῦτα γίνεσθαι (Luke 21:7).

[150] Bultmann, *History*, p. 129; Wellhausen, J. Weiss, and Klostermann, *ad loc.*

correct! Even Mark 13:14*b* is correctly interpreted by Luke 21:21, at least from Luke's viewpoint. Mark views this verse as a summons to flight, or as justification for the Christians' flight which has already occurred. For Mark, it was to occur in view of the imminent end, which he thought was linked to and recognized in the siege of Jerusalem (cf. Mark 13:2, 3-4, 14*a*). If we omit any thought of the end from Mark 13:14, flight before the besieging armies remains.[151] For Luke, the tribulation which Mark (13:17-19) viewed as a very first step toward the end was already fulfilled (Luke 21:22-23). Indeed, the content of Luke 21:24*a* exceeds Mark; but in the last analysis—and seen in retrospect [152]—it merely concretizes the general utterance in Mark 13:19.

Perhaps we can describe Luke's alteration more precisely. Not only does he break up Mark's consolidation, but he *reads his source as a description of events in chronological sequence.* Hence his aim is not to correct what he thinks is Mark's apocalyptic perspective, but, chiefly, at least, to interpret that perspective from a later time. He must *also* make a few corrections, for he sees things more clearly "after the event" than Mark (to Luke's way of thinking) could see them.

So, Mark 13:21-23, e.g., must be deleted, for *Luke* is obliged to regard it as duplicating what he already noted in this connection[153] in 21:8.[154] Here too we find support for our conten-

---

[151] Some have seen a reference here to the flight toward Pella (Rengstorf, *Das Evangelium nach Lukas, Das Neue Testament Deutsch,* 4te Auflage [Göttingen: Vandenhoeck & Ruprecht, 1949], *ad loc.*). J. Weiss (*Die Schriften des Neuen Testaments,* I, *ad loc.*) actually thinks these very verses may contain the "oracle." This is hardly correct. The topical connection is rightly seen. But we have tried to show that Mark antedates the oracle (cf. above, study two, 3*b*). Luke, of course, might contain the earliest form of the de-eschatologized oracle.

[152] Cf. Klostermann, *Das Lukasevangelium, ad loc.*

[153] But in another context this expression is not out of place. Cf. Luke 17:21. On Luke's Parousia discourse, see below.

[154] Mark 13:15-16 is also deleted in this context, but appears in 17:31 "in a much more suitable place" (J. Weiss, *Die Schriften des Neuen Testaments,* I, 468).

tion that Luke reads his exemplar on his own terms. This is further clear from the beginning of 21:12: πρὸ δὲ τούτων πάντων. We cannot be absolutely certain,[155] but in light of the structure and in view of the question in 21:7, verses 21: 10-11 must refer to the war and accompanying events (cf. 21: 20 ff.) leading up to the siege and conquest of the city. Since Luke clearly intends to connect the two events, he must set 21:12-17 ahead chronologically.[156] Of course, we may not take this to mean that later on persecutions will not also occur; but *these* persecutions preceding the siege and conquest of the city are already past.[157] For this reason we may ask *whether in Luke's context* 21:18-19 imply that the community was preserved throughout the persecution. This hypothesis is all but proven by the fact that the εἰς τέλος in Mark 13:13b is lacking in Luke 21:19. Hence Luke no longer refers to *future* suffering.[158] Moreover 21:28 also indicates this.

Accordingly, the entire first part of Luke's "apocalypse" no longer speaks of the last things. Its content is limited to the period up to Jerusalem's destruction. Whatever Mark saw in it of the final happening is eliminated.

Now Luke turns to the Parousia; but not, as has been maintained,[159] without "setting up a temporal connection." Rather,

[155] Primarily because of the σημεῖα ἀπ' οὐρανοῦ (vs. 11b).

[156] Moreover, the new introduction to the discourse in vs. 10 is striking: τότε ἔλεγεν αὐτοῖς. This suggests that we interpret vss. 8-9 as referring to actual events which must occur (in Luke's case: which had to occur), but do not signify the end, for (vss. 10-11) they have been predicted. Vss. 10-11 would then be the general prediction of events which took place (vss. 8-9), and in vss. 12 ff. are prefixed by the πρὸ δὲ τούτων πάντων.

[157] J. Weiss (*Die Schriften des Neuen Testaments*, I, *ad loc.*) is of the opinion that the evangelist is referring to the persecutions which he records in Acts, particularly the experiences of Peter and Paul. Wellhausen, *Das Evangelium Lucae* (Berlin: Georg Reimer, 1904), p. 117, notes the similarity of expressions in Luke 21:15 and Acts 6:10. "Stephen is the prototype of a witness."

[158] Contra Rengstorf, *Das Evangelium nach Lukas*, on 21:19.

[159] Rengstorf, *op. cit., ad loc.*

he introduces his own time into vs. 24b. This not only renders the ἐν ἐκείναις ταῖς ἡμέραις (Mark 13:24) superfluous, but actually false. Luke accordingly deletes it. What is yet to occur is purely future. Despite his own extensive formulation, there are Markan overtones. The terrors of the previous section prove to be part of the past. At any rate, they have nothing to do with the end. At the end, distress will come upon the nations (21:25), while the Christians will be able to raise their heads (vs. 28).[160] The events themselves will break in upon the οἰκουμένη (vs. 26).[161]

The adjoining parables are set off from the foregoing by means of a special introduction: καὶ εἶπεν παραβολὴν αὐτοῖς (21:29). Though the "discourse" runs on to vs. 36 and the connection between vss. 37-38 and Mark 13:3 is still recognizable, Luke nevertheless intends to create a seam here. The admonition to watchfulness remains, of course, though the evangelist no longer awaits the end as imminent. Luke's own conclusion makes one final reference to the Parousia as "the Parousia for the whole earth" (vs. 35).[162] It is no longer an event in Galilee, nor in Jerusalem (antichrist) and Galilee (Parousia).

But how do we interpret vs. 32 from out of Luke's own situation? Mark 13:30 is repeated almost word for word,[163] but no longer seems to fit the third evangelist's own time.[164]

[160] Wellhausen thinks that the "older idea" shines through here, that it is not Jesus' death but rather the Parousia which brings redemption, that Mark 13:24-27, in contrast, is "totally Christianized" (Das Evangelium Lucae, p. 118). This is hardly correct. Luke's point of view must be understood precisely from a later time. Busch's criticism of Wellhausen (op. cit., p. 11, n. 2) completely bypasses the real issue.

[161] "It should be noted that the cosmic upheaval does not affect the elect; on the contrary it brings them liberation" (Conzelmann, op. cit., p. 130).

[162] Wellhausen, Das Evangelium Lucae, ad loc.

[163] Luke deletes the ταῦτα, "as a result of which the saying does not refer to the matters that have just been mentioned, but to the whole of the Divine Plan" (Conzelmann, op. cit., p. 131).

[164] Thus Wellhausen and Klostermann, ad loc.

Attempts have been made to interpret this verse to mean that Luke thought of *his* generation.[165] But in Mark's case it was assumed that the γενεά refers to the Jewish race,[166] chiefly because an unfulfilled prophecy presented insuperable difficulties.[167]

When we keep in mind the oldest evangelist's point of view, not only is there nothing to prevent our assuming he was thinking of the generation still alive; this interpretation, if materially possible, is actually required here.

The position of the αὔτη points to Hebrew origin.[168] The phrase ἡ γενεά αὔτη may be a "rendering of the rabbinic הדר הזה," in which הד, as generally, is to be understood in the sense of "contemporaries" [Zeitgenossenschaft] (or "age" or "age of man").[169] So, nothing hinders our taking for granted the exegesis assumed for Mark.

Naturally, Luke *may* have taken this verse from his exemplar without noting that it no longer suits his time or point of view. But that is improbable in view of his systematic procedure elsewhere.[170] There is a more probable explanation. The

---

[165] Thus (as a possibility) J. Weiss, *Die Schriften des Neuen Testaments*, I, *ad loc.*, who for the rest leaves the question open.

[166] Busch, *op. cit.*, p. 134; similarly Schniewind, *Das Evangelium nach Markus, ad loc.* Wohlenberg refers the ταῦτα πάντα merely to the signal preceding the end (*op. cit., ad loc.*); on the other hand, B. Weiss refers them to the events predicted in Mark 13:24-27 (*op. cit.*, pp. 204-5).

[167] Lightfoot, who points up certain parallels between Mark 13 and Mark 14–15, believes that the passion narrative, provisionally at least, marks the fulfillment of this saying, which now "becomes much less difficult than is usually supposed." "A first fulfilment at any rate was not far off, which was itself regarded as a sign, a seal of assurance, and a sacrament of the ultimate fulfilment" (*The Gospel Message of St. Mark*, p. 54).

[168] Blass-Debrunner, § 292.

[169] Büchsel's article on "Γενεά" in Kittel, *op. cit.*, I, 662-63.

[170] Luke's abbreviation of Mark 9:1 in 9:27 would contradict this. He deletes "come" and "thus enables us to regard the βασιλεία τοῦ θεοῦ as including the fellowship of many believers with God" (Lohmeyer, *Das Evangelium des Markus*, p. 172). The third evangelist sees the problem very clearly. Cf. also Conzelmann, *op. cit.*, p. 56.

195

term γενεά in "the sense of the 'totality of those living as contemporaries' is not found in Greek." [171] Luke could very well interpret this verse in Mark to mean a race of the same descent, i.e., the Jews. He did not need to hesitate taking it over into his Gospel.[172] Examination of the total relationship of the separate Gospels would thus resolve a hotly disputed issue.

Let us summarize. Luke has broken up Mark's consolidation and writes a *vita Jesu*. But he already reads his source in this fashion. For him, the "prophetic-apocalyptic" predictions in Mark 13 are utterances of the historical Jesus. But he views them after their partial fulfillment in the community. For this reason, we can actually speak of *vaticinia* where Luke is concerned, for he even reshapes the materials contained *within* the traditional pieces and, in fact, *ex eventu*. But we ought to be aware that this evaluation is not quite to the point. Jesus indeed predicted (this is how Luke reads Mark) what was to come. The past proves that he was correct. Luke thus stands between fulfilled prophecy and a fulfillment yet to come. In a certain sense, the fact that something has already occurred confirms the trustworthiness of utterances dealing with what is yet to come.

In *this* sense we can agree with Wellhausen's oft-cited opinion,[173] that Luke "brought the prophecy up to date after the original time for its fulfillment had passed and it had become evident that the Messiah and the end had not come with the destruction of the holy city." But we do not come to grips with Luke's alteration if, as Wellhausen adds, we regard it as "prolonging the change," as is "typical of apocalyptic in general."

---

[171] Kittel, *op. cit.*, I, 663.

[172] Conzelmann thinks "humanity" in general is referred to (*op. cit.*, p. 131). In any case, Luke's very appropriation of this verse from Mark shows that he reads his exemplar on *his* terms. The characterization of his predecessors in his prologue also indicates this. He regards them as doing precisely what he does.

[173] Wellhausen, *Das Evangelium Lucae*, p. 118.

It is true that Luke makes "corrections" by adjusting the prophecy to the event or by describing it after the event. The most serious manipulation is his removal of the expectation of the Parousia from any connection with Jerusalem's destruction.[174] But this correction is in the service of an interpretation which he had to face and master "after the event." Then too, we may not forget that he reads Mark as a *vita* in light of his own time and thus concretizes the sayings of the "historical Jesus," for his own new situation. Luke will scarcely have been aware that his reconstruction altered the entire character of Mark's Gospel and that he created a totally different kind of "Gospel" with essentially identical material. But even if he was aware of it, he could hardly have proceeded in any other way—as a Greek of the second or third generation. He simply *must* draw this sharp contrast between past and future, because he is experiencing his own time as a sequence of events. The result is an epoch all its own. Finally, Luke also broadens the scope: The Parousia encounters the whole earth simultaneously.

[174] But Luke's removal of the "last things" from this context does not mean he dispenses with them altogether. In essence, the second half of the question in Mark 13:4, absent from Luke 21:7, recurs in Luke 17:20 (special source). This introduces Luke's own speech on the coming of the Son of man. Mark 13:15-16, 21-23 are also included (cf. Luke 17:31 and 21). We shall not engage in detailed interpretation here. But this much should be noted: This first speech on the coming even more sharply detaches the Parousia from the events around Jerusalem. What happens near the city and what happens to the city itself are not a "sign" of the imminent end. This corresponds exactly with Luke's reformulation of Mark 13:7 (the end) in 21:9. But in contrast to Mark, the demand for a sign is flatly rejected here (on Luke 17:21, cf. Conzelmann, *op. cit.*, pp. 120-21). The threefold division of epochs reappears in 17:22 ff. Jesus spoke these words in the past. The caesura lies in vs. 25. In the present (Luke's own time), men desire to see one of the days of the Son of man, a desire of which deceivers make use (vss. 22-23). Then men will "fall asleep" (vss. 26-29). But this is dangerous, for the day of the Son of man comes—later to be sure, but it comes—suddenly (vss. 24, 31). Therefore: "Watch" (vss. 33-37).

Against this background, Mark clearly appears again. Whereas for Luke the present is one *part* of a record which otherwise includes past and future, Mark's Gospel is a unified proclamation to the evangelist's own time. Whereas Luke extends the lines out into the world, Mark focuses the decisive event upon his own area.

2. Matthew

When we compare the alterations of the first and third evangelists, we see both similarity and complete dissimilarity. If we begin by inquiring into the time of Matthew's composition, we encounter the startling fact that chap. 24 is scarcely ever used in evidence. It is rather on the basis of 22:7 that the Gospel is assumed to have originated after A.D. 70.[175] The problem, of course, is that Matt. 24 is largely oriented to Mark 13 and would really have required alteration because of the new situation.

Johannes Weiss[176] already noted that "in its connection with the following discourse" only the introduction to the chapter (vss. 1-3) really "poses difficulties; there is not a single line in the discourse itself which could not have been written by Matthew, and after the year A.D. 70." This might be the beginning to a solution of the problem.

We must note the context first of all. In keeping with his style, Matthew has created a speech complex in chaps. 23–25 which connects topically related units. This is clearly the case with chap. 25, following as it does upon chap. 24.[177] But the

[175] Among others, cf. Jülicher, *Einleitung in das Neue Testament,* 7te Auflage (Tübingen: J. C. B. Mohr, 1931), pp. 285-86; Feine-Behm-Kümmel, *Introduction to the New Testament,* trans. A. J. Mattill, Jr. (Nashville: Abingdon Press, 1965), p. 84; Wikenhauser, *op. cit.,* p. 197.

[176] J. Weiss, *Die Schriften des Neuen Testaments,* I, 350.

[177] The command to make the most of the time follows the Parousia discourse. If we compare this with Mark 13:33-37, we see the shift in emphasis. In Mark, several motifs are interwoven—among others, the motif of the proper performance of the assigned task. But the secondary frame-

discourse against scribes and Pharisees also leads up to chap. 24. The unity of the scene is, of course, destroyed by 24:1-3. This may be due to Matthew's exemplar (Mark), and yet the theme of chaps. 24–25, compared with chap. 23, is somewhat out of place. Still, 23:37 ff.[178] prepares for the prediction of destruction in 24:2. Hence these ideas must be *topically* related to the preceding chapter. In a sense, that chapter is Matthew's final climax.

Verse 3 actually introduces a new discourse which treats entirely of the Parousia still to come, but whose date is completely open and no longer connected with historical utterances. This is shown at once in the question which clearly picks up and develops the second part of Mark 13:4. What is stated almost cryptically in Mark (τί τὸ σημεῖον, ὅταν μέλλῃ ταῦτα συντελεῖσθαι πάντα) is paired and given a double thrust in Matt. 24:3 (. . . τί τὸ σημεῖον τῆς παρουσίας καὶ συντελείας τοῦ αἰῶνος). Now comes the question regarding the Parousia. But this is a Matthaean alteration. Only Matthew uses the term παρουσία and only in this chapter. In this fashion he states the theme of the following discourse.

Thus in Matthew as well there is a seam which separates past and future. But it is not due (as in Luke) to a caesura set elsewhere in time. It is due rather to a topical arrangement into two complexes. In the reshaping of Mark the same goal is achieved, but by different means. And now we can state by way of anticipation that as far as we can tell, just this is typical of Matthew. He makes topical rather than temporal

---

work (vss. 33, 37) shows clearly the direction in which Mark intends the parable to be understood: "Watch!" (On this, cf. Jeremias, *The Parables of Jesus*, pp. 39 ff.; p. 40, n. 78.)

[178] Schniewind believes that in 23:37 Jerusalem is the "personification of the entire nation" (*Das Evangelium nach Matthäus*, p. 237). This may have been the original meaning in one source (cf. Luke 11:49). It was no longer so for Luke (cf. Luke 13:34 with 13:33); it could hardly be so for Matthew in his context and joined to 24:2.

divisions. The question now is: How are they to be described? [179]

Matthew's compositional work provides the beginning of an answer to this question. In his *mt.* Gospel, Mark 13:9-13 is set in the context of the tenth *mt.* chapter. The question has been raised as to whether these verses are prophecies (from the speech source?) which Mark inserted into his discourse *ad vocem*

---

[179] We should at least take note of one verse in chap. 23. Matt. 23:36 is usually related to the foregoing section in vss. 34-35, due evidently to the corresponding division of the entire section in Luke (Matt. 23:34-36 corresponds to Luke 11:49-51, and Matt. 23:37-39 to Luke 13:34-35). Schniewind (*Das Evangelium nach Matthäus,* p. 237) asks why all this (he connects vs. 36 with vss. 34-35) should come upon precisely this generation. This would conceal "the greatest guilt of this generation, i.e., the guilt of having killed the Messiah." Schniewind sees the solution in interpreting "generation" as "kind of man." But John who speaks of the "Jews" as the "enemies of Jesus," can hardly be cited in support of this interpretation. First of all, John is speaking expressly of the "Jews" and, secondly, not of the Jews as a nation but rather as Jesus' enemies without regard to their racial origin (cf. Bultmann, *Das Evangelium des Johannes,* p. 59, *passim*). But this reinterpretation of γενεά is no more necessary to Matthew than to Mark. The problem is solved when we realize that Luke has "falsely" partitioned his source here. Since he actually understood the γενεά to mean the Jews (see above), and does not state that all this will "come" upon this γενεά (Matt. 23:36) but will rather be "required" of it (Luke 11:51*b*), he could view this verse as a conclusion. In Matthew, on the other hand, it is also to be connected with what precedes; that is, to other guilt is now added the truly great guilt, i.e., the rejection of Jesus. But the punishment ("your house is forsaken and desolate") will come upon this generation (now living). This fits perfectly the following prediction of the temple's destruction which (for Matthew) has come upon this generation. On the other hand, 23:39 also prepares for the Parousia which is dealt with exclusively in 24:3 ff. Whatever meaning this verse had in Matthew's and Luke's source, for Matthew it is a "proof" that Jesus' prediction has come true. (In addition, he introduces 23:34 ff.— certainly an alteration of his source, cf. Luke 11:49— as a [scriptural] quotation.) It is clear, then, that Matthew writes after the temple's destruction. His transition from the complex in chap. 23 to that in chaps. 24-25 is much broader than 24:1-3 (4). But within this transitional section (23:34–24:4) he separates (via the caesura following 24:2) the Parousia from the event which already occurred near Jerusalem. This separation in turn is not temporal but "topical." To the "epoch" of rejection and its punishment is contrasted the "epoch" of the Parousia (cf. 23:39).

παραδιδόναι, or whether Matthew anticipates them in 10:17-22.[180] The latter idea is the more probable. When Matthew finds pieces in Mark *and* Q, he usually gives a dual account.[181] But in his reproduction of Mark in chap. 24, he inserts vss. 10-12 "as a substitute." [182] In addition, the absence of Mark 13:10 in Matthew's parallel (10:17-22) points to an anticipation, since the phrase εἰς πάντα τὰ ἔθνη (Mark 13:10) appears with slight variation at the end of Matt. 10:18. At the same time, Mark 13:10 is retained in Matthew's Parousia discourse, again with a typical variation. Matthew 24:14 then concludes: τότε ἥξει τὸ τέλος. As regards subject matter, this is scarcely an important deviation from the πρῶτον of Mark, and yet it makes of the end an independent event which *follows* this proclamation.

Once again we take a brief backward glance. We saw that by inserting 13:10 into the context of vss. 9-11, Mark reinterprets the "framework" and gives it a new climax, but that he also views the prophecy in vs. 10 as fulfilled in his lifetime. Luke has eliminated from this complex the idea of the end and in chap. 21 (vss. 5-24) created an epoch which temporally precedes the end. Matthew operates in similar fashion, but without keeping in mind the element of time. He breaks up the Markan consolidation by a topical arrangement. The two sources which Mark reworked (13:9, 11; and 13:10) again take on independent status. Their meaning is once more closer to the original than the meaning they had in Mark's consolidation. Matthew retains Mark 13:10, loosed from the context of 13:9-13, within the setting of the Parousia discourse

---

[180] Klostermann, *Das Markusevangelium*, p. 134.

[181] Feine-Behm-Kümmel, *op. cit.*, pp. 51-52. In addition, the term θλῖψις indicates that Matt. 24:9a is a redactional summary substituted for the section which was broken off. But vs. 9b (cf. Mark 13:13a) again picks up the broken thread.

[182] Bultmann, *History*, p. 122. Bultmann also calls attention to the fact that vss. 10-12 in part contain variations. Cf. vs. 10 with Matt. 10:21= Mark 13:12; vs. 11 with Matt. 24:24= Mark 13:22.

(24:14). The gospel shall now be preached to the whole οἰκουμένη.[183]

On the other hand, Matt. 24:14 has also affected the anticipated section—Mark 13:9, 11-13—and, as stated, by way of Matt. 10:18. Here the αὐτοῖς might well refer to the "Jews," [184] while the τοῖς ἔθνησιν in this context are the governors and kings. One of Mark's ideas is thereby retained, but it is no longer a matter of preaching with missionary intent (as in Mark 13:10). Rather, the "sole purpose of this testimony is to incriminate the adversary." [185] But, and this should be noted, this is in a way only one incident encountering the disciples in their preaching. We can see something else here. Matthew also retains the element of contemporaneity in the utterances of Mark 13:5-13. He eliminates only the idea of the end to which Mark connects them, not, as in Luke, by shifting the seam (cf. Mark 13:3 with Luke 21:24), but by dividing them into two complexes. This means that what Mark says will happen just before the Parousia has become a permanent state of affairs for Matthew.[186]

The evangelist refers to all this in a quite different context, long before the discourse on the return of the Son of man.[187]

---

[183] This expansion of course collides with other statements in Matthew, e.g., with 10:5, 23. But this is no counterargument, for none of the evangelists proceeds "consistently" to the last. Tradition and redaction collide, and when they do, they enable us to get an insight into the evangelist's point of view. In Matthew's case, 28:19 above all should be referred to.

[184] Klostermann, *Das Matthäusevangelium*, ad loc.; Strathmann in Kittel, op. cit., IV, 503.

[185] Strathmann, loc. cit. But it does not have this meaning in Mark's context (contra Strathmann).

[186] That this is actually Matthew's point of view is indicated by his conclusion (28:20) but also, as we stated, by chap. 25. The watchfulness motif (Mark 13:33-37) is changed to the motif of "making the most of the time," faithful stewardship, etc.

[187] Again this indicates similarity with Luke's procedure. Since Luke divides chap. 21 differently by introducing the temporal, he must extract the Parousia sayings from the second part of Mark's discourse, and attaches them to a special Parousia discourse (chap. 17).

He has marked off "topical epochs" which reflect the idea of time (Matt. 10: present; Matt. 24–25: future), though they are not, as in Luke, determined by time but must be described according to content. The epoch of mission with its persecutions is separated from the "epoch" of the Parousia.

It can thus be shown that in contrast to Mark 13, Matt. 24 more rigorously develops this feature. It is introduced in the disciples' question (24:3) already referred to. The μέλλειν (vs. 6) more clearly marks the wars and rumors of war as future events. The πάντα δὲ ταῦτα (vs. 8) more clearly makes what precedes a "sign" to be awaited (cf. also vs. 33). The hatred is no longer the hatred of all (Mark 13:13a) but more specifically of all nations (vs. 9b).[188] The βδέλυγμα τῆς ἐρημώσεως (24:15) is no longer connected with Jerusalem's destruction;[189] it is a prophecy once more and with express reference to Daniel. And, it is no longer construed as masculine, and is again a "sign" to be awaited,[190] a sign of which men can read (in Daniel!).[191]

It is clear, then, that Matthew does offer a genuine Parousia discourse which leads step by step to 24:26-31 and gives in advance the signs which should precede the Parousia. Does this point to increased abuses in Matthew's time (cf. vs. 12)? In that case he would have good reason for the insertion in vs. 30, since "the appearance of the Son of man is . . . a joyful sign that the tribulation is now coming to an end."[192] But

[188] Loisy (according to Klostermann, *Das Markusevangelium, ad loc.*) thinks, e.g., of Nero. But this would not suit Matthew's view. He is not thinking of a contemporary Caesar but of the future. Yet, the mission situation is clear. Hatred comes from the οἰκουμένη.

[189] J. Weiss, *Die Schriften des Neuen Testaments*, I, ad loc.

[190] Contra Wellhausen, *Das Evangelium Matthaei* (Berlin: Georg Reimer, 1904), p. 126.

[191] The ἐν τόπῳ ἁγίῳ (vs. 15) is added as a supplement from Dan. 9:27. For Matthew (as a Jewish Christian?), is the temple a holy place even after Jerusalem's destruction?

[192] Wellhausen, *Das Evangelium Matthaei, ad loc.*

until that time it is necessary to be faithful stewards of the gifts received (chap. 25).

We summarize. Despite all the similarity, the alterations of the first evangelist clearly differ from those of the third. Matthew suppresses the imminent expectation of the Parousia, still discernible in the traditional pieces he appropriated (above all, in vs. 34). He does this by loosing the present situation from its immediate connection with the end so as to form a separate complex. This gives to what remains the exclusive character of a Parousia discourse which in turn is set in a larger speech complex. In a sense Matthew too creates a temporal sequence, but in such a way as to juxtapose groups of related material. Hence we find no "seam" in the Lukan sense. This points to something further. The Gospel of Matthew reflects the period of the missionizing church. But the "missionary speeches" rest on the same footing and arise out of the same situation. They can deal with the present, can have as their content the fate of the missionizing disciples. They can treat of future events, such as the Parousia, and from them derive consequences for the present (Matt. 25). But what the church has to proclaim is always attributed to Jesus. He said it and says it again today, for he is with his own to the close of the age.

Against this background, what is typical of Mark emerges clearly again. Matthew's juxtaposition of complexes turns out to be a dismantling of Mark's consolidation. Actually, this dismantling at times comes closer to the original traditional material than did Mark's arrangement. The oldest evangelist focused the disparate material with its various aims and goals upon *one* point. But Matthew allows these goals to appear side by side again.

E. Summary

The result of our investigation of Mark 13 is that the evangelist actually proceeds as we assumed. The Gospel of Mark is *one* sermon; chap. 13 is a portion of it woven into the whole. The material from the tradition is reworked and adjusted to the concrete, present situation. The imminent expectation of the Parousia determines the tenor of the whole.[193] The Risen Lord is speaking.

MK.

The Gospel of Matthew, on the other hand, is a *collection* of sermons. The situation from which they arise is far more difficult to determine; for, in contrast to Mark, it is not so

Mt.

[193] At this point we should briefly note Mark 9:1 (and parallels). Günther Bornkamm has given the τίνες special stress and from it wished to conclude that the "community has already experienced the delay of the Parousia, and yet its confident hope in the coming Son of man is not extinguished" (*In Memoriam E. Lohmeyer*, p. 118). This would of course suit Mark's situation, particularly since we may be certain that the evangelist affixed this verse to the previous series of sayings (Sundwall, *op. cit.*, p. 57; Fr. Hauck, *Das Evangelium des Markus* (Leipzig: Deichert Verlag, 1931), *ad loc.*; Lohmeyer, *Das Evangelium des Markus, ad loc.*; Kümmel, *Promise and Fulfilment*, p. 25). But whether we may read these ideas out of the τίνες is highly questionable. Is not this phrase in essence the same as Mark 13:30? If this generation will not pass away before all these things take place, then we may not construe the word to mean *all* who are alive. A reflection in this direction might read too much into a saying which merely aims to express the nearness of the Parousia. But something else seems more important here. Kümmel thinks this saying must belong to the oldest tradition, "because the fact that this prediction was not realized must have caused such serious difficulties that they would have hardly been created" (*ibid.*, p. 27). This is not true, as we have tried to show. Of course, we can interpret the verse "without regard to the context" (*ibid.*, p. 25), but then we do not arrive at the proper understanding Mark joined to the verse and unavoidably end up with the alternative: genuine (Kümmel) or community formulation (Wellhausen, *Das Evangelium Marci, ad loc.*; Bultmann, *History*, p. 121; Bornkamm, *loc. cit.*). A consensus will probably never be reached here. But in Mark, 9:1 interprets 8:38. Verse 9:1 describes the word of the coming of the Son of man in glory as an event which is near at hand. In these words, regardless of their origin, the evangelist addresses those living in his time. It is not only possible but probable that "some" who lived in Jesus' day are still among them. But this is not the main thrust of the utterance. This lies rather in the saying on the nearness of the Parousia which is stressed by combining the previous series of sayings with 9:1. This is softened in Matt. 16:28 (he substitutes a present for a perfect participle); and we may ask whether Mark 9:1 is not fulfilled in Matt. 28:18*b*, 20*b*. On Luke's rearrangement, cf. above, p. 195, n. 170.

much the situation as the *content* of the proclamation which has determined the thrust and arrangement of the traditional pieces. Still, we can say of that situation that it is the time in which the missionizing church is taking shape following its surrender of the imminent expectation. To proclamation as address is added the element of teaching. He who is always with his own even to the close of the age is speaking. And *what* he says is for Matthew identical to what the "historical Jesus" said.

LK.   Luke is a historian. From the standpoint of his own time and his own experience of that time, he writes the first "church history," beginning with Jesus.

Concluding Remarks

In his essay on the synoptic Gospels,[1] Schniewind already
stated that "our Gospels intend . . . to be understood as
kerygma for a particular situation and task. We must *determine the situation from which their charismatic kerygma is
to be interpreted.* But this understanding has not even been
achieved for *the Gospels in their present form!*" We have tried
to advance a step in this direction. In conclusion, a few things,
by way of a partial summary of results, should be drawn
together.

The way in which the evangelists conclude their Gospels is
of special significance for our inquiry into their points of
view and into the genre of their work. In this connection,
Hirsch[2] remarks that "we do not rightly know an ancient
piece of writing if we do not know its conclusion," for it is

---

[1] Schniewind, "Zur Synoptiker-Exegese," p. 153.

[2] *Op. cit.,* I, 182. On the significance of conclusions for characterizing
the individual Gospels, cf. also Lightfoot, *Locality and Doctrine in the
Gospels,* pp. 43 ff.

just there that the "inner goal of the whole" becomes clear.[3]

Clearly Luke's Gospel is the first part of a continuous work

Lk/Acts (cf. 24:49), thoroughly oriented to its second part. From the viewpoint of redaction history, the third evangelist must first of all be interpreted on the basis of Acts.[4] From this it follows that the Gospel's orientation to Jerusalem is not significant for the author's situation. What is significant is the Gospel's orientation toward a center which has primarily theological significance as the center of salvation history. The lines are all drawn *toward* this point, and *from* this point the message goes out into the world. Luke himself is situated at the end of this line of mission.

Mt. In contrast, the Gospel of Matthew is a self-contained work. The evangelist's situation can be gleaned (albeit generally) from 28:19-20: "Teaching them to observe all that I have commanded you!" These words are the inner goal of the entire *book*. This agrees perfectly with what we were able to learn of the first evangelist's point of view. The speech complexes (the "gospels") are sermons on salvation as preached in Matthew's time. They are exactly what Jesus "commanded" and what should and will be "taught" and "observed."

Mk. In contrast to his two successors, Mark stands out in bold relief. His work of course concludes with 16:8; but it also points beyond this conclusion. *In this very conclusive incon-*

---

[3] This, of course, expresses Hirsch's regret over the loss of the Markan ending, which he believes he must establish. Basically, Hirsch's assertion is correct. But precisely for this reason we must ask whether or not misunderstanding of the Markan ending led to an improper evaluation of the evangelist's point of view (and vice versa).

[4] It would be more accurate to say that Luke's situation is of course not identical with the situation reported in Acts. It is of a later date. But the way from Jerusalem to the author leads through Acts, since even the speeches in Acts "are not a historical witness to the situation in which the author has set them, but are a historical witness to the type of preaching in the author's own time." (Dibelius, "Zur Formgeschichte der Evangelien," p. 191, n. 1).

clusiveness lies the inner goal of the entire Gospel.[5] If we approach it through redaction history, it is here that we grasp the evangelist's situation and point of view with especial clarity. The orientation to Galilee and the imminent Parousia awaited there provide the motive for the Gospel's formation. Mark must therefore be interpreted against this background. He has arranged his work from his own time and for his own time.

But Mark's conclusion differs not only in form from those of the other Gospels.[6] It also indicates that the Gospel originated in a different way. The evangelist's view of Galilee from his own time gives the previously compiled material its orientation. No continuous, coherent "life of Jesus" was available to Mark. So *he* had first of all to compose in backward direction, and *we* must now interpret him in this fashion. Thus arose the Gospel "form."

Once this form came into being, Mark's successors could take over the outline. Their task lay in "extending" Mark's Gospel, read as a continuous account, into the present time. Thus (aside from the pre-histories) they wrote their Gospels within the "continuity" of the event. On the face of it, the

---

[5] Cf. the description in Lightfoot, *Locality and Doctrine in the Gospels*, pp. 66-67.

[6] Not even the Fourth Gospel is an exception. 20:31 indicates John's point of view. We see in 21:24-25 why the last chapter was added—for the sake of a desired (but unattained) completeness. The motive is anticipated in 20:30, but scarcely has special weight here since such a conclusion is traditional (cf. Bultmann, *Das Evangelium des Johannes*, p. 540, n. 3). But the situation is otherwise in 21:25. *This* might furnish the incentive for supplementation, often falsely attributed to the evangelist. The beginnings of a redaction-historical investigation of John's Gospel appear in the essay by Barrett (*op. cit.*, pp. 257 ff.). Here also attempt is made to interpret the Gospel (and the evangelist!) from out of its own time. Barrett believes it was John's intention "to effect a solution to the theological problems of his day" (*op. cit.*, p. 267). [Cf. also Barrett's *The Gospel According to St. John*, p. 21. Translators' note.] The evangelist "attempts adequately to express what the earlier tradition already contained" (*op. cit.*, p. 269). [Cf. also *The Gospel According to St. John*, p. 44. Translators' note.]

"form" of the three Gospels appears quite similar. But since the major evangelists have a totally different orientation and aim, something really new has resulted. But this is true not only of them.

The reason is that the imminent expectation of Mark and his community cannot be sustained. This means that Mark's Gospel could fulfill its task, in keeping with the evangelist's original aim, only in the period of its origin. A few years later it was already "out of date." Thus, it is *absolutely* necessary for later copyists to add a conclusion. This is technically conditioned and must be understood from the later situation. But we must realize that such a conclusion gives the *entire* Gospel a different character. It is being adjusted to Matthew and Luke. The Gospel "form" created by Mark is now replaced by *the* form offered by the major evangelists. With all their dissimilarity, these Gospels are still closely related when compared to the original Mark. But of the oldest Gospel we can flatly declare that the conclusion alone has turned the sermon into a *vita*. The new "form" of the Gospel has established itself. Mark appears alongside Matthew and Luke. We now have synoptic Gospels.

The noted remark of Justin (Apology, I, 66) e.g., indicates how early this harmonizing tendency in Gospel description set in; a tendency which to this day has scarcely been overcome. Justin reckons the Gospels among the ἀπομνημονεύματα and by this term "clearly" aims "to give non-Christians a key as to how they should understand the Scriptures which the community calls εὐαγγέλιον or εὐαγγέλια." [7] Zahn[8] thinks the term ἀπομνημονεύματα was "well chosen" and "most suitable" for "giving the literary-minded Gentile a proper idea of the nature of the Gospels." This is true, of course, only when we view such things from Justin's situation or point of view.

---

[7] J. Weiss, *Das älteste Evangelium,* p. 6.

[8] Zahn, *Geschichte des Neutestamentlichen Kanons* (Erlangen: Andreas Deichert, 1888), I, 471 (cf. J. Weiss, *loc cit.*).

Once we have done this, however, we have already glossed over what is typically Markan. For Matthew as well, this kind of description is open to suspicion. Actually, it holds true only for Luke, where we even find—initially, at least—that insistence on the reliability of the tradition so common to this type of literature.

Papias' remarks have somewhat the same goal. He would like to establish an intimate connection between the Gospel of Mark (and Matthew) and the first generation eyewitnesses. He achieves this only in regard to the isolated tradition, whereas the τάξις, in his opinion, is the evangelist's work. Dibelius' evaluation is one-sided. He thinks

these remarks indicate the Gospel writers already pass for independent authors rather than transmitters of tradition. But this is the judgment of a sophisticated Christendom which interprets the process of Gospel origins individualistically and thus ignores the synoptic relationship as well as the mosaic-like character of the oldest Gospels.[9]

From the standpoint of form history, this evaluation can readily be appreciated. We then can question whether the material is attributable to Peter. *Here,* certainly, the individualistic view demands too much. And yet, does it not spring from the true awareness (*contra* Dibelius) that the Gospels themselves are each the work of one man?

By distinguishing traditional material from τάξις, Papias in a way anticipated the results of K. L. Schmidt's *Der Rahmen der Geschichte Jesu.* Papias' evaluation of the material has been corrected by form history. But it is significant that he even raises the problem of τάξις! By coming to a rather negative judgment, he indicates he is already applying a later,

[9] "Zur Formgeschichte der Evangelien," p. 189; cf. also Dibelius' "Evangelienkritik und Christologie," *Botschaft und Geschichte,* Gesammelte Aufsätze, herausgegeben von Günther Bornkamm (Tübingen: J. C. B. Mohr, 1953-1956), I, 343-44.

Lukan type of inquiry to Mark's Gospel. But if we *cannot* derive chronological sequence from Mark's Gospel (Papias), and if, moreover, we believe we can prove such sequence was not even intended, then the question arises as to the motives involved in the formation of the Gospel's framework. *In that event* very little is to be gained by dismantling the framework in purely historical fashion (Papias/K. L. Schmidt), or by dissociating "the Gospels' status in the history of literature" from other literary efforts.[10] These procedures, albeit very necessary, have only negative value so long as the genre of these pieces is not defined in a positive way. It makes little difference whether parallels can be found, or whether this "genre" is present in only one exemplar at any given time.

Again we strongly emphasize that we must not assume the compositions of the "Synoptists" (and John) are of the same genre because they are all called "Gospels." From *this* viewpoint we must simply state that *there are no "Synoptic" Gospels.*

Why did several Gospels emerge? It is unlikely that one Gospel intended to displace an earlier one. Rather, each successor to Mark set himself the task of " 'doing better' than his predecessors." [11] Naturally, that word "better" is not a judgment as to value. It is an "exegetical judgment," commensurate to the needs of a later time. The old concern is to be expressed anew, brought up to date. Mark's successors are his exegetes, but in and by this exegesis they intend to preach—by an exegesis strongly oriented to their own time. Redaction history attempts to lift from this exegesis the Gospel's situation-in-life.

Now we will have to say that in the end Luke "won out"!

[10] K. L. Schmidt, "Die Stellung der Evangelien in der allgemeinen Literaturgeschichte," *Eucharisterion,* Studien zur Religion und Literatur des alten und neuen Testaments (Göttingen: Vandenhoeck & Ruprecht, 1923) , 2. Teil, pp. 50 ff.

[11] Oscar Cullmann, "Die Pluralität der Evangelien als theologisches Problem im Altertum," *Theologische Zeitschrift,* 1. Jahrgang (1945), 30.

This is not surprising, for the experience of time cannot be reversed. It is natural, then, that his successors should read Mark in *their own* way. From there it is only a very short step to a harmony of the Gospels (including the fourth Gospel). The result of this attempt however, is not a harmony, but rather a fifth Gospel which arranges the given material according to interests corresponding to the "new author's" point of view. For the most part these interests are purely historical. And this is what throws in doubt all those attempts beginning with Tatian and climaxing in the "harmony" of the passion stories in our hymnals. A glimpse into the relationship between our Gospels, into the history of their redaction, can but warn us against an uncritical use of such later works (e.g., for preaching).

In any case, it seems advisable for the present to overestimate rather than underestimate the gulf between the individual "Gospels." Though Mark is the creator of this kind of literature, his successors have so far distanced themselves from him that it would be no exaggeration to describe their compositions as having entirely different character. Again we must emphasize that this is not a judgment as to value. What is important is that exegesis keep this in mind and allow for it.

If this removes Mark's Gospel from the characterization of a later time, its proximity to Paul becomes all the clearer.

Till now, a comparison of Mark with Paul was *bound* to encounter difficulties, since it was not *Mark* who was compared with Paul, but rather the material Mark transmitted. After detailed investigation, Werner, e.g., asserted that "any influence of Pauline theology upon the Gospel of Mark is entirely out of the question." [12] But this judgment probably relates to the fact that Werner never compares the evangelist but only the tradition he presented. Naturally, the evangelist made

[12] Werner, "Der Einfluss paulinischer Theologie im Markusevangelium," p. 209.

changes here as well; but this must be determined before any comparison is made. For,

if two entities are to be compared and their inner relation to one another determined, then the elementary prerequisite should be fulfilled in such a way that the nature and peculiarity (!) of each can be held to be unequivocally and clearly defined.[13]

Since we are only just beginning to define the uniqueness of Mark, very little can be said for the present. Examination of the "Paulinisms" in Mark seems a dubious enterprise in any case. Whether there are any Paulinisms beside the term εὐαγγέλιον must remain an open question for now. And then there is always the question whether they are not ideas the earliest Christians held in common.

Still, there is a kinship, not in the material primarily, but in the structure of the proclamation—we could almost say, in the structure of the gospel. This is clear when we take the kerygma as starting point. In Paul, any direct historical interest recedes into the background.

The real object of the apostle's faith and preaching is not Jesus as he lived on earth, but the κύριος or Χριστός in heaven, who appeared in Jesus, is now active in the Spirit, chiefly among his own, and will come again in the immediate future.[14]

This *Kyrios*, believed, proclaimed, and identical with the earthly Jesus, is at once the proclamation's source and its point of departure, so far as in the Spirit he is active in the church.

From out of this kerygma developed "the literary form: Gospel." [15] It is important to see that Mark takes up the

---

[13] *Ibid.*, p. 29.

[14] Von Soden, "Das Interesse des apostolischen Zeitalters an der evangelischen Geschichte," *Theologische Abhandlungen für C. v. Weizsäcker* (Freiburg i. Breisgau: J. C. B. Mohr, 1892) , p. 118.

[15] Bultmann, *Theology of the New Testament,* I, 86.

Pauline fundamentals. For him, also, Christ is the proclamation's source and point of departure. In contrast to Paul, Mark does not speak (as far as we can tell, at least) of the "Exalted" but rather of the "Risen Lord." But this does not alter the structure. It is this Risen Lord from whom Mark's proclamation must be viewed. Since he is in Galilee or has advanced toward it, all that Mark presents in the way of "reports" from his life is directed toward that spot. So we can flatly state that Galilee establishes the identity of the now Risen Lord with the earthly Jesus, just as the awaited Parousia, likewise in Galilee, secures his identity with the one who is to return.

Bultmann is probably correct in stating that the kerygma was expanded by "visualization." [16] And, as form history has shown, this took place *prior* to Mark. But we must recognize that Mark neither gives the sum total of such visualizations nor can be regarded as one stage in a gradual development leading up to Matthew and Luke. Rather, the proclamation of the isolated pieces runs parallel to Mark and beyond.

Mark, in fact, begins in a totally new way.[17] He proceeds, as does Paul, from the *Kyrios*. But what is unique is that he does not, as Paul, develop his message conceptually, but by visualization.[18] For this purpose he appropriates pieces of the tradition known to him and shapes them anew into *one* proclamation, *one* gospel.

When we consider how little interest early Christianity apparently had in a "life of Jesus," we will probably have to admit that a Gospel could emerge only in this way. Of course, it is idle to ask what Matthew and Luke would have done without their Markan exemplar. It is idle to ask how Luke's "life of Jesus" would have looked had he not found the outline

[16] *Ibid.*

[17] Bultmann does not sufficiently take this into account (*ibid.*). But cf. his observations on Mark, *History*, pp. 338 ff.

[18] I Cor. 15, e.g., is a certain preliminary stage, though using other means.

and important traditional material already shaped by Mark. But a glance at the further development of this material indicates that Mark checked a process of disintegration which would have come with the fragmenting of the tradition.

Mark may have checked still another process of disintegration, viz., the gnosticizing of Paul's message. It is at least doubtful whether the Pauline epistles (despite such passages as Phil. 2:5-11 and II Cor. 8:9) would have had sufficient weight to counteract the tendency to mythologizing, or to prevent the loss of a historical connection.

Mark ties together the two "strands" of primitive Christian preaching: The Pauline kerygma and the (so-called) synoptic tradition. In both strands we find the paradox inherent in the connection between the eschatological and the historical event, though with varying emphasis. Whereas Paul is basically content to assert the "that" of Jesus' humanity, the individual tradition here is more graphic. But even here we may not ignore what form history has demonstrated, viz., that this tradition is not concerned with the biographical but with the kerygmatic. Once again, therefore, Mark proves to be the consolidator. Later on this consolidation is broken up once more.

This, then, defines Mark's "place." As a thoroughly unique theologian, he occupies a position between Paul and the anonymous tradition on the one hand, and the later evangelists on the other. And though it may be too much to describe him as the "theological center" of the New Testament, his considerably central position among the theologians of primitive Christianity should not be overlooked. Though till now the influence of his successors may be greater than his, we may still inquire whether it is not Mark who deserves the greater attention.

Index of Biblical Passages

217

Index of Modern Authors

221